SMITH'S GUIDE™ TO CHAPTER 7 BANKRUPTCY

FOR PRISONERS

$

SMITH'S GUIDE™
to
Chapter 7 Bankruptcy

for
Prisoners

includes **UPDATED** *forms!*

By
Zachary A. Smith

redbat books

redbat books
2014

First Edition, June 2014
Updated forms (pgs 253–415), April 2018

ISBN-10: 0989592421
ISBN-13: 978-0-9895924-2-0
Library of Congress Control Number: 2014943639

Published by
redbat books
2901 Gekeler Lane
La Grande, OR 97850
www.redbatbooks.com

Text set in Chaparral Pro.

Book design by Kristin Summers, redbat design | www.redbatdesign.com

To the memory of my father, Charles B. Smith

TABLE OF CONTENTS

<3> Preparation of Bankruptcy Petition *(cont.)*

<4> Schedules

DISCLAIMER

This book is not an alternative to professional assistance by an attorney. This book does not provide licensed, professional legal advice. Its author is not a lawyer; its text is for informational purposes only. The material contained herein is not intended to substitute for professional assistance by an attorney. Never disregard professional legal advice, and never delay seeking it or hiring an attorney to represent you, because of anything you read in this book. It is the responsibility of you, the reader, to seek out and secure legal advice on how to proceed within the federal bankruptcy courts.

The information in this book has been carefully researched, and all efforts have been made to ensure accuracy. The author and publisher assume no responsibility for any damages or losses incurred during, or as a result of, the application of the information presented here. All information should be carefully studied and clearly understood before taking any action based on the contents of this book. The reader assumes full responsibility for the consequences of his or her own actions, filings and strategic decisions.

INTRODUCTION

On August 28, 2005, my father died unexpectedly. I received a small inheritance from his estate, which I used to cover expenses in litigating my criminal appeals, and the remaining amount ($450) was deposited in my offender account for discretionary spending. On February 2, 2007, after some tax forms arrived for me in the mail, the State of Missouri filed a suit against me under the Missouri Incarceration Reimbursement Act (MIRA). I was, however, successful in securing a dismissal of the State's suit, on a statute of limitations defense.

The State appealed the decision, and the circuit court's dismissal was overturned. On remand, the court entered judgment against me, ordering the Missouri Department of Corrections to collect 90% of any money deposited into my offender account by friends or family. I immediately appealed, arguing that the State's suit was barred by the principles of *res judicata* and *collateral estoppel*. However, the appellate court affirmed the circuit court's judgment.

Seeing that the MIRA issue in state court was getting me nowhere, I started to research United States Bankruptcy Code and found a loophole. Under 11 U.S.C. §523(a)(7), a debt for a fine, penalty, or forfeiture payable to and for the benefit of a government unit is exempted from discharge if it is not compensation for actual pecuniary loss. The three requirements for a non-dischargeable debt under the Code are: (1) that it be a fine, penalty, or forfeiture; (2) that it is payable to and for the benefit of a government unit; and (3) that it is not compensation for actual pecuniary loss. See *Kelly V. Robinson, 479 U.S. 36, 51, 101 S.Ct. 353 (1986)*.

In determining whether a civil penalty is compensation for actual pecuniary loss, the court must consider the following. First, does calculation of the penalty bear any relationship to the costs incurred by the government? Second, must the penalty collected be used to mitigate the particular damage caused by the violation? And third, did the government suffer any actual pecuniary loss? See *Arizona V. Ott (in re Ott), 218 B.R. 118 (Bankr. W.D.Wash. 1998)*.

Any creditor seeking an exception to dischargeability bears the burden of proof by a preponderance of the evidence [see *Grogan V. Garner, 498 U.S. 279, 111 S.Ct. 654 (1991)*] and that exceptions to discharge are strictly construed against the objecting creditor and liberally in favor of the debtor [see *In re Bugna, 33 F.3d 1054 (9th Cir. 1994)*].

Since the MIRA statute was enacted for reimbursement for actual incarceration costs, I filed a Chapter 7 bankruptcy petition on September 14, 2010, and was granted a discharge on March 11, 2011. My account was clear of any MIRA seizures until September 2012, when the state seized $45 from my account. I filed a motion for contempt with bankruptcy court, arguing that the state violated the discharge injunction. The court ruled that the MIRA judgment was void with respect to all costs accrued as of the bankruptcy filing, but held the judgment remained valid as to future reimbursement costs and that the costs incurred by the state since my bankruptcy petition were not dischargeable debts.

I appealed and lost; the Eighth Circuit Court of Appeals affirmed the lower court's decision on February 5, 2013, in *Smith V. Missouri, 530 Fed.Appx. 616 (8th Cir. 2013)*.

However, whiling litigating the bankruptcy case, the Missouri Court of Appeals handed down decisions in *State ex rel. Koster V. Cowin, 390 S.W.3d 239 (Mo.App.WD. 2013)* and *State ex rel. Koster V. Wadlow, 398 S.W.3d 591 (Mo.App.WD. 2013)* that held the attorney general's office could not be reimbursed with assets that were not known and identified at the time of the MIRA hearing—meaning the attorney general could not impose future costs for incarceration against a prisoner unless the money was shown to come from a current stream of income that existed when the MIRA judgment was entered.

I filed a motion under 74.06(b), citing these two cases. The state conceded, filing a satisfaction of judgment motion in the Cole County Circuit Court on October 16, 2013. All liens against my account were removed.

Filing for bankruptcy will not discharge debts imposed by all states, because the statutes are worded differently in each. But you will be granted an automatic stay from all creditors while your bankruptcy proceeding is pending, enabling you to receive money on your account until the disposition of your case.

Because all SMITH'S GUIDE books are made to be as helpful as possible, at the end of each chapter you will find completed examples of the forms you are required to file in order to begin your bankruptcy case. You will also find blank forms at the end of this book, which you may remove, fill out, and file with the bankruptcy court in your district.

Of course, this book is not just for the types of government debts discussed above, it is for the prisoner who has outstanding debts from life before prison and wants a fresh start upon release. It is my intent for this book to prove an invaluable resource guide for you and any other prisoner who needs financial freedom from their past debts.

ZA Smith

—Zachary A. Smith

$ <1> OVERVIEW OF BANKRUPTCY

Bankruptcy Process

Under Article I, Section A, of the United States Constitution, Congress enacted the Bankruptcy Code in 1978. The Bankruptcy Code, codified as title 11 of the United States Code, has been amended a number of times since being enacted. It governs all bankruptcy cases. The process can be complex and confusing without adequate guidance and proper instructions.

The procedural aspects of the bankruptcy process are governed by the Federal Rules of Bankruptcy Procedure and local rules of each bankruptcy court. The Bankruptcy Rules contain a set of official forms for use in bankruptcy cases (a set of forms for filing a chapter 7 are provided in this hook). The Bankruptcy Code and Bankruptcy Rules (as well as local rules) set forth the legal procedures for dealing with your financial debts.

There is a bankruptcy court for each judicial district in the United States. Each state has one or more districts. There are ninety bankruptcy districts across the United States. The bankruptcy courts are each usually equipped with their own clerk's office.

The court official with decision-making power over federal bankruptcy cases is the United States bankruptcy judge, a judicial officer of the United States district court. The bankruptcy judge may decide any matter connected with a bankruptcy case, such as eligibility to file or whether you should receive a discharge of your debts. Most of the bankruptcy process is administrative, however, and is conducted away from the courthouse. In cases under chapter 7, this administrative process is carried out by a trustee who is appointed to oversee the case.

A debtor's involvement with the bankruptcy judge is usually very limited. As a typical chapter 7 debtor, you will not appear in court and will not see the bankruptcy judge unless an objection is raised in the case. The only proceeding for which you must appear is the meeting of creditors, which is usually held at the offices of the U.S. trustee. This meeting is informally called a "341 meeting" because section 341 of the Bankruptcy Code requires you to attend this meeting so that creditors can question you about debts and any property you own. Of course, your personal appearance will have to be waived due to your incarceration, and you will attend this meeting via phone to be examined by the trustee and any creditors who wish to examine you. (This will be discussed in another chapter.) The 341 meeting is merely a formality, not an interrogation. Creditors rarely attend or file objections.

A fundamental goal of the federal bankruptcy laws enacted by Congress is to give debtors (i.e., you) a financial "fresh start" from burdensome debts. In *Local Loan Co. V. Hunt, 292 U.S. 234, 244 (1934),* the Supreme Court made this point about the purpose of the bankruptcy law:

> [I]t gives to the honest but unfortunate debtor...a new opportunity in life and a clear field for future effort, unhampered by the pressure and discouragement of preexisting debt.

This goal is accomplished through the bankruptcy discharge, which releases you from personal liability from specific debts and prohibits creditors from ever taking any action against you to collect those debts.

Chapter 7 of the Bankruptcy Code, entitled "Liquidation," contemplates an orderly, court-supervised procedure by which a trustee takes over the assets of the debtor's estate, reduces them to cash, and makes distributions to creditors, subject to the debtor's right to retain certain exempt property and the rights of secured creditors. Because there is usually little or no nonexempt property in most chapter 7 cases, there may not be an actual liquidation of the debtor's assets. These cases are called "no-asset cases."

Most cases filed by prisoners will be no-assets cases. A creditor holding an unsecured claim will get a distribution from the bankruptcy estate only if the case is an asset case and the creditor files a proof of claim with the bankruptcy court. In most chapter 7 cases, if the debtor is an individual, he or she receives a discharge that releases him or her from personal liability for certain dischargeable debts. The debtor normally receives a discharge just a few months after the petition is filed. Amendments to the Bankruptcy Code enacted in the Bankruptcy Abuse Prevention and Consumer Protection Act of 2005 require the application of a "means test" to determine whether individual consumer debtors qualify for relief under chapter 7. If such a debtor's income is in excess of a certain threshold, the debtor may not be eligible for chapter 7 relief. However, that shouldn't be an issue for those incarcerated.

Discharge in Bankruptcy

A bankruptcy discharge releases a debtor from personal liability for certain specified types of debts. In other words, you are no longer legally required to pay any debts that are discharged. The discharge is a permanent order prohibiting your creditors from taking any form of collection action on discharged debts (in prison or upon your release), including legal action and communications with you, such as telephone calls, letters, or personal contacts. Although you are not personally liable for discharged debts, a valid lien (i.e., a charge upon specific property to secure payment of a debt) that has not been avoided (i.e., made unenforceable) in the bankruptcy case will remain after the bankruptcy case. Therefore, a secured creditor may enforce the lien to recover the property secured by the lien. Examples of secured debts are the mortgage on a debtor's house and the loan that finances the purchase of the debtor's automobile.

The timing of the discharge varies depending on the chapter under which the case is filed. In a chapter 7 (liquidation) case, the court usually grants the discharge promptly on expiration of the time fixed for filing a complaint objecting to discharge and the time fixed for filing a motion to dismiss the case for substantial abuse (which is 60 days following the first date set for the 341 meeting). Typically, this occurs about four months after the date you file the petition with the clerk of the bankruptcy court. The court may deny you a discharge in a chapter 7 if you fail to complete an instructional course concerning financial management. (This will be discussed in another chapter, see Table of Contents.) The Bankruptcy Code provides limited exceptions to the "financial management" requirement if the U.S. trustee or bankruptcy administrator determines there are inadequate educational programs available, or if you are disabled or incapacitated or on active military duty in a combat zone. And no, being in prison doesn't qualify as a "combat zone"—although it should.

Unless there is litigation involving objections to the discharge, you will usually receive a discharge automatically. You will also automatically receive a stay of collection actions by your creditors, pursuant to Bankruptcy Code §362, upon filing your petition. (More on this later.) The Federal Rule of Bankruptcy Procedure provide for the clerk of the bankruptcy court to mail a copy of the order of discharge to all creditors, the U.S. trustee, the trustee in the case, and, if one exists, the trustee's attorney. You and your attorney (if you happen to hire one) also receive copies of the discharge order. The notice, which is simply a copy of the final order of discharge, is not specific as to those debts determined by the court to be non-dischargeable (i.e., not covered by the discharge). The notice informs creditors generally that the debts owed to them have been discharged and that they should not attempt any further collection. They are cautioned in the notice that continuing collection efforts could subject them to punishment for contempt. Any inadvertent failure on the part of the clerk to send you or any creditor a copy of the discharge order promptly within the time required by the rules does not affect the validity of the order.

Dischargeable and Nondischargeable Debts

Not all debts are discharged. The debts discharged vary under each chapter of the Bankruptcy Code. Section 523(a) of the code specifically excepts various categories of debts from the discharge granted to individual debtors. Therefore, you must still repay those debts after bankruptcy. Congress has determined that these types of debts are not dischargeable for public policy reasons (based either on the nature of the debt or the fact that the debts were incurred due to improper behavior, such as the debtor's drunken driving).

There are nineteen categories of debt from discharge under chapter 7. The exceptions to discharge apply automatically if the language prescribed by section 523 (a) applies. The most common types of nondischargeable debts are certain types of tax claims, debts not set forth by the debtor on the lists and schedules the debtor must file with the court, debts for spousal or child support or alimony, debts for willful and malicious injuries to person or property, debts to governmental units for fines and penalties, debts for most government funded or guaranteed educational loans or benefit overpayments, debts for personal injury caused by the debtor's operation of a motor vehicle while intoxicated, debts owed to certain tax-advantaged retirement plans, and debts for certain condominium or cooperative housing fees.

The types of debts described in sections 523(a) (2), (4), and (6) (obligations affected by fraud or maliciousness) are not automatically excepted from discharge. Creditors, however, must ask the court to determine that these debts are excepted from discharge. In the absence of an affirmative request by the creditor and the granting of the request by the court, the types of debts set out in sections 523(a) (2), (4), and (6) will be discharged.

A slightly broader discharge of debts is available to a debtor in a chapter 13 case than in a chapter 7 case. Debts dischargeable in a chapter 13, but not in a chapter 7, include debts for willful and malicious injury to property, debts incurred to pay non-dischargeable tax obligations, and debts arising from property settlements in divorce or separation proceedings. Although a chapter 13 debtor usually receives a discharge only after completing all payment required by the court-approved (i.e., "confirmed") repayment plan, there are some limited circumstances under which the debtor may request the court to grant a "hardship discharge" even though the debtor had failed to complete plan payments. Such a discharge is available only to a debtor whose failure to complete plan payments is due to circumstances beyond the debtor's control. The scope of a chapter 13 hardship discharge is similar to that in a chapter 7 case with regard to the types of debts that are excepted from the discharge. A hardship discharge also is available in a chapter 12 if the failure to complete plan payments is due to circumstances for which the debtor should not justly be held accountable. For informational purposes only—and to avoid any confusion—a chapter 13 is designed for those who have a regular source of income, and enables a debtor to keep available assets, such as a house. However, most prisoners do not have a regular source of income, so chapter 13 is not a subject of this book.

Creditor's Objection to Discharge

In chapter 7 cases, the debtor does not have an absolute right to a discharge. An objection to the debtor's discharge may be filed by a creditor, by the trustee in the case, or by the U.S. trustee. Shortly after the case is filed, creditors receive a notice that sets forth important information, including the deadline for objecting to the discharge. To object to the debtor's discharge, a creditor must file a complaint in the bankruptcy court before the deadline set out in the notice. Filing a complaint starts a lawsuit referred to in bankruptcy law as an "adversary proceeding."

The court may deny a chapter 7 discharge for any of the reasons described in section 727(a) of the Bankruptcy Code, including failure to provide requested tax documents; failure to complete a course on personal financial management; transfer or concealment of property with intent to hinder, delay, or defraud creditors; destruction or concealment of books or records; perjury and other fraudulent acts; failure to account for the loss of assets; violation of a court order or an earlier discharge in an earlier case commenced within certain time frames (discussed below) before the petition was filed. If the issue of your right to a discharge goes to trial, the objecting party has the burden of proving all the facts essential to the objection.

The court will deny a discharge in a later chapter 7 case if you received a discharge under chapter 7 or chapter 11 in a case filed within eight years before the second petition is filed. The court will also deny a chapter 7 discharge if you previously received a discharge in a chapter 12 or chapter 13 case filed within six years before the date of the filing of the second case unless (1) you paid all "allowed unsecured" claims in the earlier case in full, or (2) you made payments under the plan in the earlier case totaling at least 70 percent of the allowed unsecured claims and your plan was proposed in good faith and the payments represented your best effort. You are ineligible for discharge under chapter 13 if you received a prior discharge in a chapter 7, 11, or 12 case filed four years before the current case, or in a chapter 13 case filed two years before the current case.

Revocation of Discharge

The court may revoke a discharge under certain circumstances. For example, a trustee, creditor, or the U.S. trustee may request that the court revoke your discharge in a chapter 7 case based on allegations that you: obtained the discharge fraudulently; failed to disclose the fact that you acquired or became entitled to acquire property that would constitute property of the bankruptcy estate; committed one of several acts of impropriety described in section 727(a) (6) of the Bankruptcy Code; failed to explain any misstatements discovered in an audit of the case; or failed to provide documents or information requested in an audit of the case. Typically, a request to revoke a debtor's discharge must be filed within one year of the discharge or, in some cases, before the date that the case is closed. The court will decide whether such allegations are true and, if so, whether to revoke the discharge.

Paying a Discharged Debt

A debtor who has received a discharge may voluntarily repay any discharged debt. You may repay a discharged debt even though payment of that debt can no longer be legally enforced. Sometimes a debtor agrees to repay a debt because it is owed to a family member or represents an obligation to an individual for when the debtor's reputation is important, such as a family doctor or attorney.

Collection Attempts by Creditors After Debt Discharge

If a creditor attempts collection efforts on a discharged debt, you can file a motion with the court, reporting the action and asking that the case be reopened to address the matter. The bankruptcy court will often reopen a case to ensure that the discharge is not violated. The discharge constitutes a permanent statutory injunction prohibiting creditors from taking any action designed to collect a discharged debt, including the filing of a lawsuit. A creditor can be sanctioned by the court for violating the discharge injunction. The normal sanction for violating the discharge injunction is civil contempt, which is often punishable by a fine.

Discriminatory Treatment Prohibited

The law provides express prohibitions against discriminatory treatment of debtors by both governmental units and private employers. A governmental unit or private employer may not discriminate against a person solely because the person was a debtor, was insolvent before or during the case, or has not paid a debt that was discharged in the case. The law prohibits the following forms of governmental discrimination: terminating an employee; discriminating with respect to hiring; or denying, revoking, suspending, or declining to renew a license, franchise, or similar privilege. A private employer may not discriminate with respect to employment if the discrimination is based solely upon the bankruptcy filing. This information most likely won't apply to prisoners, but it is best to be informed.

Obtaining Copy of Discharge Order

If you lose or misplace the discharge order, another copy can be obtained by contacting the clerk of the bankruptcy court that entered the order. The clerk will charge a fee for searching the court records and there will be additional fees for making and certifying copies. If the case has been closed and archived, there will also be a retrieval fee and obtaining the copy will take longer.

The discharge order may be available electronically. The PACER system provides the public with electronic access to selected case information through a personal computer located in many clerk's offices. A debtor can also access PACER. Users must set up an account to acquire access to PACER, and must pay a per-page fee to download and copy documents filed electronically.

$

‹2› PREPETITION CREDIT COUNSELING REQUIREMENT

Services Available from Credit Counseling Agencies

With limited exceptions, 11 U.S.C. §109(h) of the Bankruptcy Code requires that all individual debtors who file for bankruptcy relief receive a briefing that outlines the available opportunities for credit counseling and provides assistance in performing a budget analysis. The briefing must be giving within 180 days *before* the bankruptcy filing. The briefing may be conducted by telephone and must be provided by a nonprofit budget/credit counseling agency approved by the United States trustee or bankruptcy administrator.

A debtor is not entitled to a waiver of the credit briefing requirement of 11 U.S.C. §109(h) because of his or her imprisonment; incarceration is not a disability under the statute. Complaints concerning the refusal of a credit counseling agency to offer a credit briefing by mail or free of charge should be directed to the United States trustee's officer, which is responsible for administering the counseling program.

A credit counseling briefing takes anywhere from thirty minutes to an hour to complete, so you will need to have telephone access for that amount of time. Most credit counseling services require the briefing be conducted via telephone. The Institute for Financial Literacy; 260 Western Ave., Suite 1, South Portland, ME 04106; (207) 879-0389; has a program set up for the incarcerated. The charge is $50 for the prepetition credit counseling, and $50 for the postpetition personal financial management. You may obtain both services for free, if you can demonstrate your inability to pay. All approved credit counseling agencies must provide their services without regard to the debtor's ability to pay the fees in accordance with 11 U.S.C. §111(c)(2)(h). You will need to write or call the agencies listed in this chapter for more information.

The credit counseling agency you use will send you a certificate when you complete the credit counseling briefing. With that certificate you will be ready to prepare and file a petition for bankruptcy.

In addition, after filing a bankruptcy petition, you will be required to complete a financial management instructional course before you can receive a discharge. You can use the same credit counseling agency as before. In fact, it would be best to make this arrangement during the prepetition credit counseling briefing. In the section below is a list of approved credit counseling agencies. You may use the services of any of them, even if they are not located in the bankruptcy district you'll be filing your petition in.

Approved Credit Counseling Agencies

1st Choice Credit Counseling & Financial Education
2049 Marco Drive
Camarillo, CA 93010
(877) 692-5669
English and Spanish

A 123 Credit Counselors, Inc.
703 Waterford Way (NW 62nd Ave.)
Suite 220
Miami, FL 33126
(305) 269-9201 or 1-888-412-2123
English and Spanish

Advisory Credit Management, Inc.
5769 West Sunrise Blvd.
Plantation, FL 33313
(800) 786-3940
English and Spanish

Allen Credit and Debt Counseling Agency
195 Brook Street East
Wessington, SD 57381
(888) 415-8173
English and Spanish (Interpreter Only)

Alliance Credit Counseling, Inc.
13777 Ballantyne Corporate Pl.
Suite 100
Charlotte, NC 28277
(888) 594-9596
English and Spanish

American Consumer Credit Counseling, Inc.
130 Rumford Avenue
Suite 202
Newton, MA 02466
(866) 826-6924
English and Spanish

Pacific Institute for Development and Education, Inc.
6230 Wilshire Blvd.
Suite 1763
Los Angeles, CA 90048
(800) 845-7171
English and Spanish

Black Hills Children's Ranch, Inc.
1644 Concourse Drive
Rapid City, SD 57703
(605) 348-1608
English and Spanish

Children's and Family Service d/b/a/ Family Service Agency
535 Marmion Avenue
Youngstown, OH 44502
(303) 782-5664
English and Spanish

ClearPoint Financial Solutions, Inc.
8000 Franklin Farms Drive
Richard, VA 23229
(804) 222-4660; (877) 422-9044
English and Spanish

Community Credit Counseling, Inc.
101 N. Lynnhaven Road
Suite 303
Virginia Beach, VA 23452
(800) 531-5124

Comprehensive Credit Counseling of Rural Services of Indiana, Inc.
60918 US 31 South
South Bend, IN 46614
(800) 288-6581

Consumer Credit Counseling of Springfield, Missouri, Inc.
1515 S. Glenstone
Springfield, MO 65804
(417) 889-7474

Consumer Credit Counseling Service of Greater San Antonio
6851 Citizens Parkway
Suite 100
San Antonio, TX 78229
(210) 979-4300

Consumer Credit Counseling Service of Orange County, Inc.
1920 Old Tustin Avenue
Santa Ana, CA 92832
(888) 289-8230
English and Spanish

Consumer Credit Counseling Service of San Francisco
595 Market Street
Suite 1500
San Francisco, CA 94105
(800) 777-7526
English and Spanish

Consumer Credit Counseling Service of the Midwest, Inc.
4500 East Broad Street
Columbus, OH 43213
Known to work with the incarcerated

Consumer Financial Education Foundation of America, Inc.
2 North 20th Street
Suite 1030
Birmingham, AL 35203
(205) 321-2822; (866) 684-8171

CredAbility f/k/a Consumer Credit Counseling Service of Greater Atlanta, Inc.
100 Edgewood Avenue
Suite 1800
Atlanta, GA 30303
(866) 672-2227
English and Spanish

Credit Advisers Foundation
1818 South 72nd Street
Omaha, NE 68124
(402) 393-3100; (800) 625-7725
English and Spanish

Credit Card Management Services, Inc.
4611 Okeechobee Blvd.
Suite 114
West Palm Beach, FL 33417
(800) 920-2262
English and Spanish

Credit Counseling of Arkansas, Inc.
1111 Zion Road
Fayetteville, AR 72703
(479) 521-8877; (800) 889-4916
English and Spanish

Cricket Debt Counseling
10121 SE Sunnyside Road
Suite 300
Clackamas, OR 97015
(866) 719-0400
English and Spanish
Known to work with the incarcerated

Debt Education and Certification Foundation
112 Goliad Street
Suite D
Benbrook, TX 76126
(866) 859-7323
English and Spanish

Debt Reduction Services, Inc.
6213 N. Cloverdale Road
Suite 100
Boise, ID 83713
(208) 378-0200; (877) 688-3328
English and Spanish

Family Financial Education Foundation
724 Front Street
Suite 340
Evanston, WY 82930
(307) 789-2010; (888) 292-4333
English and Spanish

Financial Fitness Services, Inc.
1226 Linn Street
Suite C
Sikeston, MO 63801
(888) 471-9737

Forbes & Newhard Credit Solutions, Inc.
7505 Tiffany Springs Parkway
Suite 130
Kansas City, MO 64153
(816) 442-7036; (866) 351-0322

Garden State Consumer Credit Counseling, Inc.
225 Willowbrook Road
Freehold, NJ 07728
(732) 409-6281; (800) 992-4557
English and Spanish

Granite Lake Educational Resources
111 West Cataldo
Suite 200
Spokane, WA 99201
(509) 325-2511; (866) 366-0599
English and Spanish

GreenPath, Inc.
38505 Country Club Drive
Suite 210
Farminton Hills, MI 48331
(800) 630-6718
English and Spanish

Hummingbird Credit Counseling and Education, Inc.
3737 Glenwood Avenue
Suite 100
Raleigh, NC 27612
(800) 645-4959
English and Spanish

InCharge Education Foundation, Inc.

21201 Park Center Drive
Suite 310
Orlando, FL 32835
(866) 729-0049
English and Spanish

Institute for Financial Literacy, Inc.

260 Western Ave.,
Suite 1
South Portland, ME 04106
(207) 879-0389
Known to work with the incarcerated

Money Management International, Inc.

9009 West Loop South
Suite 700
Houston, TX 77096
(877) 964-2227
English and Spanish

National Financial Literacy Foundation, Inc.

555 Winderley Place
Suite 300
Maitland, FL 32751
(877) 380-6353
English and Spanish

Springboard Nonprofit Consumer Credit Management, Inc.

4351 Latham Street
Riverside, CA 92501
(951) 781-0114; (888) 425-3453
English and Spanish

Stand Sure Credit Counseling, a/k/a/ Biblical Financial Concepts, Inc.

124 Oakridge Drive
Oneonta, AL 35121
(205) 421-1590

Take Charge America, Inc.
20620 North 19th Avenue
Phoenix, AZ 85027
(623) 266-6100; (866) 750-9634
English and Spanish

The Kingdom Ministries, Inc.
6094 Apple Tree Drive
Suite 11
Memphis, TN 38115
(901) 552-5131

The Mesquite Group, Inc.
600 Six Flags Drive
Suite 400
Arlington, TX 76011
(817) 769-4069

Free Annual Credit Report

It is advisable to obtain a credit report before you file for bankruptcy. You are entitled to receive one free copy per year, depending on what state you're in. Your credit report should show who your creditors are and how much you owe them. However, not all debts will be stated in the credit report. Write to the following addresses with documentation of your identity. Signed letters from your caseworker may be used as documentary proof.

Experian
P.O. Box 2002
Allen, TX 75013

Equifax Information Services, LLC
Disclosure Department
P.O. Box 740241
Atlanta, GA 30374

TransUnion
P.O. Box 1000
Chester, PA 19022

Free Annual Credit Report per the Fact Act
P.O. Box 105281
Atlanta, GA 30348

Federal Income Tax Returns

You may be required to submit copies of your income tax returns, if you've ever filed. You may request copies for the last two years from the address below.

Internal Revenue Service
United States Department of the Treasury
Philadelphia, PA 19255-1498

<3> PREPARATION OF BANKRUPTCY PETITION

Voluntary Petition

Official Form B1, known as a "voluntary petition" must be used by you to begin a bankruptcy case. Filing this petition is how you declare bankruptcy. It also generally operates to stop action by creditors to collect their debt, a feature of the bankruptcy process, pursuant to Section 362 of the Bankruptcy Code.

The voluntary petition provides the bankruptcy court with basic information needed to begin your case. Although some of the information asked for in Official Form R1 will he requested in greater detail in the schedules and statements that you must also file (discussed in next chapter), the court needs certain information immediately to make a rough estimate of the resources needed to handle the case, to monitor multiple filings, to assign cases to judges, and to compile certain statistical information.

Applicable Law and Rules

Filing a voluntary petition with a bankruptcy court under chapter 7 starts your bankruptcy case, according to 11 U.S.C. §§301, 302. It also constitutes an "order for relief," as defined by 11 U.S.C. §§301(b), 302(a). If filing jointly, a joint case is started by the filing of a single petition by you and your spouse, 11 U.S.C. §302(a). If you are married, it is not necessary for your spouse to also file; you may file separately.

Rule 1002 of the Federal Rules of Bankruptcy Procedure (which I sometimes refer to herein as simply "Rules") requires a petition to be filed with the clerk of the court. The case should be filed in an appropriate bankruptcy court location (venue), based on the criteria established in section 1408 of title 28 of the United States Code.

In addition to the petition, Bankruptcy Rule 1007 and 11 U.S.C. §521 say that the filing of a bankruptcy case requires the filing of schedules listing your property and debts, a statement of financial affairs, a statement of "current monthly income" by you with primarily consumer debts, and several other documents. These documents include a mailing list (matrix) containing the names and addresses of the creditors and others who should receive notice from the court in the case. You must submit to the court a statement of your full Social Security Number. Rule 1007(f) indicates the requirements concerning the format of the mailing list are set by the local bankruptcy courts. Information about the requirements of the court in which your case will be filed can be obtained by contacting the clerk's office or visiting the court's website. (Links to the bankruptcy courts' local rules, and additional information, are posted at http://www.uscourts.gov/rules/bk-localrules.html.).

A list of the documents to be filed in a bankruptcy case under chapter 7 can be found in Form B200, "Required Lists, Schedules, Statements and Fees." This form is posted under "Procedural Forms and Instructions" in the bankruptcy forms section of the Judiciary's' website, at http://www.uscourts.gov/bkforms/. Of course, all the required forms are provided at the back of this book; however, a bankruptcy court may require additional documents by local rule. You may determine what the particular court's requirements are by contacting the clerk's office or by checking the court's local rules. Most court clerks will send you the necessary forms if your petition does not contain every document that particular bankruptcy court requires.

If the schedules and other documents are not prepared and ready to be filed at the same time the petition is filed, Rule 1007(c) allows 14 days for completing and filing most of them. However, Rule 1007 demands that the mailing list, an individual debtor's statement of Social Security Number, and Exhibit D to Official Form B1 (individual Debtor's Statement of Compliance with Credit Counseling Requirement) must accompany the petition. It is best to file all the required documents all at once.

By signing, filing, or submitting a petition, schedule, statement, or other paper with the court, you are certifying—to the best of your knowledge, information and belief, formed after a reasonable investigation under the circumstances—that the petition, schedule, statement, or other paper is not being presented to the court for any improper purpose, such as causing unnecessary delay or to harass. After giving notice and an opportunity to respond, the court may impose sanctions for violations of the rules under 11 U.S.C. §§707(b)(4)(A) and (B), and Federal Rules of Bankruptcy Procedure Rule 9011(c).

Before a bankruptcy case is commenced by you, whose debts are primarily consumer debts (debts incurred by individuals primarily for personal, family, or household purposes, according to 11 U.S.C. §101(8).) the clerk must give you written notice containing a brief description of chapters 7, 11, 12, and 13; the general purpose, costs and benefits of proceeding under each chapter; and a brief description of the types of services available from credit counseling agencies.

11 U.S.C. §342(b) states that the notice also must contain statements informing you that a person who knowingly and fraudulently conceals assets or makes a false statement under penalty of perjury in connection with a bankruptcy case is subject to fines, imprisonment, or both, and that all information supplied by you in connection with a bankruptcy case is subject to examination by the Attorney General.

The signature field for you on Official Form B1 includes a declaration that, although you are filing under chapter 7 as a person with primarily consumer debts, you are aware of your right to proceed under chapter 11, 12, or 13, and aware of the relief available under each chapter. This field also provides for you to declare that you obtained and read the notice given under §342(b) of the Code.

In addition to the petition, lists, schedules, and statements, Rule 1006(a) and 28 U.S.C. §1930(a) require every petition to be accompanied by the filing fee required by law. Other fees have been prescribed in the Bankruptcy Court Miscellaneous Fee Schedule issued in accordance with section 1930(b) of title 28, and some of these also are payable at the time of filing the petition. Rule 1006(b) allows you to file an application to pay the filing fee in installments. If you meet certain eligibility requirements, 28 U.S.C. §1930(f) says you may apply for a waiver of the filing fee 28 U.S.C. §1930(f). An example is provided at the end of this chapter, and a clean copy for your use is provided at the back of this book.

With certain exceptions and limitation set forth in section 362(a) of the Bankruptcy Code, the filing of a petition "operates as a stay, applicable to all entities." This stay takes effect automatically, immediately upon the filing of a petition. The automatic stay essentially places a freeze on the collection of debts incurred before the filing of the petition. Creditors must cease all existing collection activities against you and your property, and they are forbidden from initiating new ones. Section 362(b) provides a list of exceptions to the stay, and other subsections provide additional exceptions and limitations, particularly with respect to expired leases of residential real property and successive cases filed by one debtor or involving a single piece of real property.

It is important to remember that the filing of a bankruptcy case is a public transaction. Per 11 U.S.C. §101 and 107, and 28 U.S.C. §586, the information on file with the court, with the exception of your Social Security Number and tax returns, will remain open to review by any entity, including any person, estate, trust governmental unit, and the United States trustee (an official of the United States Department of Justice). In addition to being available for review in the clerk's office, papers filed in cases also may be viewed over the Internet by subscribers to the federal courts' PACER service and similar services of the local court.

You have a right to amend a voluntary petition as a matter of course at any time before the case is closed. Rule 1009 (a) requires you to give notice of any amendment to the trustee and to any entity affected by the amendment.

Directions for Preparing Petition

While preparing your petition, you should refer to the example provided at the end of this chapter.

United States Bankruptcy Court

You must identify the judicial district in which you intend to file the petition. The example was filed in the Western District of Missouri. To find the name and address of your judicial district, you may refer to the local telephone directory, which should have a listing under "United States Government." Alternatively, ask the law clerk at your institution. If you have such resources, have a friend or family member use the court locator at http://www.uscourts.gov/courtlinks/. The locator can search for bankruptcy courts by zip code, city and state, judicial circuit, county and state, or area code. It can also search nationwide. The counties which comprise each federal judicial district are set out in sections 81 through 131 of title 28 of the United States Code. Your institutional law library should contain a directory. After checking, if you are still uncertain about the correct district or the correct name of the district, you should verify with the bankruptcy court clerk's office in your area before proceeding.

Names/Identification Numbers

Rule 1005 requires you to include your "name, employer identification number [if any], last four digits of the Social Security Number, any other individual-taxpayer identification number, and all other names used" within the eight years prior to filing the petition. Examples of other names used by you include trade names, names used in doing business, former married name(s), and maiden name (if used within the eight years prior to filing the petition). These should be stated in the space provided. If there is not sufficient room for all such names on the form, you will need to list them on a separate sheet of paper and attach it to your petition. Your name should also be placed at the top of the second and third pages of Official Form B1. (See example petition.)

Separate spaces are provided for the name, address, and other information of joint debtors filing bankruptcy together in a joint case. Only a husband and wife may file a joint bankruptcy case, per 11 U.S.C. §302. If the bankruptcy case is filed by one person, a corporation, or a partnership, the "joint debtor" spaces on the petition should be left blank.

Complete information helps creditors to (1) correctly identify the debtor when they receive notices and orders from the court, (2) comply with the automatic stay, (3) file a proof of claim, and (4) exercise other rights given to them by the Bankruptcy Code. It is important to make sure that all creditors know about the bankruptcy proceeding and are allowed to exercise their rights in the case. A debt owed to a creditor who is not given proper notice of the bankruptcy may not be discharged or forgiven, and you may continue to be liable for payment of that debt despite having completed your bankruptcy case. Therefore, it is essential to provide not only your current legal name(s) but all name(s) used by you and any joint debtor during the previous eight-year period.

Addresses/Locations of Principal Assets

This form requires both a street address and any separate mailing addresses used by you, as well as any separate addresses used by a joint debtor. Thus, you must include the complete street address (and mailing address, if different) in the appropriate boxes. You must state the county of your residence in the box provided.

Type of Debtor

A debtor can be an individual (which includes both individuals in a joint case), a corporation (including LLCs and LLPs), or a partnership. You must check one box. If you do not fit into any of the categories listed, a box labeled "other" is provided, together with a space in which to state the type of entity. Being incarcerated, you should check the first box.

Nature of Business/Tax-Exempt Entity

Being incarcerated, you should check the "other" box.

Chapter of Bankruptcy Code Under Which the Petition is Filed

11 U.S.C. §109(h) says that only a person, ("person" is defined by section 101 of the Bankruptcy Code as including an individual, partnership, or corporation) that resides or has a domicile, place of business, or property in the United States, or is a municipality, may be a debtor in a bankruptcy case. Section 109 describes additional eligibility requirements for individual debtors as well as the specific requirements for filing under various chapters. To be eligible under any chapter, you must obtain a briefing from an approved nonprofit budget and credit counseling agency within the 180 days prior to your filing of the petition. Section 109(h) contains certain very narrow exceptions to this requirement. When a case is filed under a particular chapter, various rights and duties arise for both you and your creditors. Although the case can be converted to another chapter later in the proceeding, it is important to file under the chapter that best suits your needs and under which you are legally eligible to file. A brief summary of the requirements of each chapter follows.

Chapter 7: A person (individual, partnership, or corporation, but not a governmental unit) may be a debtor under chapter 7 only if that person is not a railroad, insurance company, bank, small-business investment company, credit union, or certain similar entity, as specified in §109(b) of the Code. Stockbrokers and commodity brokers can file only under this chapter, which contains special provisions governing their cases. Special provisions also apply to "health care business" debtors, as defined in section 101 (27A) of the Code.

Chapter 9: Only a municipality or municipal corporation authorized by state law to file bankruptcy may be a debtor under chapter 9, according to 11 U.S.C. §109(c).

Chapter 11: 11 U.S.C. §109(d) states that only a debtor under chapter 7 (but not a stockbroker or commodity broker), or a railroad, may be a debtor under chapter 11.

Chapter 12: 11 U.S.C. §109(f) dictates that only a "family farmer," as defined in §101(18), or a "family fisherman," as defined in section 101(19A), with regular annual income may be a debtor under chapter 12.

Chapter 13: Relief under chapter 13 is limited to an individual, or individual and spouse, with regular income, whose debts on the date of filing petition are within the monetary limit set forth in §109(e) of the Bankruptcy Code. These dollar limits are adjusted for inflation every three years according to a formula prescribed in §104(a) of the Code.

In August 2009, those limits were $336,900 for unsecured debts (i.e., debts for which a creditor does not have a lien, or, if the property on which a creditor had a lien is not worth enough to pay the creditor in full, that portion of the debt which exceeds the value of any pledged property [collateral] and $1,010,650 for secured debts (i.e., those for which a creditor has a lien on property of the debtor [collateral] that gives the creditor the right to be paid from that property before creditors without a lien on the property). Examples of unsecured debts are credit card bills and unpaid doctor bills. Example of secured debts are the mortgage on a debtor's house and the loan that finances the purchase of the debtor's automobile. If the debt(s) or account(s) is/are contingent or unliquidated, chapter 13 may be available even to a debtor whose creditors assert that the debtor owes amounts higher than the limits set forth in the Code. (A claim is contingent if the debtor's liability depends on the occurrence of a certain event, such as where the debtor is a cosigner on another person's loan who fails to pay. A claim is unliquidated when the amount owed has not been determined.)

Chapter 15: According to 11 U.S.C. §1504, a case under chapter 15 is commenced when a "foreign representative" files a petition for recognition of a "foreign proceeding." (Definitions of these terns are defined in section 1502 of the Code.) The type of foreign proceeding affects the authority that the foreign representative can exercise later. Accordingly, the foreign representative must specify whether the foreign proceeding is "main" or "nonmain." Once a court in the United States has granted recognition of the foreign proceeding, the foreign representative of a foreign main proceeding may file a voluntary case for the debtor under any other chapter for which the debtor is eligible.

For the purposes of an incarcerated individual with consumer debts, the checkbox for chapter 7 should be marked.

Nature of Debts

Depending on the circumstances of the case, you should indicate whether the debts are primarily consumer debts or primarily business debts. A consumer debt is defined in section 101(8) of the Bankruptcy Code as a debt incurred by someone primarily for a personal, family, or household purpose. A business debt is one incurred to start or continue a business or profession. Even in a case filed by an individual or married couple, if a debt is primarily related to the operation of a business, the debtor should check the box marked "Business." Being incarcerated, most debts you have incurred will likely be consumer debts; therefore, you should check the box marked "Consumer Debts."

Filing Fees

Starting a bankruptcy case requires the payment of filing fees. Fees for a chapter 7 include the $245 filing fee, a $39 administrative fee, and a $15 trustee surcharge, for a total fee of $299.*

Section 1930(a)(7) permits an individual debtor to pay the filing fees in installments. Section 1930(f) authorizes the court to waive a debtor's filing fees if the court determines that the debtor meets the criteria set forth in §1930(f). This criteria is not difficult to meet for incarcerated debtors.

With respect to paying the fees in installments, the rule limits the number of installments to a maximum of four, with the final installment due not later than 120 days after the filing of the petition. The court can extend the time for paying any installment, but you must file a motion explaining the reason an extension is needed. In any case, the last installment must be paid not later than 180 days after the filing of the petition.

---

*   Current fees may vary

With respect to waiving the fees, section 1930(f) sets a ceiling on your income to be eligible for a waiver. If you receive less than $50 a month, you most likely meet the eligibility requirement. By law, the judge may waive the fees only if your income is less than 150 percent of the official poverty line applicable to your family size and you are unable to pay the fees in installments. If you are uncertain, you may obtain information about the poverty guidelines at www.uscourts.gov or from the bankruptcy clerk in your district.

To pay the fees in installments, Official Form B3A must be completed and filed with the petition. To apply for a waiver of the filing fees, Official Form B3B must be completed and filed with the petition. Copies of Forms B3A and B3B are provided at the back of the book. Examples are also provided at the end of this chapter.

Check the appropriate box on your petition to indicate if the fees are being paid, or if an application to pay in installments or to waive the fees is being filed.

Chapter 11 Debtor

You will leave this field blank because you are filing under chapter 7.

Statistical/Administrative Information

This section requests that you predict whether funds will be available for distribution to unsecured creditors by checking one of the two boxes provided. On the basis of this estimate, the clerk may notify creditors in a chapter 7 case that it appears there are no assets from which they may be paid, and it is not necessary for them to file claims unless later notified by the clerk to do so, as per Rules 2002(e) and 3002(c)(5).

You are also asked to indicate in the boxes provided the estimated number of creditors, amount of assets, and amount of liabilities. This information is used by the clerk to complete statistical reports that are required by law and to advise the court on what to expect from the case, in terms of size and judicial time.

Prior Bankruptcy Case Filed within Last 8 Years

A chapter 7 discharge order eliminates your legal obligation to pay any debts (with some exceptions) that existed on the date your bankruptcy case was filed. Under Section 72(a)(8) of the Bankruptcy Code, you are not entitled to a chapter 7 discharge if you were granted a discharge in a chapter 7 or 11 case that began within 8 years prior to the beginning of the current case.

If you've never filed for bankruptcy, just write or type "N/A," as in the example.

Pending Bankruptcy Case Filed by Any Spouse, Partner or Affiliate of This Debtor

Information about any pending bankruptcy cases related to your case signals the clerk to assign the case to the judge to whom any such related case has been assigned. You should report the name of any spouse, partner, or affiliate who has a pending case (one that has not been closed) under the heading "Name of Debtor." You should include that case number, the date that petition was filed, your relationship with that case, the district where that case is pending, and that judge assigned to the case in the spaces provided.

If none of this applies to your situation, simply write or type "N/A."

Exhibit A

You are only required to complete and file Exhibit A if you are a corporation requesting relief under chapter 11. Leave this field blank.

Exhibit B

Leave the Exhibit B field blank also, unless you're represented by an attorney.

Exhibit C

Exhibit C requires you to disclose whether you own or have possession of any property that poses or is alleged to pose a threat of imminent and identifiable harm to public health or safety. You must check the box marked "Yes" or "No" according to the facts of your case. If any such property exists, you must complete and attach Exhibit C describing the property, its location, and any potential danger it poses. Checking "Yes" will alert the United States trustee and any person selected as trustee in your case that immediate precautionary action may be necessary.

Exhibit D

You must receive a briefing from an approved nonprofit budget- and credit-counseling agency within 180 days prior to filing your bankruptcy case. Refer to chapter 2 of this book if you have not complied with this requirement.

Rule 1007(b)(3) requires you to complete and file a statement concerning compliance with the credit counseling requirement. You make the required statement by checking one of the five statements on Exhibit D to Official Form B1. Each spouse in a joint case must complete a separate Exhibit D. The form for Exhibit D includes a warning about the requirement to obtain counseling and the consequences of failing to fulfill this requirement. It further provides checkboxes and instructions concerning the additional documents that are required in particular circumstances, in order to minimize the number of cases the court must dismiss for ineligibility. If you have received the required counseling, you should check the first box and file copies of the certificate from the credit counseling agency, along with any debt repayment plan developed through the agency, with Exhibit D. If you have received the counseling but have not yet received the certificate from the agency, you should check the second box and file copies of the certificate and any debt repayment plan within 14 days. If exigent circumstances or one of the other limited exceptions set out in section 109(h)(2) and (h)(4) applies to you, you should check the appropriate box and follow the instructions in that box.

Information Regarding the Debtor—Venue

You should file your bankruptcy case in the federal judicial district that governs the correctional center at which you have been incarcerated for at least 180 days. Check the first box.

Statement by a Debtor Who Resides as a Tenant of Residential Property

Being incarcerated, you should leave this section blank.

Signatures

The signature page of the form is where you request relief in accordance with the chapter of the Bankruptcy Code specified on the first page of the petition. Signing indicates to the court that you, in fact, are requesting relief under the Bankruptcy Code. Signing and filing a petition makes it a legally effective document. In addition, by signing the petition, you are declaring, under the penalty of perjury, that the information in the petition is true and correct. (See 28 U.S.C. §1746 and Federal "Rules of Bankruptcy Procedure Rule 1008 for more information.)

You must sign the petition in the appropriate signature field on page 3, you should sign in the "Individual/Joint" section.

Signature of Attorney

Unless you are represented by an attorney, you should leave this section blank.

Signature of a Foreign Representative

You should leave this section blank unless it applies to your situation.

Signature of Non-Attorney Bankruptcy Petition Preparer

Being incarcerated, you most likely are preparing your own petition; therefore, you should leave this section blank.

PREPARATION OF BANKRUPTCY PETITION

Example Voluntary Petition

B1 (Official Form 1) (4/10)

UNITED STATES BANKRUPTCY COURT Western District of Missouri	VOLUNTARY PETITION

Name of Debtor (if individual, enter Last, First, Middle): Smith, Zachary, Adrian	Name of Joint Debtor (Spouse) (Last, First, Middle):
All Other Names used by the Debtor in the last 8 years (include married, maiden, and trade names): N/A	All Other Names used by the Joint Debtor in the last 8 years (include married, maiden, and trade names):
Last four digits of Soc. Sec. or Individual-Taxpayer I.D. (ITIN)/Complete EIN (if more than one, state all): XXX-XX-1234	Last four digits of Soc. Sec. or Individual-Taxpayer I.D. (ITIN)/Complete EIN (if more than one, state all):
Street Address of Debtor (No. and Street, City, and State): Crossroads Corr. Center 1115 East Pence Road Cameron, MO 64429 ZIP CODE	Street Address of Joint Debtor (No. and Street, City, and State): ZIP CODE
County of Residence or of the Principal Place of Business: Dekalb County	County of Residence or of the Principal Place of Business:
Mailing Address of Debtor (if different from street address): Same as above ZIP CODE	Mailing Address of Joint Debtor (if different from street address): ZIP CODE
Location of Principal Assets of Business Debtor (if different from street address above): Same as above ZIP CODE	

Type of Debtor (Form of Organization) (Check one box.)
- [X] Individual (includes Joint Debtors) *See Exhibit D on page 2 of this form.*
- [ ] Corporation (includes LLC and LLP)
- [ ] Partnership
- [ ] Other (If debtor is not one of the above entities, check this box and state type of entity below.)

Nature of Business (Check one box.)
- [ ] Health Care Business
- [ ] Single Asset Real Estate as defined in 11 U.S.C. § 101(51B)
- [ ] Railroad
- [ ] Stockbroker
- [ ] Commodity Broker
- [ ] Clearing Bank
- [X] Other

Tax-Exempt Entity (Check box, if applicable.)
- [ ] Debtor is a tax-exempt organization under Title 26 of the United States Code (the Internal Revenue Code).

Chapter of Bankruptcy Code Under Which the Petition is Filed (Check one box.)
- [X] Chapter 7
- [ ] Chapter 9
- [ ] Chapter 11
- [ ] Chapter 12
- [ ] Chapter 13
- [ ] Chapter 15 Petition for Recognition of a Foreign Main Proceeding
- [ ] Chapter 15 Petition for Recognition of a Foreign Nonmain Proceeding

Nature of Debts (Check one box.)
- [X] Debts are primarily consumer debts, defined in 11 U.S.C. § 101(8) as "incurred by an individual primarily for a personal, family, or household purpose."
- [ ] Debts are primarily business debts.

Filing Fee (Check one box.)
- [ ] Full Filing Fee attached.
- [ ] Filing Fee to be paid in installments (applicable to individuals only). Must attach signed application for the court's consideration certifying that the debtor is unable to pay fee except in installments. Rule 1006(b). See Official Form 3A.
- [X] Filing Fee waiver requested (applicable to chapter 7 individuals only). Must attach signed application for the court's consideration. See Official Form 3B.

Chapter 11 Debtors
Check one box:
- [ ] Debtor is a small business debtor as defined in 11 U.S.C. § 101(51D).
- [ ] Debtor is not a small business debtor as defined in 11 U.S.C. § 101(51D).

Check if:
- [ ] Debtor's aggregate noncontingent liquidated debts (excluding debts owed to insiders or affiliates) are less than $2,343,300 (*amount subject to adjustment on 4/01/13 and every three years thereafter*).

Check all applicable boxes:
- [ ] A plan is being filed with this petition.
- [ ] Acceptances of the plan were solicited prepetition from one or more classes of creditors, in accordance with 11 U.S.C. § 1126(b).

Statistical/Administrative Information
- [ ] Debtor estimates that funds will be available for distribution to unsecured creditors.
- [X] Debtor estimates that, after any exempt property is excluded and administrative expenses paid, there will be no funds available for distribution to unsecured creditors.

THIS SPACE IS FOR COURT USE ONLY

Estimated Number of Creditors

[X] 1-49	[ ] 50-99	[ ] 100-199	[ ] 200-999	[ ] 1,000-5,000	[ ] 5,001-10,000	[ ] 10,001-25,000	[ ] 25,001-50,000	[ ] 50,001-100,000	[ ] Over 100,000

Estimated Assets

[X] $0 to $50,000	[ ] $50,001 to $100,000	[ ] $100,001 to $500,000	[ ] $500,001 to $1 million	[ ] $1,000,001 to $10 million	[ ] $10,000,001 to $50 million	[ ] $50,000,001 to $100 million	[ ] $100,000,001 to $500 million	[ ] $500,000,001 to $1 billion	[ ] More than $1 billion

Estimated Liabilities

[ ] $0 to $50,000	[ ] $50,001 to $100,000	[X] $100,001 to $500,000	[ ] $500,001 to $1 million	[ ] $1,000,001 to $10 million	[ ] $10,000,001 to $50 million	[ ] $50,000,001 to $100 million	[ ] $100,000,001 to $500 million	[ ] $500,000,001 to $1 billion	[ ] More than $1 billion

Example Voluntary Petition (cont.)

B1 (Official Form 1) (4/10)   Page 2

Voluntary Petition *(This page must be completed and filed in every case.)*	Name of Debtor(s): Smith, Zachary, Adrian

All Prior Bankruptcy Cases Filed Within Last 8 Years (If more than two, attach additional sheet.)

Location Where Filed: N/A	Case Number:	Date Filed:
Location Where Filed: N/A	Case Number:	Date Filed:

Pending Bankruptcy Case Filed by any Spouse, Partner, or Affiliate of this Debtor (If more than one, attach additional sheet.)

Name of Debtor: N/A	Case Number:	Date Filed:
District: N/A	Relationship:	Judge:

Exhibit A	Exhibit B (To be completed if debtor is an individual whose debts are primarily consumer debts.)
(To be completed if debtor is required to file periodic reports (e.g., forms 10K and 10Q) with the Securities and Exchange Commission pursuant to Section 13 or 15(d) of the Securities Exchange Act of 1934 and is requesting relief under chapter 11.) ☐ Exhibit A is attached and made a part of this petition.	I, the attorney for the petitioner named in the foregoing petition, declare that I have informed the petitioner that [he or she] may proceed under chapter 7, 11, 12, or 13 of title 11, United States Code, and have explained the relief available under each such chapter. I further certify that I have delivered to the debtor the notice required by 11 U.S.C. § 342(b). X _____ Signature of Attorney for Debtor(s) (Date)

Exhibit C

Does the debtor own or have possession of any property that poses or is alleged to pose a threat of imminent and identifiable harm to public health or safety?

☐   Yes, and Exhibit C is attached and made a part of this petition.

☒   No.

Exhibit D

(To be completed by every individual debtor. If a joint petition is filed, each spouse must complete and attach a separate Exhibit D.)

☒   Exhibit D completed and signed by the debtor is attached and made a part of this petition.

If this is a joint petition:

☐   Exhibit D also completed and signed by the joint debtor is attached and made a part of this petition.

Information Regarding the Debtor - Venue
(Check any applicable box.)

☒   Debtor has been domiciled or has had a residence, principal place of business, or principal assets in this District for 180 days immediately preceding the date of this petition or for a longer part of such 180 days than in any other District.

☐   There is a bankruptcy case concerning debtor's affiliate, general partner, or partnership pending in this District.

☐   Debtor is a debtor in a foreign proceeding and has its principal place of business or principal assets in the United States in this District, or has no principal place of business or assets in the United States but is a defendant in an action or proceeding [in a federal or state court] in this District, or the interests of the parties will be served in regard to the relief sought in this District.

Certification by a Debtor Who Resides as a Tenant of Residential Property
(Check all applicable boxes.)

☐   Landlord has a judgment against the debtor for possession of debtor's residence. (If box checked, complete the following.)

_____
(Name of landlord that obtained judgment)

_____
(Address of landlord)

☐   Debtor claims that under applicable nonbankruptcy law, there are circumstances under which the debtor would be permitted to cure the entire monetary default that gave rise to the judgment for possession, after the judgment for possession was entered, and

☐   Debtor has included with this petition the deposit with the court of any rent that would become due during the 30-day period after the filing of the petition.

☐   Debtor certifies that he/she has served the Landlord with this certification. (11 U.S.C. § 362(l)).

Example Voluntary Petition (cont.)

B1 (Official Form) 1 (4/10)	Page 3

Voluntary Petition *(This page must be completed and filed in every case.)*	Name of Debtor(s): Smith, Zachary, Adrian

Signatures

Signature(s) of Debtor(s) (Individual/Joint)	Signature of a Foreign Representative

I declare under penalty of perjury that the information provided in this petition is true and correct.
[If petitioner is an individual whose debts are primarily consumer debts and has chosen to file under chapter 7] I am aware that I may proceed under chapter 7, 11, 12 or 13 of title 11, United States Code, understand the relief available under each such chapter, and choose to proceed under chapter 7.
[If no attorney represents me and no bankruptcy petition preparer signs the petition] I have obtained and read the notice required by 11 U.S.C. § 342(b).
 	
I request relief in accordance with the chapter of title 11, United States Code, specified in this petition.
 	
Zachary Adrian Smith
X _____
  Signature of Debtor
 	
X _____
  Signature of Joint Debtor
 	
  Telephone Number (if not represented by attorney)
  N/A
  Date X-XX-XXXX
	I declare under penalty of perjury that the information provided in this petition is true and correct, that I am the foreign representative of a debtor in a foreign proceeding, and that I am authorized to file this petition.
	
	(Check only one box.)
	
	☐ I request relief in accordance with chapter 15 of title 11, United States Code. Certified copies of the documents required by 11 U.S.C. § 1515 are attached.
	
	☐ Pursuant to 11 U.S.C. § 1511, I request relief in accordance with the chapter of title 11 specified in this petition. A certified copy of the order granting recognition of the foreign main proceeding is attached.
	
	X _____
	  (Signature of Foreign Representative)
	
	_____
	  (Printed Name of Foreign Representative)
	
	_____
	  Date

Signature of Attorney*	Signature of Non-Attorney Bankruptcy Petition Preparer

X _____
  Signature of Attorney for Debtor(s)
 	
  Printed Name of Attorney for Debtor(s)
 	
  Firm Name
 	
_____
_____
  Address
 	
  Telephone Number
 	
  Date
 	
*In a case in which § 707(b)(4)(D) applies, this signature also constitutes a certification that the attorney has no knowledge after an inquiry that the information in the schedules is incorrect.
	I declare under penalty of perjury that: (1) I am a bankruptcy petition preparer as defined in 11 U.S.C. § 110; (2) I prepared this document for compensation and have provided the debtor with a copy of this document and the notices and information required under 11 U.S.C. §§ 110(b), 110(h), and 342(b); and, (3) if rules or guidelines have been promulgated pursuant to 11 U.S.C. § 110(h) setting a maximum fee for services chargeable by bankruptcy petition preparers, I have given the debtor notice of the maximum amount before preparing any document for filing for a debtor or accepting any fee from the debtor, as required in that section. Official Form 19 is attached.
	
	_____
	  Printed Name and title, if any, of Bankruptcy Petition Preparer
	
	  Social-Security number (If the bankruptcy petition preparer is not an individual, state the Social-Security number of the officer, principal, responsible person or partner of the bankruptcy petition preparer.) (Required by 11 U.S.C. § 110.)

Signature of Debtor (Corporation/Partnership)	

I declare under penalty of perjury that the information provided in this petition is true and correct, and that I have been authorized to file this petition on behalf of the debtor.
 	
The debtor requests the relief in accordance with the chapter of title 11, United States Code, specified in this petition.
 	
X _____
  Signature of Authorized Individual
 	
  Printed Name of Authorized Individual
 	
  Title of Authorized Individual
 	
  Date
	_____
	  Address
	X _____
	
	_____
	  Date
	
	Signature of bankruptcy petition preparer or officer, principal, responsible person, or partner whose Social-Security number is provided above.
	
	Names and Social-Security numbers of all other individuals who prepared or assisted in preparing this document unless the bankruptcy petition preparer is not an individual.
	
	If more than one person prepared this document, attach additional sheets conforming to the appropriate official form for each person.
	
	A bankruptcy petition preparer's failure to comply with the provisions of title 11 and the Federal Rules of Bankruptcy Procedure may result in fines or imprisonment or both. 11 U.S.C. § 110; 18 U.S.C. § 156.

Instruction for Waiver of Filing Fee

B 3B (Official Form 3B) (12/07)

APPLICATION FOR WAIVER OF THE CHAPTER 7 FILING FEE
FOR INDIVIDUALS WHO CANNOT PAY THE FILING FEE
IN FULL OR IN INSTALLMENTS

The court fee for filing a case under chapter 7 of the Bankruptcy Code is $299.

If you cannot afford to pay the full fee at the time of filing, you may apply to pay the fee in installments. A form, which is available from the bankruptcy clerk's office, must be completed to make that application. If your application to pay in installments is approved, you will be permitted to file your petition, generally completing payment of the fee over the course of four to six months.

If you cannot afford to pay the fee either in full at the time of filing or in installments, you may request a waiver of the filing fee by completing this application and filing it with the Clerk of Court. A judge will decide whether you have to pay the fee. By law, the judge may waive the fee only if your income is less than 150 percent of the official poverty line applicable to your family size and you are unable to pay the fee in installments. You may obtain information about the poverty guidelines at www.uscourts.gov or in the bankruptcy clerk's office.

Required information. Complete all items in the application, and attach requested schedules. Then sign the application on the last page. If you and your spouse are filing a joint bankruptcy petition, you both must provide information as requested and sign the application.

Example Application to Pay Filing Fee in Installments

B 3A (Official Form 3A) (12/07)

UNITED STATES BANKRUPTCY COURT

In re ___Zachary Adrian Smith___ ,   Case No. _____
          Debtor

Chapter ___7___

APPLICATION TO PAY FILING FEE IN INSTALLMENTS

1. In accordance with Fed. R. Bankr. P. 1006, I apply for permission to pay the filing fee amounting to $ __74.75__ in installments.

2. I am unable to pay the filing fee except in installments.

3. Until the filing fee is paid in full, I will not make any additional payment or transfer any additional property to an attorney or any other person for services in connection with this case.

4. I propose the following terms for the payment of the Filing Fee.*

    $ __74.75__   Check one ☒   With the filing of the petition, or
                                       ☐   On or before _____

    $ __74.75__   on or before __XX-XX-XX__

    $ __74.75__   on or before __XX-XX-XX__

    $ __74.75__   on or before __XX-XX-XX__

*   The number of installments proposed shall not exceed four (4), and the final installment shall be payable not later than 120 days after filing the petition. For cause shown, the court may extend the time of any installment, provided the last installment is paid not later than 180 days after filing the petition. Fed. R. Bankr. P. 1006(b)(2).

5. I understand that if I fail to pay any installment when due, my bankruptcy case may be dismissed and I may not receive a discharge of my debts.

                                         Zachary A. Smith   XX-XX-XX

_____   _____
Signature of Attorney   Date   Signature of Debtor   Date
                                         (In a joint case, both spouses must sign.)

Name of Attorney   _____
                                         Signature of Joint Debtor (if any)   Date

---

DECLARATION AND SIGNATURE OF NON-ATTORNEY BANKRUPTCY PETITION PREPARER (See 11 U.S.C. § 110)

    I declare under penalty of perjury that: (1) I am a bankruptcy petition preparer as defined in 11 U.S.C. § 110; (2) I prepared this document for compensation and have provided the debtor with a copy of this document and the notices and information required under 11 U.S.C. §§ 110(b), 110(h), and 342(b); (3) if rules or guidelines have been promulgated pursuant to 11 U.S.C. § 110(h) setting a maximum fee for services chargeable by bankruptcy petition preparers, I have given the debtor notice of the maximum amount before preparing any document for filing for a debtor or accepting any fee from the debtor, as required under that section; and (4) I will not accept any additional money or other property from the debtor before the filing fee is paid in full.

_____   _____
Printed or Typed Name and Title, if any, of Bankruptcy Petition Preparer   Social-Security No. (Required by 11 U.S.C. § 110.)
If the bankruptcy petition preparer is not an individual, state the name, title (if any), address, and social-security number of the officer, principal, responsible person, or partner who signs the document.

_____

Address

x_____   _____
Signature of Bankruptcy Petition Preparer   Date

Names and Social-Security numbers of all other individuals who prepared or assisted in preparing this document, unless the bankruptcy petition preparer is not an individual:

If more than one person prepared this document, attach additional signed sheets conforming to the appropriate Official Form for each person.
A bankruptcy petition preparer's failure to comply with the provisions of title 11 and the Federal Rules of Bankruptcy Procedure may result in fines or imprisonment or both. 11 U.S.C. § 110; 18 U.S.C. § 156.

Example Order Approving Payment of Filing Fee in Installments

B 3A (Official Form 3A) (12/07) - Cont.

UNITED STATES BANKRUPTCY COURT

In re Zachary Adrian Smith   ,   Case No. 10-50921-jwv7
           Debtor

Chapter   7

ORDER APPROVING PAYMENT OF FILING FEE IN INSTALLMENTS

☒   IT IS ORDERED that the debtor(s) may pay the filing fee in installments on the terms proposed in the foregoing application.

☒   IT IS ORDERED that the debtor(s) shall pay the filing fee according to the following terms:

$ __74.75__   Check one ☑ With the filing of the petition, or
                         ☐ On or before _____

$ __74.75__   on or before XX-XX-XX _____

$ __74.75__   on or before XX-XX-XX _____

$ __74.75__   on or before XX-XX-XX _____

☒   IT IS FURTHER ORDERED that until the filing fee is paid in full the debtor(s) shall not make any additional payment or transfer any additional property to an attorney or any other person for services in connection with this case.

BY THE COURT

Date: __XX-XX-XX__   /s/ Jerry W. Venters _____
                                 United States Bankruptcy Judge

Example Application for Waiver of Filing Fee

B 3B (Official Form 3B) (12/07) -- Cont.

UNITED STATES BANKRUPTCY COURT

In re: Zachary Adrian Smith   Case No. _____
              Debtor(s)   (if known)

APPLICATION FOR WAIVER OF THE CHAPTER 7 FILING FEE
FOR INDIVIDUALS WHO CANNOT PAY THE FILING FEE IN FULL OR IN INSTALLMENTS

Part A. Family Size and Income

1. Including yourself, your spouse, and dependents you have listed or will list on Schedule I (Current Income of Individual Debtors(s)), how many people are in your family? (Do not include your spouse if you are separated AND are not filing a joint petition.) ___1___

2. Restate the following information that you provided, or will provide, on Line 16 of Schedule I. Attach a completed copy of Schedule I, if it is available.

    Total Combined Monthly Income (Line 16 of Schedule I): $ 8.50 _____

3. State the monthly net income, if any, of dependents included in Question 1 above. Do not include any income already reported in Item 2. If none, enter $0.

                                                                          $ 0 _____

4. Add the "Total Combined Monthly Income" reported in Question 2 to your dependents' monthly net income from Question 3.

                                                                          $ 8.50 _____

5. Do you expect the amount in Question 4 to increase or decrease by more than 10% during the next 6 months? Yes ___ No X__

    If yes, explain.

Part B. Monthly Expenses

6. EITHER (a) attach a completed copy of Schedule J (Schedule of Monthly Expenses), and state your total monthly expenses reported on Line 18 of that Schedule, OR (b) if you have not yet completed Schedule J, provide an estimate of your total monthly expenses.

                                                                 $ 8.50 _____

7. Do you expect the amount in Question 6 to increase or decrease by more than 10% during the next 6 months? Yes ___ No _X_
    If yes, explain.

Part C. Real and Personal Property

EITHER (1) attach completed copies of Schedule A (Real Property) and Schedule B (Personal Property), OR (2) if you have not yet completed those schedules, answer the following questions.

8. State the amount of cash you have on hand. $ 8.50 _____

9. State below any money you have in savings, checking, or other accounts in a bank or other financial institution.

Bank or Other Financial Institution:	Type of Account such as savings, checking, CD:	Amount:
Inmate account	Inmate acount	$ 8.50
_____	_____	$ _____

Example Application for Waiver of Filing Fee (cont.)

B 3B (Official Form 3B) (12/07) -- Cont.

10. State below the assets owned by you. **Do not list ordinary household furnishings and clothing.**

Home	Address: N/A _____	Value: $ _____ Amount owed on mortgages and liens: $ _____
Other real estate	Address: N/A _____ _____	Value: $ _____ Amount owed on mortgages and liens: $ _____
Motor vehicle	Model/Year: N/A _____ _____	Value: $ _____ Amount owed: $ _____
Motor vehicle	Model/Year: N/A _____ _____	Value: $ _____ Amount owed: $ _____
Other	Description_____ N/A _____ _____	Value: $ _____ Amount owed: $ _____

11. State below any person, business, organization, or governmental unit that owes you money and the amount that is owed.

Name of Person, Business, or Organization that Owes You Money	Amount Owed
N/A _____	$ _____
_____	$ _____

Part D. Additional Information.

12. Have you paid an **attorney** any money for services in connection with this case, including the completion of this form, the bankruptcy petition, or schedules? Yes ___ No _X_
If yes, how much have you paid? $ _____

13. Have you promised to pay or do you anticipate paying an **attorney** in connection with your bankruptcy case? Yes ___ No _x_
If yes, how much have you promised to pay or do you anticipate paying? $ _____

14. Have you paid **anyone other than an attorney** (such as a bankruptcy petition preparer, paralegal, typing service, or another person) any money for services in connection with this case, including the completion of this form, the bankruptcy petition, or schedules? Yes ___ No _X_
If yes, how much have you paid? $ _____

15. Have you promised to pay or do you anticipate paying **anyone other than an attorney** (such as a bankruptcy petition preparer, paralegal, typing service, or another person) any money for services in connection with this case, including the completion of this form, the bankruptcy petition, or schedules?
Yes ___ No _X_
If yes, how much have you promised to pay or do you anticipate paying? $ _____

16. Has anyone paid an attorney or other person or service in connection with this case, on your behalf?
Yes ___ No _X_

   If yes, explain.

Example Application for Waiver of Filing Fee (cont.)

B 3B (Official Form 3B) (12/07) -- Cont.

17. Have you previously filed for bankruptcy relief during the past eight years? Yes ___ No X__

Case Number (if known)	Year filed	Location of filing	Did you obtain a discharge? (if known)
_____	_____	_____	Yes ____ No ____ Don't know ____
_____	_____	_____	Yes ____ No ____ Don't know ____

18. Please provide any other information that helps to explain why you are unable to pay the filing fee in installments.

    I am incarcerated and only receive $8.50 a month from the Missouri Department of Corrections.

19. I (we) declare under penalty of perjury that I (we) cannot currently afford to pay the filing fee in full or in installments and that the foregoing information is true and correct.

Executed on: ___X-XX-XXXX_____   ___Zachary Adrian Smith___
                  Date   Signature of Debtor

             _____   _____
                  Date   Signature of Codebtor

DECLARATION AND SIGNATURE OF BANKRUPTCY PETITION PREPARER (See 11 U.S.C. § 110)

I declare under penalty of perjury that: (1) I am a bankruptcy petition preparer as defined in 11 U.S.C. § 110; (2) I prepared this document for compensation and have provided the debtor with a copy of this document and the notices and information required under 11 U.S.C. §§ 110(b), 110(h), and 342(b); and (3) if rules or guidelines have been promulgated pursuant to 11 U.S.C. § 110(h) setting a maximum fee for services chargeable by bankruptcy petition preparers, I have given the debtor notice of the maximum amount before preparing any document for filing for a debtor or accepting any fee from the debtor, as required under that section.

_____   _____
Printed or Typed Name and Title, if any, of Bankruptcy Petition Preparer   Social-Security No. (Required by
                                                                                  11 U.S.C. §110.)
If the bankruptcy petition preparer is not an individual, state the name, title (if any), address, and social-security number of the officer, principal, responsible person, or partner who signs the document.

_____

_____
Address

x_____   _____
Signature of Bankruptcy Petition Preparer   Date

Names and Social-Security numbers of all other individuals who prepared or assisted in preparing this document, unless the bankruptcy petition preparer is not an individual:

If more than one person prepared this document, attach additional signed sheets conforming to the appropriate Official Form for each person.
A bankruptcy petition preparer's failure to comply with the provisions of title 11 and the Federal Rules of Bankruptcy Procedure may result in fines or imprisonment or both. 11 U.S.C. § 110; 18 U.S.C. § 156.

Example Order Granting Waiver of Filing Fee

B 3B (Official Form 3B) (12/07) -- Cont.

UNITED STATES BANKRUPTCY COURT

In re: <u>Zachary Adrian Smith</u>   Case No. <u>10-50921-jwv7</u>
Debtor(s)

ORDER ON DEBTOR'S APPLICATION FOR WAIVER OF THE CHAPTER 7 FILING FEE

Upon consideration of the debtor's "Application for Waiver of the Chapter 7 Filing Fee," the court orders that the application be:

[x] GRANTED.

> This order is subject to being vacated at a later time if developments in the administration of the bankruptcy case demonstrate that the waiver was unwarranted.

[ ] DENIED.

> The debtor shall pay the chapter 7 filing fee according to the following terms:
>
> $ _____ on or before _____
>
> $ _____ on or before _____
>
> $ _____ on or before _____
>
> $ _____ on or before _____
>
> Until the filing fee is paid in full, the debtor shall not make any additional payment or transfer any additional property to an attorney or any other person for services in connection with this case.
>
> IF THE DEBTOR FAILS TO TIMELY PAY THE FILING FEE IN FULL OR TO TIMELY MAKE INSTALLMENT PAYMENTS, THE COURT MAY DISMISS THE DEBTOR'S CASE.

[ ] SCHEDULED FOR HEARING.

> A hearing to consider the debtor's "Application for Waiver of the Chapter 7 Filing Fee" shall be held on _____ at _____ am/pm at _____.
> (address of courthouse)
>
> IF THE DEBTOR FAILS TO APPEAR AT THE SCHEDULED HEARING, THE COURT MAY DEEM SUCH FAILURE TO BE THE DEBTOR'S CONSENT TO THE ENTRY OF AN ORDER DENYING THE FEE WAIVER APPLICATION BY DEFAULT.

BY THE COURT:

DATE: <u>X-XX-XXXX</u>   <u>/s/ Jerry W. Venters</u>
United States Bankruptcy Judge

Example Exhibit D—Individual Debtor's Statement of Compliance

B 1D (Official Form 1, Exhibit D) (12/09)

UNITED STATES BANKRUPTCY COURT

In re Zachary Adrian Smith   Case No._____

        Debtor   (if known)

EXHIBIT D - INDIVIDUAL DEBTOR'S STATEMENT OF COMPLIANCE WITH CREDIT COUNSELING REQUIREMENT

Warning: You must be able to check truthfully one of the five statements regarding credit counseling listed below. If you cannot do so, you are not eligible to file a bankruptcy case, and the court can dismiss any case you do file. If that happens, you will lose whatever filing fee you paid, and your creditors will be able to resume collection activities against you. If your case is dismissed and you file another bankruptcy case later, you may be required to pay a second filing fee and you may have to take extra steps to stop creditors' collection activities.

Every individual debtor must file this Exhibit D. If a joint petition is filed, each spouse must complete and file a separate Exhibit D. Check one of the five statements below and attach any documents as directed.

☑ 1. Within the 180 days **before the filing of my bankruptcy case**, I received a briefing from a credit counseling agency approved by the United States trustee or bankruptcy administrator that outlined the opportunities for available credit counseling and assisted me in performing a related budget analysis, and I have a certificate from the agency describing the services provided to me. *Attach a copy of the certificate and a copy of any debt repayment plan developed through the agency.*

☐ 2. Within the 180 days **before the filing of my bankruptcy case**, I received a briefing from a credit counseling agency approved by the United States trustee or bankruptcy administrator that outlined the opportunities for available credit counseling and assisted me in performing a related budget analysis, but I do not have a certificate from the agency describing the services provided to me. *You must file a copy of a certificate from the agency describing the services provided to you and a copy of any debt repayment plan developed through the agency no later than 14 days after your bankruptcy case is filed.*

Example Exhibit D—Individual Debtor's Statement of Compliance (cont.)

❏ 3. I certify that I requested credit counseling services from an approved agency but was unable to obtain the services during the seven days from the time I made my request, and the following exigent circumstances merit a temporary waiver of the credit counseling requirement so I can file my bankruptcy case now. *[Summarize exigent circumstances here.]*

If your certification is satisfactory to the court, you must still obtain the credit counseling briefing within the first 30 days after you file your bankruptcy petition and promptly file a certificate from the agency that provided the counseling, together with a copy of any debt management plan developed through the agency. Failure to fulfill these requirements may result in dismissal of your case. Any extension of the 30-day deadline can be granted only for cause and is limited to a maximum of 15 days. Your case may also be dismissed if the court is not satisfied with your reasons for filing your bankruptcy case without first receiving a credit counseling briefing.

❏ 4. I am not required to receive a credit counseling briefing because of: *[Check the applicable statement.] [Must be accompanied by a motion for determination by the court.]*

❏ Incapacity. (Defined in 11 U.S.C. § 109(h)(4) as impaired by reason of mental illness or mental deficiency so as to be incapable of realizing and making rational decisions with respect to financial responsibilities.);
❏ Disability. (Defined in 11 U.S.C. § 109(h)(4) as physically impaired to the extent of being unable, after reasonable effort, to participate in a credit counseling briefing in person, by telephone, or through the Internet.);
❏ Active military duty in a military combat zone.

❏ 5. The United States trustee or bankruptcy administrator has determined that the credit counseling requirement of 11 U.S.C. § 109(h) does not apply in this district.

I certify under penalty of perjury that the information provided above is true and correct.

Signature of Debtor: <u>Zachary Adrian Smith</u>

Date: <u>X-XX-XXXX</u>

Example Motion for Stay of Collection Actions by Creditors

UNITED STATES STATES BANKRUPTCY COURT
WESTERN DISTRICT OF MISSOURI

IN RE: Zachary Adrian Smith,)
)
             Debtor.   )
) Case No. 10-50921-7
)

MOTION FOR STAY OF COLLECTION ACTIONS BY CREDITORS

COMES NOW the Debtor, Zachary A. Smith, and respectfully requests this Court to grant Debtor a stay of collection actions by the creditor pursuant to Bankruptcy Code §362. In support of motion, Debtor states the following.

1. On January 20, 2009, the Cole County Circuit Court entered judgment in favor of the plaintiff State of Missouri, ordering Rodney Kueffer, Inmate Treasurer of the Department of Corrections, to pay to plaintiff State of Missouri, Inmate Incarceration Reimbursement Act Revolving Fund, P.O. Box 899, Jefferson City, Missouri 65102, 90% of any and all deposits to Smith's inmate account for costs of care incurred by the plaintiff.

2. Debtor respectfully requests this Court to enter a stay, pursuant to Bankruptcy Code §362, and prohibit Rodney Kueffer, Inmate Treasurer of the Department of Corrections, 2729 Plaza Drive, P.O. Box 236, Jefferson City, MO 65102; Telephone: 573-751-2389; Fax: 573-751-4099, from taking any further collection actions against Debtor's inmate account until the resolution of these bankruptcy proceedings.

For the foregoing reasons, Smith prays this Court grant the requested relief. He further prays for any other and further relief which this Court may deem just and proper under the circumstances.

Example Motion for Stay of Collection Actions by Creditors (cont.)

Respectfully submitted,

ZACHARY SMITH, #521163
Crossroads Corr. Center
1115 E. Pence Road
Cameron, MO 64429

Debtor

CERTIFICATE OF SERVICE

I hereby certify that a copy of the foregoing was mailed, postage prepaid, this 22 day of november , 2010, to; Bruce E. Strauss, Bankruptcy Trustee, 1044 Main Street, 4th Floor, Kansas City, MO 64105.

Debtor

Example of How to Create a Matrix

HOW TO CREATE A MATRIX
FOR PRO SE DEBTOR PAPER FILING

1. Prepare a typed list of all your creditors (mailing matrix).

2. The matrix must include the name of the creditor, the address, and the city, state and zip code.

3. The list should be in a single column format with a 1 inch left margin.

4. Single-space the creditors   but . . .

5. Double-space between creditors but do not separate a creditor from the address. The full name and address of a creditor should be on one page.

6. The city, state and zip must be all on the same line.

7. Use an ordinary font such as Times New Roman or Arial.

Here is an example:

        ABC Corporation
        1200 Main Street
        Anywhere, MO 60000

        Mr. and Mrs. XYZ
        2100 Maple Drive
        Anywhere, MO 60000

        H&M Business Supply
        1010 Elm Boulevard
        Anywhere, MO 60000

8. You may use either a typewriter or a computer.

9. If using a computer, do not use hard returns.

Example Debtor's Mailing Matrix of Creditors

UNITED STATES BANKRUPTCY COURT

In re Zachary Adrian Smith,   )
)
                           Debtor,   ) Case No._____
)
) Chapter 7

DEBTOR'S MAILING MATRIX OF CREDITORS

Chris Koster, Attorney General of the State of Missouri
P.O. Box 899
Jefferson City, Missouri 65102

Missouri Department of Corrections
Rodney Kueffer, Inmate Treasurer of the Department of Corrections
2729 Plaza Drive
P.O. Box 236
Jefferson City, Missouri 65102

Truman Medical Center
2600 Holmes Street
Kansas City, Missouri 64108

Respectfully submitted,

Zachary Adrian Smith
Debtor

Date: XX-XX-XXXX

\<4\> SCHEDULES

General Instructions

The first page of your schedules and the first page of any amendments thereto must contain a caption. Subsequent pages should be identified with your name and case number unless the schedules are filed with the petition, in which instance the case number should be left blank.

Schedules D, E, and F have been designed for the listing of each claim only once. Even when a claim is secured only in part or entitled to priority only in part, it still should be listed only once. A claim that is secured in whole or in part should be listed on Schedule D only, and a claim that is entitled to priority in whole or in part should be listed on Schedule E only. Do not list the same claim twice. If a creditor has more than one claim, such as claims arising from separate transactions, each claim should be scheduled separately.

Review the specific instruction for each schedule before completing the schedule.

Summary of Schedules and Statistical Summary of Certain Liabilities

The Summary of Schedules is designed to help you make sure that all required schedules are in order, and have been completed. Indicate as to each schedule whether that schedule is attached and state the number of pages in each. Report the totals from Schedules A, B, D, E, F, I, and J in the boxes provided. Add the amounts from Schedules A and B to determine the total amount of your assets. Add the amount of all claims from Schedules D, E, and F to determine the total amount of your liabilities. You also must complete the Statistical Summary of Certain Liabilities and Related Data when filing a case under chapter 7, 11, or 13.

The Summary of Schedules and Statistical Summary of Certain Liabilities and Related Data should only be completed after you've completed all the schedules. See the example at the end of this chapter.

Schedule A—Real Property

On Schedule A, list all real property in which you have any legal, equitable, or future interest, including all property owned as a cotenant, community property, or that you have a life estate. Include any property to which you hold rights and powers exercisable for your own benefit. If you are married, state whether you, your spouse, both, or the marital community own the property by placing an H, W, J, or C in the column labeled "Husband, Wife, Joint, or Community." If you hold no interest in real property, write "None" under "Description and Location of Property."

Do not include interests in executory contracts and unexpired leases on this schedule. List them in Schedule G—Executory Contracts and Unexpired Leases.

If an entity claims to have a lien or hold a secured interest in any of your property, state the amount of the secured claim. See Schedule D. If no entity claims to hold a secured interest in the property, write "None" in the column labeled "Amount of Secured Claim."

If you are filing as an individual or if a joint petition is filed, state the amount of any exemption claimed in the property only in Schedule C—Property Claimed as Exempt.

Schedule B—Personal Property

On Schedule B, list all your personal property of whatever kind. If you do not have property in one or more of the categories, place an X in the appropriate position in the column labeled "None." If additional space is needed in any category, attach a separate sheet properly identified with the case name, case number (if schedules are filed after filing the petition), and the number of the category. If you are married, state whether you, your spouse, both, or the marital community own the property by placing an H, W, J, or C in the column labeled "Husband,Wife, Joint, or Community." If you are filing as an individual or a joint petition is filed, state the amount of any exemptions claimed only in Schedule C—Property Claimed as Exempt.

Do not list interests in executory contracts and unexpired leases on this schedule. List them in Schedule G—Executory Contracts and Unexpired Leases.

If the property is being held for you by someone else, state that person's name and address under "Description and Location of Property." If the property is being held for a minor child, simply state the child's initials and the name and address of the child's parent or guardian, such as "A.B., a minor child, by John Doe, guardian." Do not disclose the child's name, per 11 U.S.C. §112 and Federal Rule of Bankruptcy Procedure 1007(m).

Schedule C—Property Claimed as Exempt

Unless you own a homestead or receive payments from Foreign Service Retirement and Disability, Social Security, Injury or Death Compensation from War Risk Hazards, Wages of Fishermen, Seamen, and Apprentices, Civil Service Retirement Benefits, Railroad Retirement Act Annuities and Pensions, or other property that falls within the exempt property set forth in 11 U.S.C. §522(b)(2) and (3), you should leave this form blank.

Schedule D—Creditors Holding Secured Claims

State the name, mailing address (including zip code}, and last four digits of any account number of all entities holding claims secured by property of yours as of the date of filing of the petition.

The complete account number of any account you have with a creditor is useful to the trustee and the creditor and may be provided if you choose to do so. List creditors holding all types of secured interests such as judgment liens, garnishments, statutory liens, mortgages, deeds of trust, and other security interests.

Try to list creditors in alphabetical order. If a minor child is the creditor, state the child's initials and the name and address of the child's parent or guardian, such as "A.B., a minor child, by John Doe, guardian." As mentioned previously, do not disclose the child's name. If all secured creditors will not fit on the page, use the continuation sheet provided.

If any entity other than a spouse in a joint case may be jointly liable on a claim, place an X in the column labeled "Codebtor." Include this entity on the appropriate schedule of creditors and complete Schedule H—Codebtors. As before, if yours is a joint petition, state whether you, your spouse, or both, or the marital community may be liable on each claim by placing an H, W, J, or C in the column labeled "Husband, Wife, Joint, or Community."

If the claim is contingent, place an X in the column labeled "Contingent." If the claim is unliquidated, place an X in the column labeled "Unliquidated." If the claim is disputed, place an X in the column labeled "Disputed." You may need to place an X in more than one of these three columns.

Total the columns labeled "Amount of Claim Without Deducting Value of Collateral" and "Unsecured Portion, if Any" in the boxes labeled "Total(s)" on the last sheet of the completed schedule. Also report the total from the column labeled "Amount of Claim Without Deducting Value of Collateral" on the Summary of Schedules and, if you are an individual with primarily consumer debts, report the total from the column labeled "Unsecured Portion, if Any" on the Statistical Summary of Certain Liabilities and Related Data.

If you don't have any creditors holding secured claims to report on Schedule D, check the appropriate box and leave the rest of the form blank.

Schedule E—Creditors Holding Unsecured Priority Claims

A complete list of claims entitled to priority, listed separately by type of priority, is to be set forth on these sheets. Only holders of unsecured claims entitled to priority should be listed in this schedule. In the boxes provided on the attached sheets, state the name, mailing address (including zip code), and last four digits of the account number, if any, of all entities holding priority claims against you or your property, as of the date of the filing of the petition. Use a separate continuation sheet for each type of priority, and label each with the type of priority.

Again, the complete account number of any account you have with a creditor is useful to the trustee and the creditor, so provide it if you wish. If a minor child is a creditor, state the child's initials and the name and address of the child's parent or guardian, such as "A.B., a minor child, by John Doe, guardian." Remember not to disclose the child's name.

If any entity other than a spouse in a joint case may be jointly liable on a claim, place an X in the column labeled "Codebtor," include the entity on the appropriate schedule of creditors, and complete Schedule H—Codebtor. For joint petitions, state whether you, your spouse, both, or the marital community may be liable on each claim by placing an H, W, J, or C in the column labeled "Husband, Wife, Joint, or Community." If the claim is contingent, place an X in the column labeled "Contingent." If the claim is unliquidated, place an X in the column labeled "Unliquidated." If the claim is disputed, place an X in the column labeled "Disputed." As before, you may have to place an X in more than one of these columns.

Report the total of claims and amounts entitled to priority listed on each sheet in the boxes labeled "Subtotals." On the last sheet of Schedule E, report the total of all claims and amounts entitled to priority on this schedule in the box labeled "Total." Report this total on the Summary of Schedules also.

When you are an individual debtor with primarily consumer debts, you'll also report the total amounts entitled to priority on the Statistical Summary of Certain Liabilities and Related Data.

On each sheet, report the listed total of amounts not entitled to priority in the box labeled "Subtotals." On the last sheet of the completed schedule, report the listed total of all Schedule E amounts not entitled to priority in the box labeled "Totals." If you are an individual debtor with primarily consumer debts, you'll also report this total on the Statistical Summary of Certain Liabilities and Related Data.

If you have no creditors holding unsecured priority claims to report, check the box so indicated and leave the rest of the form blank.

As for "Types of Priority Claims," check the appropriate box(es) if claims in that category are listed on your attached sheets.

Schedule F—Creditors Holding Unsecured Nonpriority Claims

State the name, mailing address (including zip code), and at least the last four digits of any account number, of all entities holding unsecured claims without priority against you or your property, as of the date of filing of the petition. Provide the complete account number of any account you have with the creditor only if you choose to. As in prior schedules, if a minor child is a creditor, state only the child's initials and the name and address of the child's parent or guardian, such as "A.B., a minor child, by John Doe, guardian." Do not include claims listed in Schedules D and E. If all of the creditors will not fit on the page, use the continuation sheet.

If any entity other than a spouse in a joint case may be jointly liable on a claim, place an X in the column labeled "Codebtor," include the entity on the appropriate schedule of creditors, and complete Schedule H—Codebtors. If yours is a joint petition, state whether you, your spouse, both, or the marital community may be liable on each claim by placing an H, W, ,J, or C in the column labeled "Husband, Wife, Joint, or Community ."

If the claim is contingent, place an X in the column labeled "Contingent." If the claim is unliquidated, place an X in the column labeled "Unliquidated." If the claim is disputed, place an X in the column labeled "Disputed." You may of course need to place an X in multiple columns.

Total all claims listed on the schedule and report the sum in the box labeled "Total" on the last sheet of the completed schedule. Report the total also on the Summary of Schedules and also if you are an individual debtor with primarily consumer debts, on the Statistical Summary of Certain Liabilities and Related Data.

If you have no creditors holding unsecured claims to report on Schedule F, check that box and leave the rest of the form blank.

Schedule G—Executory Contracts and Unexpired Leases

Describe all executory contracts (of any nature) and all unexpired leases of real or personal property. Include any timeshare interests. State the nature of your interest in the contract (i.e., "Purchaser," "Agent," etc.). State whether you are the lesser or lessee of a lease. Provide the names and complete mailing addresses of all other parties to each lease or contract described. As on previous schedules, if a minor child is a party to one of the leases or contracts, state the child's initials and the name and address of the child's parent or guardian.

If you do not have any executory contracts or unexpired leases, check the appropriate box and leave the rest of the form blank.

Schedule H—Codebtors

Provide the information requested concerning any person or entity, other than a spouse in a joint case, that is also liable on any debts listed by you in the schedules of creditors. Include all guarantors and cosigners. If you now reside or formerly resided in a community property state, commonwealth, or territory (including Alaska, Arizona, California, Idaho, Louisiana, Nevada, New Mexico, Puerto Rico, Texas, Washington, or Wisconsin) within the eight-year period immediately preceding the commencement of the case, identify the name of any spouse and/or former spouse who resided with you in the community property state, commonwealth, or territory. Include all names used by the nondebtor spouse during the eight years immediately preceding the commencement of this case. Of course, if a minor child is a codebtor or a creditor, state only the child's initials and the name and address of the child's parent or guardian.

If you have no codebtors, check the box thus indicated and leave the rest of the form blank.

Schedule I—Current Income of Individual Debtor(s)

The "Spouse" column must be completed in all cases filed by joint debtors and by every married debtor, whether or not a joint petition is filed. The exception is only for spouses who are separated at the time of a filing as an individual. Do not state the name of any minor child. The average monthly income calculated here may differ from the current monthly income calculated on Forms 22A, 22B, and 22C. This is acceptable.

Schedule J—Current Expenditures of Individual Debtor(s)

Complete Schedule J by estimating the average or projected monthly expenses of you and your family at time case is filed. Prorate any payments made biweekly, quarterly, semi-annually, or annually to show monthly rate. The average monthly expenses calculated on this form are permitted to differ from the deductions from income allowed on Form 22A or 22C.

If a joint petition is filed and your spouse maintains a separate household, check the box so indicated. Then complete a separate schedule of expenditures labeled "Spouse."

Declaration Concerning Debtor's Schedules

When all the schedules are completed, sign and date the Declaration Concerning Debtor's Schedules, thereby declaring under the penalty of perjury that you have read the foregoing summary and schedules, consisting of X number of sheets, and that they are true and correct to the best of your knowledge, information, and belief.

Example Summary of Schedules

B6 Summary (Official Form 6 - Summary) (12/07)

United States Bankruptcy Court

In re Zachary Adrian Smtih _____ ,

         Debtor

Case No. _____

Chapter _____7_____

SUMMARY OF SCHEDULES

Indicate as to each schedule whether that schedule is attached and state the number of pages in each. Report the totals from Schedules A, B, D, E, F, I, and J in the boxes provided. Add the amounts from Schedules A and B to determine the total amount of the debtor's assets. Add the amounts of all claims from Schedules D, E, and F to determine the total amount of the debtor's liabilities. Individual debtors also must complete the "Statistical Summary of Certain Liabilities and Related Data" if they file a case under chapter 7, 11, or 13.

NAME OF SCHEDULE	ATTACHED (YES/NO)	NO. OF SHEETS	ASSETS	LIABILITIES	OTHER
A - Real Property	Yes.	1	$ 0		
B - Personal Property	Yes.	3	$ 0		
C - Property Claimed as Exempt	Yes.	1	0		
D - Creditors Holding Secured Claims	Yes.	1	0	$ 0	
E - Creditors Holding Unsecured Priority Claims (Total of Claims on Schedule E)	Yes.	3	0	$100,000, plus $15,000 every year.	
F - Creditors Holding Unsecured Nonpriority Claims	Yes.	2	0	$ 105,000	
G - Executory Contracts and Unexpired Leases	Yes.	1	0	0	
H - Codebtors	Yes.	1	0	0	
I - Current Income of Individual Debtor(s)	Yes.	1			$ 8.50
J - Current Expenditures of Individual Debtors(s)	Yes.	1			$ 8.50
TOTAL		15	$ 0	$ 205,000	

63

SCHEDULES

Example Statistical Summary of Certain Liabilities and Related Data

B 6 Summary (Official Form 6 - Summary) (12/07)

United States Bankruptcy Court

In re Zachary Adrian Smith_____ ,   Case No. _____

        Debtor

                                Chapter __7__

STATISTICAL SUMMARY OF CERTAIN LIABILITIES AND RELATED DATA (28 U.S.C. § 159)

If you are an individual debtor whose debts are primarily consumer debts, as defined in § 101(8) of the Bankruptcy Code (11 U.S.C. § 101(8)), filing a case under chapter 7, 11 or 13, you must report all information requested below.

☐ Check this box if you are an individual debtor whose debts are NOT primarily consumer debts. You are not required to report any information here.

This information is for statistical purposes only under 28 U.S.C. § 159.

Summarize the following types of liabilities, as reported in the Schedules, and total them.

Type of Liability	Amount
Domestic Support Obligations (from Schedule E)	$ 0
Taxes and Certain Other Debts Owed to Governmental Units (from Schedule E)	$ 0
Claims for Death or Personal Injury While Debtor Was Intoxicated (from Schedule E) (whether disputed or undisputed)	$ 0
Student Loan Obligations (from Schedule F)	$ 0
Domestic Support, Separation Agreement, and Divorce Decree Obligations Not Reported on Schedule E	$ 0
Obligations to Pension or Profit-Sharing, and Other Similar Obligations (from Schedule F)	$ 0
TOTAL	$ 0

State the following:

Average Income (from Schedule I, Line 16)	$ 8.50
Average Expenses (from Schedule J, Line 18)	$ 8.50
Current Monthly Income (from Form 22A Line 12; OR, Form 22B Line 11; OR, Form 22C Line 20)	$ 8.50

State the following:

1. Total from Schedule D, "UNSECURED PORTION, IF ANY" column		$ 0
2. Total from Schedule E, "AMOUNT ENTITLED TO PRIORITY" column.	$ 100,000	
3. Total from Schedule E, "AMOUNT NOT ENTITLED TO PRIORITY, IF ANY" column		$ 10%
4. Total from Schedule F		$ 105,000
5. Total of non-priority unsecured debt (sum of 1, 3, and 4)		$ 105,000

64

Example Schedule A—Real Property

B6A (Official Form 6A) (12/07)

In re Zachary Adrian Smith   ,   Case No. _____
              Debtor   (If known)

SCHEDULE A - REAL PROPERTY

Except as directed below, list all real property in which the debtor has any legal, equitable, or future interest, including all property owned as a co-tenant, community property, or in which the debtor has a life estate. Include any property in which the debtor holds rights and powers exercisable for the debtor's own benefit. If the debtor is married, state whether the husband, wife, both, or the marital community own the property by placing an "H," "W," "J," or "C" in the column labeled "Husband, Wife, Joint, or Community." If the debtor holds no interest in real property, write "None" under "Description and Location of Property."

Do not include interests in executory contracts and unexpired leases on this schedule. List them in Schedule G - Executory Contracts and Unexpired Leases.

If an entity claims to have a lien or hold a secured interest in any property, state the amount of the secured claim. See Schedule D. If no entity claims to hold a secured interest in the property, write "None" in the column labeled "Amount of Secured Claim."

If the debtor is an individual or if a joint petition is filed, state the amount of any exemption claimed in the property only in Schedule C - Property Claimed as Exempt.

DESCRIPTION AND LOCATION OF PROPERTY	NATURE OF DEBTOR'S INTEREST IN PROPERTY	HUSBAND, WIFE, JOINT, OR COMMUNITY	CURRENT VALUE OF DEBTOR'S INTEREST IN PROPERTY, WITHOUT DEDUCTING ANY SECURED CLAIM OR EXEMPTION	AMOUNT OF SECURED CLAIM
None.				

Total➤   0

(Report also on Summary of Schedules.)

Example Schedule B—Personal Property

B 6B (Official Form 6B) (12/07)

In re _Zachary Adrian Smith_____,   Case No. _____
           Debtor   (If known)

SCHEDULE B - PERSONAL PROPERTY

      Except as directed below, list all personal property of the debtor of whatever kind. If the debtor has no property in one or more of the categories, place an "x" in the appropriate position in the column labeled "None." If additional space is needed in any category, attach a separate sheet properly identified with the case name, case number, and the number of the category. If the debtor is married, state whether the husband, wife, both, or the marital community own the property by placing an "H," "W," "J," or "C" in the column labeled "Husband, Wife, Joint, or Community." If the debtor is an individual or a joint petition is filed, state the amount of any exemptions claimed only in Schedule C - Property Claimed as Exempt.

      Do not list interests in executory contracts and unexpired leases on this schedule. List them in Schedule G - Executory Contracts and Unexpired Leases.

If the property is being held for the debtor by someone else, state that person's name and address under "Description and Location of Property." If the property is being held for a minor child, simply state the child's initials and the name and address of the child's parent or guardian, such as "A.B., a minor child, by John Doe, guardian." Do not disclose the child's name. See, 11 U.S.C. §112 and Fed. R. Bankr. P. 1007(m).

TYPE OF PROPERTY	N O N E	DESCRIPTION AND LOCATION OF PROPERTY	HUSBAND, WIFE, JOINT, OR COMMUNITY	CURRENT VALUE OF DEBTOR'S INTEREST IN PROPERTY, WITH-OUT DEDUCTING ANY SECURED CLAIM OR EXEMPTION
1. Cash on hand.	X			
2. Checking, savings or other financial accounts, certificates of deposit or shares in banks, savings and loan, thrift, building and loan, and homestead associations, or credit unions, brokerage houses, or cooperatives.	X			
3. Security deposits with public utilities, telephone companies, landlords, and others.	X			
4. Household goods and furnishings, including audio, video, and computer equipment.	X			
5. Books; pictures and other art objects; antiques; stamp, coin, record, tape, compact disc, and other collections or collectibles.	X			
6. Wearing apparel.	X			
7. Furs and jewelry.	X			
8. Firearms and sports, photographic, and other hobby equipment.	X			
9. Interests in insurance policies. Name insurance company of each policy and itemize surrender or refund value of each.	X			
10. Annuities. Itemize and name each issuer.	X			
11. Interests in an education IRA as defined in 26 U.S.C. § 530(b)(1) or under a qualified State tuition plan as defined in 26 U.S.C. § 529(b)(1). Give particulars. (File separately the record(s) of any such interest(s). 11 U.S.C. § 521(c).)	X			

Example Schedule B—Personal Property (cont.)

B 6B (Official Form 6B) (12/07) -- Cont.

In re   Zachary Adrian Smith   ,   Case No. _____
       Debtor   (If known)

SCHEDULE B - PERSONAL PROPERTY
(Continuation Sheet)

TYPE OF PROPERTY	NONE	DESCRIPTION AND LOCATION OF PROPERTY	HUSBAND, WIFE, JOINT, OR COMMUNITY	CURRENT VALUE OF DEBTOR'S INTEREST IN PROPERTY, WITHOUT DEDUCTING ANY SECURED CLAIM OR EXEMPTION
12. Interests in IRA, ERISA, Keogh, or other pension or profit sharing plans. Give particulars.	X			
13. Stock and interests in incorporated and unincorporated businesses. Itemize.	X			
14. Interests in partnerships or joint ventures. Itemize.	X			
15. Government and corporate bonds and other negotiable and non-negotiable instruments.	X			
16. Accounts receivable.	X			
17. Alimony, maintenance, support, and property settlements to which the debtor is or may be entitled. Give particulars.	X			
18. Other liquidated debts owed to debtor including tax refunds. Give particulars.	X			
19. Equitable or future interests, life estates, and rights or powers exercisable for the benefit of the debtor other than those listed in Schedule A – Real Property.	X			
20. Contingent and noncontingent interests in estate of a decedent, death benefit plan, life insurance policy, or trust.	X			
21. Other contingent and unliquidated claims of every nature, including tax refunds, counterclaims of the debtor, and rights to setoff claims. Give estimated value of each.	X			

Example Schedule B—Personal Property (cont.)

B 6B (Official Form 6B) (12/07) -- Cont.

In re ___Zachary Adrian Smith_____,   Case No. _____
                    Debtor   (If known)

SCHEDULE B - PERSONAL PROPERTY
(Continuation Sheet)

TYPE OF PROPERTY	N O N E	DESCRIPTION AND LOCATION OF PROPERTY	HUSBAND, WIFE, JOINT, OR COMMUNITY	CURRENT VALUE OF DEBTOR'S INTEREST IN PROPERTY, WITH-OUT DEDUCTING ANY SECURED CLAIM OR EXEMPTION
22. Patents, copyrights, and other intellectual property. Give particulars.	X			
23. Licenses, franchises, and other general intangibles. Give particulars.	X			
24. Customer lists or other compilations containing personally identifiable information (as defined in 11 U.S.C. § 101(41A)) provided to the debtor by individuals in connection with obtaining a product or service from the debtor primarily for personal, family, or household purposes.	X			
25. Automobiles, trucks, trailers, and other vehicles and accessories.	X			
26. Boats, motors, and accessories.	X			
27. Aircraft and accessories.	X			
28. Office equipment, furnishings, and supplies.	X			
29. Machinery, fixtures, equipment, and supplies used in business.	X			
30. Inventory.	X			
31. Animals.	X			
32. Crops - growing or harvested. Give particulars.	X			
33. Farming equipment and implements.	X			
34. Farm supplies, chemicals, and feed.	X			
35. Other personal property of any kind not already listed. Itemize.	X			

_____0___ continuation sheets attached   Total▶ $ 0
(Include amounts from any continuation
sheets attached. Report total also on
Summary of Schedules.)

Example Schedule C—Property Claimed as Exempt

B 6C (Official Form 6C) (04/10)

In re Zachary Adrian Smith , Case No. _____
　　　　　　　Debtor　　　　　　　　　　　　　　　　　　　*(If known)*

SCHEDULE C - PROPERTY CLAIMED AS EXEMPT

Debtor claims the exemptions to which debtor is entitled under:　　☐ Check if debtor claims a homestead exemption that exceeds
(Check one box)　　　　　　　　　　　　　　　　　　　　　　$146,450.*
☐　11 U.S.C. § 522(b)(2)
☐　11 U.S.C. § 522(b)(3)

DESCRIPTION OF PROPERTY	SPECIFY LAW PROVIDING EACH EXEMPTION	VALUE OF CLAIMED EXEMPTION	CURRENT VALUE OF PROPERTY WITHOUT DEDUCTING EXEMPTION
None.			

* *Amount subject to adjustment on 4/1/13, and every three years thereafter with respect to cases commenced on or after the date of adjustment.*

SCHEDULES

Example Schedule D—Creditors Holding Secured Claims

B 6D (Official Form 6D) (12/07)

In re __Zachary Adrian Smith__ ,   Case No. _____
    Debtor   (If known)

SCHEDULE D - CREDITORS HOLDING SECURED CLAIMS

State the name, mailing address, including zip code, and last four digits of any account number of all entities holding claims secured by property of the debtor as of the date of filing of the petition. The complete account number of any account the debtor has with the creditor is useful to the trustee and the creditor and may be provided if the debtor chooses to do so. List creditors holding all types of secured interests such as judgment liens, garnishments, statutory liens, mortgages, deeds of trust, and other security interests.

List creditors in alphabetical order to the extent practicable. If a minor child is the creditor, state the child's initials and the name and address of the child's parent or guardian, such as "A.B., a minor child, by John Doe, guardian." Do not disclose the child's name. See, 11 U.S.C. §112 and Fed. R. Bankr. P. 1007(m). If all secured creditors will not fit on this page, use the continuation sheet provided.

If any entity other than a spouse in a joint case may be jointly liable on a claim, place an "X" in the column labeled "Codebtor," include the entity on the appropriate schedule of creditors, and complete Schedule H – Codebtors. If a joint petition is filed, state whether the husband, wife, both of them, or the marital community may be liable on each claim by placing an "H," "W," "J," or "C" in the column labeled "Husband, Wife, Joint, or Community."

If the claim is contingent, place an "X" in the column labeled "Contingent." If the claim is unliquidated, place an "X" in the column labeled "Unliquidated." If the claim is disputed, place an "X" in the column labeled "Disputed." (You may need to place an "X" in more than one of these three columns.)

Total the columns labeled "Amount of Claim Without Deducting Value of Collateral" and "Unsecured Portion, if Any" in the boxes labeled "Total(s)" on the last sheet of the completed schedule. Report the total from the column labeled "Amount of Claim Without Deducting Value of Collateral" also on the Summary of Schedules and, if the debtor is an individual with primarily consumer debts, report the total from the column labeled "Unsecured Portion, if Any" on the Statistical Summary of Certain Liabilities and Related Data.

[X] Check this box if debtor has no creditors holding secured claims to report on this Schedule D.

CREDITOR'S NAME AND MAILING ADDRESS INCLUDING ZIP CODE AND AN ACCOUNT NUMBER (See Instructions Above.)	CODEBTOR	HUSBAND, WIFE, JOINT, OR COMMUNITY	DATE CLAIM WAS INCURRED, NATURE OF LIEN, AND DESCRIPTION AND VALUE OF PROPERTY SUBJECT TO LIEN	CONTINGENT	UNLIQUIDATED	DISPUTED	AMOUNT OF CLAIM WITHOUT DEDUCTING VALUE OF COLLATERAL	UNSECURED PORTION, IF ANY
ACCOUNT NO.								
			VALUE $					
ACCOUNT NO.								
			VALUE $					
ACCOUNT NO.								
			VALUE $					
___ continuation sheets attached			Subtotal ▶ (Total of this page)				$	$
			Total ▶ (Use only on last page)				$	$
							(Report also on Summary of Schedules.)	(If applicable, report also on Statistical Summary of Certain Liabilities and Related Data.)

70

SCHEDULES

Example Schedule E—Creditors Holding Unsecured Priority Claims

B 6E (Official Form 6E) (04/10)

In re Zachary Adrian Smith , Case No._____
              Debtor   *(if known)*

SCHEDULE E - CREDITORS HOLDING UNSECURED PRIORITY CLAIMS

A complete list of claims entitled to priority, listed separately by type of priority, is to be set forth on the sheets provided. Only holders of unsecured claims entitled to priority should be listed in this schedule. In the boxes provided on the attached sheets, state the name, mailing address, including zip code, and last four digits of the account number, if any, of all entities holding priority claims against the debtor or the property of the debtor, as of the date of the filing of the petition. Use a separate continuation sheet for each type of priority and label each with the type of priority.

The complete account number of any account the debtor has with the creditor is useful to the trustee and the creditor and may be provided if the debtor chooses to do so. If a minor child is a creditor, state the child's initials and the name and address of the child's parent or guardian, such as "A.B., a minor child, by John Doe, guardian." Do not disclose the child's name. See, 11 U.S.C. §112 and Fed. R. Bankr. P. 1007(m).

If any entity other than a spouse in a joint case may be jointly liable on a claim, place an "X" in the column labeled "Codebtor," include the entity on the appropriate schedule of creditors, and complete Schedule H-Codebtors. If a joint petition is filed, state whether the husband, wife, both of them, or the marital community may be liable on each claim by placing an "H," "W," "J," or "C" in the column labeled "Husband, Wife, Joint, or Community." If the claim is contingent, place an "X" in the column labeled "Contingent." If the claim is unliquidated, place an "X" in the column labeled "Unliquidated." If the claim is disputed, place an "X" in the column labeled "Disputed." (You may need to place an "X" in more than one of these three columns.)

Report the total of claims listed on each sheet in the box labeled "Subtotals" on each sheet. Report the total of all claims listed on this Schedule E in the box labeled "Total" on the last sheet of the completed schedule. Report this total also on the Summary of Schedules.

Report the total of amounts entitled to priority listed on each sheet in the box labeled "Subtotals" on each sheet. Report the total of all amounts entitled to priority listed on this Schedule E in the box labeled "Totals" on the last sheet of the completed schedule. Individual debtors with primarily consumer debts report this total also on the Statistical Summary of Certain Liabilities and Related Data.

Report the total of amounts not entitled to priority listed on each sheet in the box labeled "Subtotals" on each sheet. Report the total of all amounts not entitled to priority listed on this Schedule E in the box labeled "Totals" on the last sheet of the completed schedule. Individual debtors with primarily consumer debts report this total also on the Statistical Summary of Certain Liabilities and Related Data.

☐ Check this box if debtor has no creditors holding unsecured priority claims to report on this Schedule E.

TYPES OF PRIORITY CLAIMS (Check the appropriate box(es) below if claims in that category are listed on the attached sheets.)

☐ **Domestic Support Obligations**

Claims for domestic support that are owed to or recoverable by a spouse, former spouse, or child of the debtor, or the parent, legal guardian, or responsible relative of such a child, or a governmental unit to whom such a domestic support claim has been assigned to the extent provided in 11 U.S.C. § 507(a)(1).

☐ **Extensions of credit in an involuntary case**

Claims arising in the ordinary course of the debtor's business or financial affairs after the commencement of the case but before the earlier of the appointment of a trustee or the order for relief. 11 U.S.C. § 507(a)(3).

☐ **Wages, salaries, and commissions**

Wages, salaries, and commissions, including vacation, severance, and sick leave pay owing to employees and commissions owing to qualifying independent sales representatives up to $11,725* per person earned within 180 days immediately preceding the filing of the original petition, or the cessation of business, whichever occurred first, to the extent provided in 11 U.S.C. § 507(a)(4).

☐ **Contributions to employee benefit plans**

Money owed to employee benefit plans for services rendered within 180 days immediately preceding the filing of the original petition, or the cessation of business, whichever occurred first, to the extent provided in 11 U.S.C. § 507(a)(5).

* Amount subject to adjustment on 4/01/13, and every three years thereafter with respect to cases commenced on or after the date of adjustment.

Example Schedule E—Creditors Holding Unsecured Priority Claims (cont.)

B 6E (Official Form 6E) (04/10) – Cont.

In re Zachary Adrian Smith_____, Case No._____
Debtor   (if known)

☐ Certain farmers and fishermen

   Claims of certain farmers and fishermen, up to $5,775* per farmer or fisherman, against the debtor, as provided in 11 U.S.C. § 507(a)(6).

☐ Deposits by individuals

   Claims of individuals up to $2,600* for deposits for the purchase, lease, or rental of property or services for personal, family, or household use, that were not delivered or provided. 11 U.S.C. § 507(a)(7).

☐ Taxes and Certain Other Debts Owed to Governmental Units

   Taxes, customs duties, and penalties owing to federal, state, and local governmental units as set forth in 11 U.S.C. § 507(a)(8).

☐ Commitments to Maintain the Capital of an Insured Depository Institution

   Claims based on commitments to the FDIC, RTC, Director of the Office of Thrift Supervision, Comptroller of the Currency, or Board of Governors of the Federal Reserve System, or their predecessors or successors, to maintain the capital of an insured depository institution. 11 U.S.C. § 507 (a)(9).

☐ Claims for Death or Personal Injury While Debtor Was Intoxicated

   Claims for death or personal injury resulting from the operation of a motor vehicle or vessel while the debtor was intoxicated from using alcohol, a drug, or another substance. 11 U.S.C. § 507(a)(10).

* Amounts are subject to adjustment on 4/01/13, and every three years thereafter with respect to cases commenced on or after the date of adjustment.

_1_ continuation sheets attached

Example Schedule E—Creditors Holding Unsecured Priority Claims (cont.)

B 6E (Official Form 6E) (04/10) – Cont.

In re Zachary Adrian Smith _____ , Case No. _____
                          Debtor   (if known)

SCHEDULE E - CREDITORS HOLDING UNSECURED PRIORITY CLAIMS
(Continuation Sheet)

Type of Priority for Claims Listed on This Sheet

CREDITOR'S NAME, MAILING ADDRESS INCLUDING ZIP CODE, AND ACCOUNT NUMBER (*See instructions above.*)	CODEBTOR	HUSBAND, WIFE, JOINT, OR COMMUNITY	DATE CLAIM WAS INCURRED AND CONSIDERATION FOR CLAIM	CONTINGENT	UNLIQUIDATED	DISPUTED	AMOUNT OF CLAIM	AMOUNT ENTITLED TO PRIORITY	AMOUNT NOT ENTITLED TO PRIORITY, IF ANY
Account No. 07ACCC00109011 Chris Koster Attorney General P.O. Box 899 Jefferson City, MO 65102			January 20, 09	X	X		$100,000 Plus $15,000	90%	10%
Account No.									
Account No.									
Account No.									

Sheet no. 1 of 1 continuation sheets attached to Schedule of Creditors Holding Priority Claims

Subtotals➤ (Totals of this page)	$ 100,000	$
Total➤ (Use only on last page of the completed Schedule E. Report also on the Summary of Schedules.)	$ 100,000 plus $15,000 every year.	
Totals➤ (Use only on last page of the completed Schedule E. If applicable, report also on the Statistical Summary of Certain Liabilities and Related Data.)		$	$

SCHEDULES

Example Schedule F—Creditors Holding Unsecured Nonpriority Claims

B 6F (Official Form 6F) (12/07)

In re Zachary Adrian Smith , Case No. _____
             Debtor   (if known)

SCHEDULE F - CREDITORS HOLDING UNSECURED NONPRIORITY CLAIMS

State the name, mailing address, including zip code, and last four digits of any account number, of all entities holding unsecured claims without priority against the debtor or the property of the debtor, as of the date of filing of the petition. The complete account number of any account the debtor has with the creditor is useful to the trustee and the creditor and may be provided if the debtor chooses to do so. If a minor child is a creditor, state the child's initials and the name and address of the child's parent or guardian, such as "A.B., a minor child, by John Doe, guardian." Do not disclose the child's name. See, 11 U.S.C. §112 and Fed. R. Bankr. P. 1007(m). Do not include claims listed in Schedules D and E. If all creditors will not fit on this page, use the continuation sheet provided.

If any entity other than a spouse in a joint case may be jointly liable on a claim, place an "X" in the column labeled "Codebtor," include the entity on the appropriate schedule of creditors, and complete Schedule H - Codebtors. If a joint petition is filed, state whether the husband, wife, both of them, or the marital community may be liable on each claim by placing an "H," "W," "J," or "C" in the column labeled "Husband, Wife, Joint, or Community."

If the claim is contingent, place an "X" in the column labeled "Contingent." If the claim is unliquidated, place an "X" in the column labeled "Unliquidated." If the claim is disputed, place an "X" in the column labeled "Disputed." (You may need to place an "X" in more than one of these three columns.)

Report the total of all claims listed on this schedule in the box labeled "Total" on the last sheet of the completed schedule. Report this total also on the Summary of Schedules and, if the debtor is an individual with primarily consumer debts, report this total also on the Statistical Summary of Certain Liabilities and Related Data..

☐ Check this box if debtor has no creditors holding unsecured claims to report on this Schedule F.

CREDITOR'S NAME, MAILING ADDRESS INCLUDING ZIP CODE, AND ACCOUNT NUMBER (See instructions above.)	CODEBTOR	HUSBAND, WIFE, JOINT, OR COMMUNITY	DATE CLAIM WAS INCURRED AND CONSIDERATION FOR CLAIM. IF CLAIM IS SUBJECT TO SETOFF, SO STATE.	CONTINGENT	UNLIQUIDATED	DISPUTED	AMOUNT OF CLAIM
ACCOUNT NO. XXXXXXXXXXX Truman Medical Center 2600 Holmes Kansas City, MO 64108			XX-XX-XX		X		$50,000
ACCOUNT NO. XXXXXXXXXXXX List any credit card debts.			XX-XX-XX		X		$20,000
ACCOUNT NO. XXXXXXXXXXXX List any utility bills.			XX-XX-XX		X		$1,000
ACCOUNT NO. XXXXXXXXXXXX List any rent owed to halfway houses, or costs for disposal or destruction of property.			XX-XX-XX		X		$2,000
					Subtotal➤		$100,000
1 continuation sheets attached			Total➤				$

(Use only on last page of the completed Schedule F.)
(Report also on Summary of Schedules and, if applicable, on the Statistical Summary of Certain Liabilities and Related Data.)

74

Example Schedule F—Creditors Holding Unsecured Nonpriority Claims (cont.)

B 6F (Official Form 6F) (12/07) - Cont.

In re ___Zachary Adrian Smith___ ,   Case No. _____
     Debtor   **(if known)**

SCHEDULE F - CREDITORS HOLDING UNSECURED NONPRIORITY CLAIMS
(Continuation Sheet)

CREDITOR'S NAME, MAILING ADDRESS INCLUDING ZIP CODE, AND ACCOUNT NUMBER (See instructions above.)	CODEBTOR	HUSBAND, WIFE, JOINT, OR COMMUNITY	DATE CLAIM WAS INCURRED AND CONSIDERATION FOR CLAIM. IF CLAIM IS SUBJECT TO SETOFF, SO STATE.	CONTINGENT	UNLIQUIDATED	DISPUTED	AMOUNT OF CLAIM
ACCOUNT NO. XXXXXXXXXXXX List any other debts.			XX-XX-XX		X		$5,000
ACCOUNT NO.							
ACCOUNT NO.							
ACCOUNT NO.							
ACCOUNT NO.							

Sheet no. _1_ of _1_ continuation sheets attached to Schedule of Creditors Holding Unsecured Nonpriority Claims

Subtotal➤ $ $5,000

Total➤ $105,000
(Use only on last page of the completed Schedule F.)
(Report also on Summary of Schedules and, if applicable on the Statistical Summary of Certain Liabilities and Related Data.)

Example Schedule G—Executory Contracts and Unexpired Leases

B 6G (Official Form 6G) (12/07)

In re Zachary Adrian Smith _____ ,　　　Case No._____
　　　　　　Debtor　　　　　　　　　　　　　　　　(if known)

SCHEDULE G - EXECUTORY CONTRACTS AND UNEXPIRED LEASES

Describe all executory contracts of any nature and all unexpired leases of real or personal property. Include any timeshare interests. State nature of debtor's interest in contract, i.e., "Purchaser," "Agent," etc. State whether debtor is the lessor or lessee of a lease. Provide the names and complete mailing addresses of all other parties to each lease or contract described. If a minor child is a party to one of the leases or contracts, state the child's initials and the name and address of the child's parent or guardian, such as "A.B., a minor child, by John Doe, guardian." Do not disclose the child's name. See, 11 U.S.C. §112 and Fed. R. Bankr. P. 1007(m).

☒ Check this box if debtor has no executory contracts or unexpired leases.

NAME AND MAILING ADDRESS, INCLUDING ZIP CODE, OF OTHER PARTIES TO LEASE OR CONTRACT.	DESCRIPTION OF CONTRACT OR LEASE AND NATURE OF DEBTOR'S INTEREST. STATE WHETHER LEASE IS FOR NONRESIDENTIAL REAL PROPERTY. STATE CONTRACT NUMBER OF ANY GOVERNMENT CONTRACT.

Example Schedule H—Codebtor

B 6H (Official Form 6H) (12/07)

In re Zachary Adrian Smith   ,   Case No. _____

         Debtor   **(if known)**

SCHEDULE H - CODEBTORS

Provide the information requested concerning any person or entity, other than a spouse in a joint case, that is also liable on any debts listed by the debtor in the schedules of creditors. Include all guarantors and co-signers. If the debtor resides or resided in a community property state, commonwealth, or territory (including Alaska, Arizona, California, Idaho, Louisiana, Nevada, New Mexico, Puerto Rico, Texas, Washington, or Wisconsin) within the eight-year period immediately preceding the commencement of the case, identify the name of the debtor's spouse and of any former spouse who resides or resided with the debtor in the community property state, commonwealth, or territory. Include all names used by the nondebtor spouse during the eight years immediately preceding the commencement of this case. If a minor child is a codebtor or a creditor, state the child's initials and the name and address of the child's parent or guardian, such as "A.B., a minor child, by John Doe, guardian." Do not disclose the child's name. See, 11 U.S.C. §112 and Fed. R. Bankr. P. 1007(m).

[X] Check this box if debtor has no codebtors.

NAME AND ADDRESS OF CODEBTOR	NAME AND ADDRESS OF CREDITOR

Example Schedule I—Current Income of Individual Debtor(s)

B6I (Official Form 6I) (12/07)

In re _Zachary Adrian Smith_____,   Case No. _____
             Debtor   (if known)

SCHEDULE I - CURRENT INCOME OF INDIVIDUAL DEBTOR(S)

The column labeled "Spouse" must be completed in all cases filed by joint debtors and by every married debtor, whether or not a joint petition is filed, unless the spouses are separated and a joint petition is not filed. Do not state the name of any minor child. The average monthly income calculated on this form may differ from the current monthly income calculated on Form 22A, 22B, or 22C.

Debtor's Marital Status: Single	DEPENDENTS OF DEBTOR AND SPOUSE	
	RELATIONSHIP(S):	AGE(S):

Employment:	None. DEBTOR	SPOUSE
Occupation	N/A	
Name of Employer	N/A	
How long employed		
Address of Employer	N/A	

INCOME: (Estimate of average or projected monthly income at time case filed)	DEBTOR	SPOUSE
	$ 8.50	$
1. Monthly gross wages, salary, and commissions (Prorate if not paid monthly)	$ 0	$
2. Estimate monthly overtime		
3. SUBTOTAL	$ 8.50	$
4. LESS PAYROLL DEDUCTIONS	0	
a. Payroll taxes and social security	$ 0	$
b. Insurance	$ 0	$
c. Union dues	$ 0	$
d. Other (Specify): _____	$ 0	$
5. SUBTOTAL OF PAYROLL DEDUCTIONS	$ 0	$
6. TOTAL NET MONTHLY TAKE HOME PAY	$ 8.50	$
7. Regular income from operation of business or profession or farm (Attach detailed statement)	$ 0	$
8. Income from real property	$ 0	$
9. Interest and dividends	$ 0	$
10. Alimony, maintenance or support payments payable to the debtor for the debtor's use or that of dependents listed above	$ 0	$
11. Social security or government assistance (Specify):_____	$ 0	$
12. Pension or retirement income	$ 0	$
13. Other monthly income (Specify):_____	$ 0	$
14. SUBTOTAL OF LINES 7 THROUGH 13	$ 8.50	$
15. AVERAGE MONTHLY INCOME (Add amounts on lines 6 and 14)	$ 8.50	$
16. COMBINED AVERAGE MONTHLY INCOME: (Combine column totals from line 15)	$ 8.50	

(Report also on Summary of Schedules and, if applicable, on Statistical Summary of Certain Liabilities and Related Data)

17. Describe any increase or decrease in income reasonably anticipated to occur within the year following the filing of this document:

I receive $8.50 once a month from the department of corrections.

Example Schedule J—Current Expenditures of Individual Debtor(s)

B6J (Official Form 6J) (12/07)

In re Zachary Adrian Smith   ,   Case No. _____

Debtor   (if known)

SCHEDULE J - CURRENT EXPENDITURES OF INDIVIDUAL DEBTOR(S)

Complete this schedule by estimating the average or projected monthly expenses of the debtor and the debtor's family at time case filed. Prorate any payments made bi-weekly, quarterly, semi-annually, or annually to show monthly rate. The average monthly expenses calculated on this form may differ from the deductions from income allowed on Form22A or 22C.

☐ Check this box if a joint petition is filed and debtor's spouse maintains a separate household. Complete a separate schedule of expenditures labeled "Spouse."

1. Rent or home mortgage payment (include lot rented for mobile home)	$ 0
a. Are real estate taxes included? Yes _____ No _____	
b. Is property insurance included? Yes _____ No _____	
2. Utilities: a. Electricity and heating fuel	$ 0
b. Water and sewer	$ 0
c. Telephone	$ 0
d. Other _____	$ 0
3. Home maintenance (repairs and upkeep)	$ 0
4. Food	$ 0
5. Clothing	$ 0
6. Laundry and dry cleaning	$ 8.50
7. Medical and dental expenses	$ 0
8. Transportation (not including car payments)	$ 0
9. Recreation, clubs and entertainment, newspapers, magazines, etc.	$ 0
10.Charitable contributions	$ 0
11.Insurance (not deducted from wages or included in home mortgage payments)	
a. Homeowner's or renter's	$ 0
b. Life	$ 0
c. Health	$ 0
d. Auto	$ 0
e. Other _____	$ 0
12. Taxes (not deducted from wages or included in home mortgage payments) (Specify) _____	$ 0
13. Installment payments: (In chapter 11, 12, and 13 cases, do not list payments to be included in the plan)	
a. Auto	$ 0
b. Other _____	$ 0
c. Other _____	$ 0
14. Alimony, maintenance, and support paid to others	$ 0
15. Payments for support of additional dependents not living at your home	$ 0
16. Regular expenses from operation of business, profession, or farm (attach detailed statement)	$ 0
17. Other _____	$ 0
18. AVERAGE MONTHLY EXPENSES (Total lines 1-17. Report also on Summary of Schedules and, if applicable, on the Statistical Summary of Certain Liabilities and Related Data.)	$ 8.50

19. Describe any increase or decrease in expenditures reasonably anticipated to occur within the year following the filing of this document:

20. STATEMENT OF MONTHLY NET INCOME

a. Average monthly income from Line 15 of Schedule I	$ 8.50
b. Average monthly expenses from Line 18 above	$ 8.50
c. Monthly net income (a. minus b.)	$ 0

Example Declaration Concerning Debtor's Schedules

B6 Declaration (Official Form 6 - Declaration) (12/07)

In re Zachary Adrian Smith ,   Case No. _____
             Debtor   (if known)

DECLARATION CONCERNING DEBTOR'S SCHEDULES

DECLARATION UNDER PENALTY OF PERJURY BY INDIVIDUAL DEBTOR

    I declare under penalty of perjury that I have read the foregoing summary and schedules, consisting of 17 sheets, and that they are true and correct to the best of my knowledge, information, and belief.

Date XX-XX-XX _____   Signature: *ZA. Smith* _____
                                                                Debtor

Date _____   Signature: _____
                                                (Joint Debtor, if any)

[If joint case, both spouses must sign.]

DECLARATION AND SIGNATURE OF NON-ATTORNEY BANKRUPTCY PETITION PREPARER (See 11 U.S.C. § 110)

    I declare under penalty of perjury that: (1) I am a bankruptcy petition preparer as defined in 11 U.S.C. § 110; (2) I prepared this document for compensation and have provided the debtor with a copy of this document and the notices and information required under 11 U.S.C. §§ 110(b), 110(h) and 342(b); and, (3) if rules or guidelines have been promulgated pursuant to 11 U.S.C. § 110(h) setting a maximum fee for services chargeable by bankruptcy petition preparers, I have given the debtor notice of the maximum amount before preparing any document for filing for a debtor or accepting any fee from the debtor, as required by that section.

_____   _____
Printed or Typed Name and Title, if any,   Social Security No.
of Bankruptcy Petition Preparer   *(Required by 11 U.S.C. § 110.)*

If the bankruptcy petition preparer is not an individual, state the name, title (if any), address, and social security number of the officer, principal, responsible person, or partner who signs this document.

_____
_____
_____
Address

X _____   _____
   Signature of Bankruptcy Petition Preparer   Date

Names and Social Security numbers of all other individuals who prepared or assisted in preparing this document, unless the bankruptcy petition preparer is not an individual:

If more than one person prepared this document, attach additional signed sheets conforming to the appropriate Official Form for each person.

A bankruptcy petition preparer's failure to comply with the provisions of title 11 and the Federal Rules of Bankruptcy Procedure may result in fines or imprisonment or both. 11 U.S.C. § 110; 18 U.S.C. § 156.

DECLARATION UNDER PENALTY OF PERJURY ON BEHALF OF A CORPORATION OR PARTNERSHIP

    I, the _____ [the president or other officer or an authorized agent of the corporation or a member or an authorized agent of the partnership] of the _____ [corporation or partnership] named as debtor in this case, declare under penalty of perjury that I have read the foregoing summary and schedules, consisting of ____ sheets (*Total shown on summary page plus 1*), and that they are true and correct to the best of my knowledge, information, and belief.

Date _____

                            Signature: _____

                                        [Print or type name of individual signing on behalf of debtor.]

[An individual signing on behalf of a partnership or corporation must indicate position or relationship to debtor.]

Penalty for making a false statement or concealing property: Fine of up to $500,000 or imprisonment for up to 5 years or both. 18 U.S.C. §§ 152 and 3571.

$

<5> STATEMENT OF CURRENT MONTHLY INCOME AND MEANS-TEST CALCULATION

Chapter 7 Statement of Current Monthly Income and Means-Test Calculation

In addition to Schedules I and J, this statement must be completed by every individual chapter 7 debtor, whether or not filing jointly. Unless the exclusion in Line 1C of the form applies, joint debtors may complete a single statement. If the exclusion in Line 1C applies, each joint filer must complete a separate statement.

Under 11 U.S.C. §707(b)(1), the court may dismiss or convert an individual's chapter 7 case if the debtor has "primarily consumer debts" and the granting of relief would be an abuse of chapter 7. Congress enacted §707(b) to address the problem of consumer debtors taking inordinate advantage of modern easy-credit practices, running up consumer debt, and then seeking discharge of that debt through chapter 7, and to give courts a means for dismissing such cases.

Bankruptcy Code 11 U.S.C. §101(8), defines consumer debts as "debt incurred by an individual primarily for personal, family, or household purpose."

Under 11 U.S.C. §707(b)(2), a case is presumptively abusive if the debtor's income, as calculated by the means-test mentioned in Chapter 1 of this book, exceeds a certain threshold. However, this should not become an issue in light of your incarceration.

In the example at the end of this chapter you will notice that the nonconsumer debts box was checked because the debts listed were not all consumer debts. The main debt listed in the example was incurred from a civil judgment by the State under the Missouri Incarceration Reimbursement Act. If your debts consist of primarily consumer debts, you will have to fill out the entire Statement of Current Monthly Income and Means-Test Calculation Form.

Example Statement of Current Monthly Income and Means-Test Calculation

B 22A (Official Form 22A) (Chapter 7) (04/10)

In re __Zachary Adrian Smith__
    Debtor(s)

Case Number: _____
         (If known)

According to the information required to be entered on this statement (check one box as directed in Part I, III, or VI of this statement):

☐ The presumption arises.
☐ The presumption does not arise.
☐ The presumption is temporarily inapplicable.

CHAPTER 7 STATEMENT OF CURRENT MONTHLY INCOME AND MEANS-TEST CALCULATION

In addition to Schedules I and J, this statement must be completed by every individual chapter 7 debtor, whether or not filing jointly. Unless the exclusion in Line 1C applies, joint debtors may complete a single statement. If the exclusion in Line 1C applies, each joint filer must complete a separate statement.

Part I. MILITARY AND NON-CONSUMER DEBTORS

1A	**Disabled Veterans.** If you are a disabled veteran described in the Declaration in this Part IA, (1) check the box at the beginning of the Declaration, (2) check the box for "The presumption does not arise" at the top of this statement, and (3) complete the verification in Part VIII. Do not complete any of the remaining parts of this statement. ☐ **Declaration of Disabled Veteran.** By checking this box, I declare under penalty of perjury that I am a disabled veteran (as defined in 38 U.S.C. § 3741(1)) whose indebtedness occurred primarily during a period in which I was on active duty (as defined in 10 U.S.C. § 101(d)(1)) or while I was performing a homeland defense activity (as defined in 32 U.S.C. §901(1)).
1B	**Non-consumer Debtors.** If your debts are not primarily consumer debts, check the box below and complete the verification in Part VIII. Do not complete any of the remaining parts of this statement. ☒ **Declaration of non-consumer debts.** By checking this box, I declare that my debts are not primarily consumer debts.

1C	**Reservists and National Guard Members; active duty or homeland defense activity.** Members of a reserve component of the Armed Forces and members of the National Guard who were called to active duty (as defined in 10 U.S.C. § 101(d)(1)) after September 11, 2001, for a period of at least 90 days, or who have performed homeland defense activity (as defined in 32 U.S.C. § 901(1)) for a period of at least 90 days, are excluded from all forms of means testing during the time of active duty or homeland defense activity and for 540 days thereafter (the "exclusion period"). If you qualify for this temporary exclusion, (1) check the appropriate boxes and complete any required information in the Declaration of Reservists and National Guard Members below, (2) check the box for "The presumption is temporarily inapplicable" at the top of this statement, and (3) complete the verification in Part VIII. **During your exclusion period you are not required to complete the balance of this form, but you must complete the form no later than 14 days after the date on which your exclusion period ends, unless the time for filing a motion raising the means test presumption expires in your case before your exclusion period ends.**
	
	☐ **Declaration of Reservists and National Guard Members.** By checking this box and making the appropriate entries below, I declare that I am eligible for a temporary exclusion from means testing because, as a member of a reserve component of the Armed Forces or the National Guard
	
	   a. ☐ I was called to active duty after September 11, 2001, for a period of at least 90 days and
	      ☐ I remain on active duty /or/
	      ☐ I was released from active duty on _____, which is less than 540 days before this bankruptcy case was filed;
	
	      OR
	
	   b. ☐ I am performing homeland defense activity for a period of at least 90 days /or/
	      ☐ I performed homeland defense activity for a period of at least 90 days, terminating on _____, which is less than 540 days before this bankruptcy case was filed.

Example Statement of Current Monthly Income and Means-Test Calculation (cont.)

B 22A (Official Form 22A) (Chapter 7) (04/10)   2

	Part II. CALCULATION OF MONTHLY INCOME FOR § 707(b)(7) EXCLUSION		
2	**Marital/filing status.** Check the box that applies and complete the balance of this part of this statement as directed. a. ☐ Unmarried. **Complete only Column A ("Debtor's Income") for Lines 3-11.** b. ☐ Married, not filing jointly, with declaration of separate households. By checking this box, debtor declares under penalty of perjury: "My spouse and I are legally separated under applicable non-bankruptcy law or my spouse and I are living apart other than for the purpose of evading the requirements of § 707(b)(2)(A) of the Bankruptcy Code." **Complete only Column A ("Debtor's Income") for Lines 3-11.** c. ☐ Married, not filing jointly, without the declaration of separate households set out in Line 2.b above. **Complete both Column A ("Debtor's Income") and Column B ("Spouse's Income") for Lines 3-11.** d. ☐ Married, filing jointly. **Complete both Column A ("Debtor's Income") and Column B ("Spouse's Income") for Lines 3-11.**			
	All figures must reflect average monthly income received from all sources, derived during the six calendar months prior to filing the bankruptcy case, ending on the last day of the month before the filing. If the amount of monthly income varied during the six months, you must divide the six-month total by six, and enter the result on the appropriate line.	**Column A** Debtor's Income	**Column B** Spouse's Income	
3	**Gross wages, salary, tips, bonuses, overtime, commissions.**	$	$	
4	**Income from the operation of a business, profession or farm.** Subtract Line b from Line a and enter the difference in the appropriate column(s) of Line 4. If you operate more than one business, profession or farm, enter aggregate numbers and provide details on an attachment. Do not enter a number less than zero. **Do not include any part of the business expenses entered on Line b as a deduction in Part V.** a. Gross receipts — $ b. Ordinary and necessary business expenses — $ c. Business income — Subtract Line b from Line a	$	$	
5	**Rent and other real property income.** Subtract Line b from Line a and enter the difference in the appropriate column(s) of Line 5. Do not enter a number less than zero. **Do not include any part of the operating expenses entered on Line b as a deduction in Part V.** a. Gross receipts — $ b. Ordinary and necessary operating expenses — $ c. Rent and other real property income — Subtract Line b from Line a	$	$	
6	**Interest, dividends and royalties.**	$	$	
7	**Pension and retirement income.**	$	$	
8	**Any amounts paid by another person or entity, on a regular basis, for the household expenses of the debtor or the debtor's dependents, including child support paid for that purpose.** Do not include alimony or separate maintenance payments or amounts paid by your spouse if Column B is completed.	$	$	
9	**Unemployment compensation.** Enter the amount in the appropriate column(s) of Line 9. However, if you contend that unemployment compensation received by you or your spouse was a benefit under the Social Security Act, do not list the amount of such compensation in Column A or B, but instead state the amount in the space below: Unemployment compensation claimed to be a benefit under the Social Security Act — Debtor $ _____ Spouse $ _____	$	$	

Example Statement of Current Monthly Income and Means-Test Calculation (cont.)

B 22A (Official Form 22A) (Chapter 7) (04/10)   3

10	**Income from all other sources.** Specify source and amount. If necessary, list additional sources on a separate page. **Do not include alimony or separate maintenance payments paid by your spouse if Column B is completed, but include all other payments of alimony or separate maintenance.** Do not include any benefits received under the Social Security Act or payments received as a victim of a war crime, crime against humanity, or as a victim of international or domestic terrorism.		
	a. $		
	b. $		
	Total and enter on Line 10	$	$
11	**Subtotal of Current Monthly Income for § 707(b)(7).** Add Lines 3 thru 10 in Column A, and, if Column B is completed, add Lines 3 through 10 in Column B. Enter the total(s).	$	$
12	**Total Current Monthly Income for § 707(b)(7).** If Column B has been completed, add Line 11, Column A to Line 11, Column B, and enter the total. If Column B has not been completed, enter the amount from Line 11, Column A.	$	

Part III. APPLICATION OF § 707(b)(7) EXCLUSION

13	**Annualized Current Monthly Income for § 707(b)(7).** Multiply the amount from Line 12 by the number 12 and enter the result.	$
14	**Applicable median family income.** Enter the median family income for the applicable state and household size. (This information is available by family size at www.usdoj.gov/ust/ or from the clerk of the bankruptcy court.) a. Enter debtor's state of residence: _____ b. Enter debtor's household size: _____	$
15	**Application of Section 707(b)(7).** Check the applicable box and proceed as directed. ☐ **The amount on Line 13 is less than or equal to the amount on Line 14.** Check the box for "The presumption does not arise" at the top of page 1 of this statement, and complete Part VIII; do not complete Parts IV, V, VI or VII. ☐ **The amount on Line 13 is more than the amount on Line 14.** Complete the remaining parts of this statement.	

Complete Parts IV, V, VI, and VII of this statement only if required. (See Line 15.)

	Part IV. CALCULATION OF CURRENT MONTHLY INCOME FOR § 707(b)(2)

16	**Enter the amount from Line 12.**	$
17	**Marital adjustment.** If you checked the box at Line 2.c, enter on Line 17 the total of any income listed in Line 11, Column B that was NOT paid on a regular basis for the household expenses of the debtor or the debtor's dependents. Specify in the lines below the basis for excluding the Column B income (such as payment of the spouse's tax liability or the spouse's support of persons other than the debtor or the debtor's dependents) and the amount of income devoted to each purpose. If necessary, list additional adjustments on a separate page. If you did not check box at Line 2.c, enter zero.	
	a. $	
	b. $	
	c. $	
	Total and enter on Line 17.	$
18	**Current monthly income for § 707(b)(2).** Subtract Line 17 from Line 16 and enter the result.	$

Part V. CALCULATION OF DEDUCTIONS FROM INCOME

Subpart A: Deductions under Standards of the Internal Revenue Service (IRS)

19A	**National Standards: food, clothing and other items.** Enter in Line 19A the "Total" amount from IRS National Standards for Food, Clothing and Other Items for the applicable household size. (This information is available at www.usdoj.gov/ust/ or from the clerk of the bankruptcy court.)	$

Example Statement of Current Monthly Income and Means-Test Calculation (cont.)

B 22A (Official Form 22A) (Chapter 7) (04/10)   4

19B	**National Standards: health care.** Enter in Line a1 below the amount from IRS National Standards for Out-of-Pocket Health Care for persons under 65 years of age, and in Line a2 the IRS National Standards for Out-of-Pocket Health Care for persons 65 years of age or older. (This information is available at www.usdoj.gov/ust/ or from the clerk of the bankruptcy court.) Enter in Line b1 the number of members of your household who are under 65 years of age, and enter in Line b2 the number of members of your household who are 65 years of age or older. (The total number of household members must be the same as the number stated in Line 14b.) Multiply Line a1 by Line b1 to obtain a total amount for household members under 65, and enter the result in Line c1. Multiply Line a2 by Line b2 to obtain a total amount for household members 65 and older, and enter the result in Line c2. Add Lines c1 and c2 to obtain a total health care amount, and enter the result in Line 19B.	

Household members under 65 years of age		Household members 65 years of age or older		
a1.	Allowance per member	a2.	Allowance per member	
b1.	Number of members	b2.	Number of members	
c1.	Subtotal	c2.	Subtotal	$

20A	**Local Standards: housing and utilities; non-mortgage expenses.** Enter the amount of the IRS Housing and Utilities Standards; non-mortgage expenses for the applicable county and household size. (This information is available at www.usdoj.gov/ust/ or from the clerk of the bankruptcy court).	$

20B	**Local Standards: housing and utilities; mortgage/rent expense.** Enter, in Line a below, the amount of the IRS Housing and Utilities Standards; mortgage/rent expense for your county and household size (this information is available at www.usdoj.gov/ust/ or from the clerk of the bankruptcy court); enter on Line b the total of the Average Monthly Payments for any debts secured by your home, as stated in Line 42; subtract Line b from Line a and enter the result in Line 20B. **Do not enter an amount less than zero.**	

a.	IRS Housing and Utilities Standards; mortgage/rental expense	$	
b.	Average Monthly Payment for any debts secured by your home, if any, as stated in Line 42	$	
c.	Net mortgage/rental expense	Subtract Line b from Line a.	$

21	**Local Standards: housing and utilities; adjustment.** If you contend that the process set out in Lines 20A and 20B does not accurately compute the allowance to which you are entitled under the IRS Housing and Utilities Standards, enter any additional amount to which you contend you are entitled, and state the basis for your contention in the space below: _____ _____ _____	$

22A	**Local Standards: transportation; vehicle operation/public transportation expense.** You are entitled to an expense allowance in this category regardless of whether you pay the expenses of operating a vehicle and regardless of whether you use public transportation. Check the number of vehicles for which you pay the operating expenses or for which the operating expenses are included as a contribution to your household expenses in Line 8. ☐ 0 ☐ 1 ☐ 2 or more. If you checked 0, enter on Line 22A the "Public Transportation" amount from IRS Local Standards: Transportation. If you checked 1 or 2 or more, enter on Line 22A the "Operating Costs" amount from IRS Local Standards: Transportation for the applicable number of vehicles in the applicable Metropolitan Statistical Area or Census Region. (These amounts are available at www.usdoj.gov/ust/ or from the clerk of the bankruptcy court.)	$

22B	**Local Standards: transportation; additional public transportation expense.** If you pay the operating expenses for a vehicle and also use public transportation, and you contend that you are entitled to an additional deduction for your public transportation expenses, enter on Line 22B the "Public Transportation" amount from IRS Local Standards: Transportation. (This amount is available at www.usdoj.gov/ust/ or from the clerk of the bankruptcy court.)	$

Example Statement of Current Monthly Income and Means-Test Calculation (cont.)

B 22A (Official Form 22A) (Chapter 7) (04/10)   5

23	**Local Standards: transportation ownership/lease expense; Vehicle 1.** Check the number of vehicles for which you claim an ownership/lease expense. (You may not claim an ownership/lease expense for more than two vehicles.) ☐ 1 ☐ 2 or more. Enter, in Line a below, the "Ownership Costs" for "One Car" from the IRS Local Standards: Transportation (available at www.usdoj.gov/ust/ or from the clerk of the bankruptcy court); enter in Line b the total of the Average Monthly Payments for any debts secured by Vehicle 1, as stated in Line 42; subtract Line b from Line a and enter the result in Line 23. **Do not enter an amount less than zero.**			

a.	IRS Transportation Standards, Ownership Costs	$
b.	Average Monthly Payment for any debts secured by Vehicle 1, as stated in Line 42	$
c.	Net ownership/lease expense for Vehicle 1	Subtract Line b from Line a. $

24	**Local Standards: transportation ownership/lease expense; Vehicle 2.** Complete this Line only if you checked the "2 or more" Box in Line 23. Enter, in Line a below, the "Ownership Costs" for "One Car" from the IRS Local Standards: Transportation (available at www.usdoj.gov/ust/ or from the clerk of the bankruptcy court); enter in Line b the total of the Average Monthly Payments for any debts secured by Vehicle 2, as stated in Line 42; subtract Line b from Line a and enter the result in Line 24. **Do not enter an amount less than zero.**

a.	IRS Transportation Standards, Ownership Costs	$
b.	Average Monthly Payment for any debts secured by Vehicle 2, as stated in Line 42	$
c.	Net ownership/lease expense for Vehicle 2	Subtract Line b from Line a. $

25	**Other Necessary Expenses: taxes.** Enter the total average monthly expense that you actually incur for all federal, state and local taxes, other than real estate and sales taxes, such as income taxes, self-employment taxes, social-security taxes, and Medicare taxes. **Do not include real estate or sales taxes.**	$
26	**Other Necessary Expenses: involuntary deductions for employment.** Enter the total average monthly payroll deductions that are required for your employment, such as retirement contributions, union dues, and uniform costs. **Do not include discretionary amounts, such as voluntary 401(k) contributions.**	$
27	**Other Necessary Expenses: life insurance.** Enter total average monthly premiums that you actually pay for term life insurance for yourself. **Do not include premiums for insurance on your dependents, for whole life or for any other form of insurance.**	$
28	**Other Necessary Expenses: court-ordered payments.** Enter the total monthly amount that you are required to pay pursuant to the order of a court or administrative agency, such as spousal or child support payments. **Do not include payments on past due obligations included in Line 44.**	$
29	**Other Necessary Expenses: education for employment or for a physically or mentally challenged child.** Enter the total average monthly amount that you actually expend for education that is a condition of employment and for education that is required for a physically or mentally challenged dependent child for whom no public education providing similar services is available.	$
30	**Other Necessary Expenses: childcare.** Enter the total average monthly amount that you actually expend on childcare—such as baby-sitting, day care, nursery and preschool. **Do not include other educational payments.**	$
31	**Other Necessary Expenses: health care.** Enter the total average monthly amount that you actually expend on health care that is required for the health and welfare of yourself or your dependents, that is not reimbursed by insurance or paid by a health savings account, and that is in excess of the amount entered in Line 19B. **Do not include payments for health insurance or health savings accounts listed in Line 34.**	$
32	**Other Necessary Expenses: telecommunication services.** Enter the total average monthly amount that you actually pay for telecommunication services other than your basic home telephone and cell phone service— such as pagers, call waiting, caller id, special long distance, or internet service—to the extent necessary for your health and welfare or that of your dependents. **Do not include any amount previously deducted.**	$
33	**Total Expenses Allowed under IRS Standards.** Enter the total of Lines 19 through 32.	$

Example Statement of Current Monthly Income and Means-Test Calculation (cont.)

B 22A (Official Form 22A) (Chapter 7) (04/10)   6

	Subpart B: Additional Living Expense Deductions **Note: Do not include any expenses that you have listed in Lines 19-32**		
34	Health Insurance, Disability Insurance, and Health Savings Account Expenses. List the monthly expenses in the categories set out in lines a-c below that are reasonably necessary for yourself, your spouse, or your dependents. a. Health Insurance — $ b. Disability Insurance — $ c. Health Savings Account — $ Total and enter on Line 34 If you do not actually expend this total amount, state your actual total average monthly expenditures in the space below: $ _____		$
35	Continued contributions to the care of household or family members. Enter the total average actual monthly expenses that you will continue to pay for the reasonable and necessary care and support of an elderly, chronically ill, or disabled member of your household or member of your immediate family who is unable to pay for such expenses.		$
36	Protection against family violence. Enter the total average reasonably necessary monthly expenses that you actually incurred to maintain the safety of your family under the Family Violence Prevention and Services Act or other applicable federal law. The nature of these expenses is required to be kept confidential by the court.		$
37	Home energy costs. Enter the total average monthly amount, in excess of the allowance specified by IRS Local Standards for Housing and Utilities, that you actually expend for home energy costs. You must provide your case trustee with documentation of your actual expenses, and you must demonstrate that the additional amount claimed is reasonable and necessary.		$
38	Education expenses for dependent children less than 18. Enter the total average monthly expenses that you actually incur, not to exceed $147.92* per child, for attendance at a private or public elementary or secondary school by your dependent children less than 18 years of age. You must provide your case trustee with documentation of your actual expenses, and you must explain why the amount claimed is reasonable and necessary and not already accounted for in the IRS Standards.		$
39	Additional food and clothing expense. Enter the total average monthly amount by which your food and clothing expenses exceed the combined allowances for food and clothing (apparel and services) in the IRS National Standards, not to exceed 5% of those combined allowances. (This information is available at www.usdoj.gov/ust/ or from the clerk of the bankruptcy court.) You must demonstrate that the additional amount claimed is reasonable and necessary.		$
40	Continued charitable contributions. Enter the amount that you will continue to contribute in the form of cash or financial instruments to a charitable organization as defined in 26 U.S.C. § 170(c)(1)-(2).		$
41	Total Additional Expense Deductions under § 707(b). Enter the total of Lines 34 through 40		$

*Amount subject to adjustment on 4/01/13, and every three years thereafter with respect to cases commenced on or after the date of adjustment.

Example Statement of Current Monthly Income and Means-Test Calculation (cont.)

B 22A (Official Form 22A) (Chapter 7) (04/10)   7

Subpart C: Deductions for Debt Payment	

42 Future payments on secured claims. For each of your debts that is secured by an interest in property that you own, list the name of the creditor, identify the property securing the debt, state the Average Monthly Payment, and check whether the payment includes taxes or insurance. The Average Monthly Payment is the total of all amounts scheduled as contractually due to each Secured Creditor in the 60 months following the filing of the bankruptcy case, divided by 60. If necessary, list additional entries on a separate page. Enter the total of the Average Monthly Payments on Line 42.

	Name of Creditor	Property Securing the Debt	Average Monthly Payment	Does payment include taxes or insurance?
a.			$	☐ yes ☐ no
b.			$	☐ yes ☐ no
c.			$	☐ yes ☐ no
			Total: Add Lines a, b and c.	$

43 Other payments on secured claims. If any of debts listed in Line 42 are secured by your primary residence, a motor vehicle, or other property necessary for your support or the support of your dependents, you may include in your deduction 1/60th of any amount (the "cure amount") that you must pay the creditor in addition to the payments listed in Line 42, in order to maintain possession of the property. The cure amount would include any sums in default that must be paid in order to avoid repossession or foreclosure. List and total any such amounts in the following chart. If necessary, list additional entries on a separate page.

	Name of Creditor	Property Securing the Debt	1/60th of the Cure Amount
a.			$
b.			$
c.			$
			Total: Add Lines a, b and c $

44 Payments on prepetition priority claims. Enter the total amount, divided by 60, of all priority claims, such as priority tax, child support and alimony claims, for which you were liable at the time of your bankruptcy filing. **Do not include current obligations, such as those set out in Line 28.** $

45 Chapter 13 administrative expenses. If you are eligible to file a case under chapter 13, complete the following chart, multiply the amount in line a by the amount in line b, and enter the resulting administrative expense.

a.	Projected average monthly chapter 13 plan payment.	$
b.	Current multiplier for your district as determined under schedules issued by the Executive Office for United States Trustees. (This information is available at www.usdoj.gov/ust/ or from the clerk of the bankruptcy court.)	X
c.	Average monthly administrative expense of chapter 13 case	Total: Multiply Lines a and b $

46 Total Deductions for Debt Payment. Enter the total of Lines 42 through 45. $

Subpart D: Total Deductions from Income	

47 Total of all deductions allowed under § 707(b)(2). Enter the total of Lines 33, 41, and 46. $

Example Statement of Current Monthly Income and Means-Test Calculation (cont.)

B 22A (Official Form 22A) (Chapter 7) (04/10)   8

Part VI. DETERMINATION OF § 707(b)(2) PRESUMPTION

48	Enter the amount from Line 18 (Current monthly income for § 707(b)(2))	$
49	Enter the amount from Line 47 (Total of all deductions allowed under § 707(b)(2))	$
50	Monthly disposable income under § 707(b)(2). Subtract Line 49 from Line 48 and enter the result	$
51	60-month disposable income under § 707(b)(2). Multiply the amount in Line 50 by the number 60 and enter the result.	$

52	**Initial presumption determination.** Check the applicable box and proceed as directed. ☐ **The amount on Line 51 is less than $7,025*** Check the box for "The presumption does not arise" at the top of page 1 of this statement, and complete the verification in Part VIII. Do not complete the remainder of Part VI. ☐ **The amount set forth on Line 51 is more than $11,725*.** Check the box for "The presumption arises" at the top of page 1 of this statement, and complete the verification in Part VIII. You may also complete Part VII. Do not complete the remainder of Part VI. ☐ **The amount on Line 51 is at least $7,025*, but not more than $11,725*.** Complete the remainder of Part VI (Lines 53 through 55).

53	Enter the amount of your total non-priority unsecured debt	$
54	Threshold debt payment amount. Multiply the amount in Line 53 by the number 0.25 and enter the result.	$

55	**Secondary presumption determination.** Check the applicable box and proceed as directed. ☐ **The amount on Line 51 is less than the amount on Line 54.** Check the box for "The presumption does not arise" at the top of page 1 of this statement, and complete the verification in Part VIII. ☐ **The amount on Line 51 is equal to or greater than the amount on Line 54.** Check the box for "The presumption arises" at the top of page 1 of this statement, and complete the verification in Part VIII. You may also complete Part VII.

Part VII: ADDITIONAL EXPENSE CLAIMS

56	**Other Expenses.** List and describe any monthly expenses, not otherwise stated in this form, that are required for the health and welfare of you and your family and that you contend should be an additional deduction from your current monthly income under § 707(b)(2)(A)(ii)(I). If necessary, list additional sources on a separate page. All figures should reflect your average monthly expense for each item. Total the expenses.

	Expense Description	Monthly Amount
a.		$
b.		$
c.		$
	Total: Add Lines a, b and c	$

Part VIII: VERIFICATION

57	I declare under penalty of perjury that the information provided in this statement is true and correct. *(If this is a joint case, both debtors must sign.)*
	
	 Date: ___XX–XX–XX___ Signature: _Z.A. Smith_
	                                                 (Debtor)
	
	 Date: _____ Signature: _____
	                                                 (Joint Debtor, if any)

**Amounts are subject to adjustment on 4/01/13, and every three years thereafter with respect to cases commenced on or after the date of adjustment.*

<6> STATEMENT OF FINANCIAL AFFAIRS; DEBTOR'S STATEMENT OF INTENTION; AND STATEMENT OF SOCIAL SECURITY NUMBER(S)

Statement of Financial Affairs

The Statement of Financial Affairs provides a summary of your financial history, transactions, and operations over certain periods of time before the commencement of your case, as specified in the questions. It is important for you to pay special attention to these different time periods referred to in the questions. For example, when a question asks you to list payments made to creditors within 90 days of the commencement of your case, that means you should list only those payments to creditors made during the 90-day period before the date of the filing of your bankruptcy petition.

The form should be cross-checked for consistency with assets listed in Schedules A, B, and G.

Questions 1 through 18 must be completed by all debtors. Questions 19 through 25 are to be completed by debtors who are or have been in business. The definition for the term "in business" is set out on page 1 of the form. If you are not or have never been in business, skip directly to the signature page after answering question 18(b).

If the answer to any question is "None," mark the box labeled "None." In the event sufficient space is not provided to fully answer any question, you should use a continuation sheet and attach it to the form. Each continuation sheet should be clearly marked with the number of the corresponding question from the form.

To indicate payments, transfers, and the like to minor children, state the child's initials and the name and address of the child's parent or guardian as instructed in Chapter 4.

Applicable Law and Rules

The Bankruptcy Code and Federal Rules of Bankruptcy Procedure require you to perform many duties. One such duty is to file a Statement of Financial Affairs. This statement must be filed at the same time as the bankruptcy petition in a voluntary case or, if the petition is accompanied by a list of all the creditors and their addresses, within 14 days after the filing of the petition. It is preferable to file your Statement of Financial Affairs with your petition.

An extension of time for filing the statement may be granted by the court only on motion for cause shown, on notice to the United States trustee, and on notice to any committee, trustee, examiner, or other party directed by the court.

At any time before the case is closed, a Statement of Financial Affairs may be amended by you as a matter of course per Federal Rules of Bankruptcy Procedure 1009(a). You must give notice of the amendment to the trustee and any entity affected by the amendment.

Question 1: Income from Employment or Operation of Business

This question requires you to state the gross amount of income received from employment, trade, profession, or from operation of your business. Include any part-time activities you conducted either as an employee or in independent trade or business. You should note that the information is required for the following two time periods: (1) from the beginning of this calendar year to the date of the commencement of the case, and (2) the two years before the calendar year in which the case is commenced. The form allows you to use a fiscal year rather than a calendar year, if necessary. The amount and source of the income should be listed for each time period. Spouses who have filed a joint petition should list the income of each spouse separately.

Question 2: Income Other Than from Employment or Operation of Business

All other income (other than from employment, trade, profession, or from operation of your business) that you received during the two years before the commencement of the case should be disclosed under question 2. This category may include, but is not limited to, income from tax refunds, Social security and other public benefit payments, alimony, child support, interest, dividends, pensions, annuities, capital gains, money judgments from lawsuits, royalties, licenses, rents, leases, and subleases. The amount and source of the income should be listed in the space provided. Again, spouses who have filed a joint petition should list the income of each spouse separately.

Question 3: Payment to Creditors

This question directs you to list payments to creditors within two specific time periods. You should include payments to creditors on secured and unsecured debts. You must complete either question 3(a) or 3(b), depending on the nature of your debts. All debtors are required to complete question 3(c).

Each creditor should be listed separately, with the date of each payment, amount of each payment, and current outstanding balance of the debt.

a. Individual or joint debtors with primarily consumer debts are required to complete question 3(a). List all payments of $600 or more on loans, installment purchases of goods or services, and other debts paid to any creditor on or within 90 days prior to the commencement of the bankruptcy case. Indicate with an asterisk (*) any payments that were made to a creditor on account of a domestic support obligation or as part of an alternative repayment schedule under a plan by an approved nonprofit budgeting and counseling agency.

b. Debtors whose debts are not primarily consumer debts are required to complete question 3(b). List all payments or other transfers of property made to any creditor on or within 90 days prior the commencement of the bankruptcy case if the aggregate value of the payment or transfer is $5,475 or more. You are required to indicate with an asterisk (*) any payments that were made to a creditor on account of a domestic support obligation or as part of an alternative repayment schedule under a plan by an approved nonprofit budgeting and counseling agency.

c. All debtors are required to complete question 3(c). List all payments made within one year prior to the commencement of the bankruptcy case to or for the benefit of a creditor who is or was an "insider." The definition of an insider appears on page 1 of the form. Specify the relationship of the creditors listed in question 3(c) to you.

Question 4: Suits, Administrative Proceedings, Execution, Garnishments, and Attachments

In question 4(a) you must list all lawsuits and administrative proceedings, to which you were a party within one year prior to filing the bankruptcy case. This includes, but is not limited to, divorce proceedings and state and federal administrative proceedings. You must list each suit or administrative proceeding and case number separately, providing a description of the nature of the proceeding, the court or agency involved, the location of the proceeding, and the status of any pending proceeding or the disposition (ultimate result) of any finalized one.

Question 5: Repossessions, Foreclosures, and Returns

You should list all property that has been repossessed by a creditor, sold at a foreclosure sale, transferred through a deed in lieu of foreclosure, or returned to the seller within one year prior to the commencement of your case. The name and address of each creditor or seller, the date of repossession, foreclosure, sale, transfer, or return, and a description and value of the property should be included. This question covers repossession or voluntary return of any personal property, such as vehicles, tools, or household goods, as well as foreclosure and sale of any real estate.

Question 6: Assignments and Receiverships

Here you should describe any assignment of property for the benefit of creditors made within the 120 days before commencement of your case. The name and address of the assignee, date of assignment, and terms of the assignment or settlement should also be described.

For question 6(b), list all property which has been in the hands of a custodian, receiver, or court-appointed official within one year prior to the commencement of your case. (This does not include a chapter 7 bankruptcy trustee.) The name and address of the custodian, name and location of the court, case title, case number, date of the order, as well as a description of the property and its value should be included.

Question 7: Gifts

You must list all gifts or charitable contributions you made within one year prior to the commencement of your case, except ordinary and usual gifts to family members that total less than $200 in value per person, and charitable contributions that total less than $100 per recipient. You must list the name and address of the person or organization, their relationship to you, date of the gift, and a description and the value of the gift. Question 7 covers cash and noncash items alike.

Question 8: Losses

You must list all losses from fire, theft, other casualty, or gambling incurred within one year prior to the commencement of your case or since the commencement of your case. You should describe the property lost, state its value, give the date of said loss, and describe the circumstances of the loss. Explain if any loss was covered by insurance in whole or in part.

Pending claims from insurance coverage should also be listed on Schedule B.

Question 9: Payments Related to Debt Counseling or Bankruptcy

This question requires you to list all payments made, or property transferred by or on behalf of you, to any person, for consultation concerning debt consolidation, relief under bankruptcy law, or preparation of a bankruptcy petition within one year prior to the commencement of your case. You are asked to include the name and address of the person or entity paid, the date of payment, the name of the payer (if other than you), the amount of money paid, and a description and value of the property.

Question 10: Other Transfers

Question 10(a) requires you to list all property (other than property transferred in the ordinary course of your business or financial affairs) transferred either absolutely or as security within two years prior to the commencement of your case. The name and address of the person or entity that received the property, and their relationship to you, should be listed. Any security interest that meets the foregoing criteria should be listed. Also include the date of the transfer, a description of the property transferred, and value that was received.

Question 10(b) requires you to list all property transferred, within ten years before commencement of your case, to a self-settled trust or similar device of which you are a beneficiary.

Question 11: Closed Financial Accounts

In question 11 you must list all financial accounts and instruments held in your name or for your benefit which were closed, sold, or otherwise transferred within one year prior to the commencement of your case. These include checking, savings, or other financial accounts, certificates of deposit, as well as any shares and share accounts held in banks, credit unions, pension funds, cooperatives, associations, brokerage house, or other financial institutions. Other examples include any Individual Retirement Accounts (IRAs), mutual funds, bonds, savings plans, and annuities. You should list the name and address of the institution, the type of account, the last four digits of the account number, the amount of the final balance, and the amount and date of any sale or closing.

Question 12: Safe Deposit Boxes

Question 12 requires you to list each safe deposit box or other box or depository in which you have or had securities, cash, or other valuables within one year prior to the commencement of your case. You are asked to include the name and address of the bank or depository, the names and addresses of those with access to the box or depository, a description of the contents, and the date of any transfer or surrender.

Question 13: Setoffs

Here you are asked to list all "setoff" made by any creditor, including a bank, against a debt or deposit of yours within the 90 days before commencement of your case. A setoff is when part or all of a debt moved by you to a creditor is canceled out by a pre-existing debt owed by the creditor to you. Since certain pre-petition setoffs taken by a creditor may be subject to recovery by the bankruptcy estate, it is important that all setoffs be accounted for in the form. You must include the name and address of the creditor, the date of setoff, and the amount of the setoff.

Question 14: Property Held for Another Person

Question 14 directs you to list all property owned by another person that you hold or control. You should list the name and address of the owner, a description of the property, its value, and the location of the property. Examples of this type of property may include property you hold or control in the capacity of a trustee or bailee, or property on consignment.

Question 15: Prior Address of Debtor

If you have moved within the three years prior to commencement of your case, you must list all premises which you occupied and vacated during that period. Spouses filing a joint petition should list any separate addresses individually, including the name used and the dates of occupancy.

STATEMENTS OF: FINANCIAL AFFAIRS, DEBTOR'S INTENTION AND SOCIAL SECURITY NUMBER(S)

Question 16: Spouses and Former Spouses

If at any time within the eight years prior to your bankruptcy case you resided with a spouse in a community property state, you are required to disclose that former spouse's name. Community property states include Alaska, Arizona, California, Idaho, Louisiana, Nevada, New Mexico, Puerto Rico, Texas, Washington, and Wisconsin.

Question 17: Environmental Information

This question requires you to provide information concerning any environmentally hazardous material or hazardous site or sites which you own, manufacture, release or may formerly have owned, manufactured, or released. These include biological, chemical, and radioactive materials. Because it is possible that an individual non-business debtor may own or have released hazardous material or property on which hazardous material exists, every debtor must answer this question. (The terms "hazardous site," and "hazardous material" are defined in question 17 on the form.) Note that there is no time limit cited; all notices, releases, and proceedings of which you have knowledge must be reported, regardless of when they occurred.

a. This question requires you to list every hazardous site for which you have received a notice from a government agency that you may be liable under, or in violation of, an environmental law. ("Environmental law" is defined within question 17 on the form.) You should give the name and address of the governmental unit that issued the notice, the date of the notice, and, if known, the name and section number(s) of the environmental law (for example, Illinois Waterways Protection Act, section 38-7.01).

b. You are required to list the name and address of any hazardous site for which you provided notice to a government agency of a release of hazardous material. In addition to the name and address of the site or sites involved, state the name and address of the governmental unit to \which notice was sent, the date of any notice, and, if known, the name and section number(s) of the environmental law under which you acted.

c. Here you must list any judicial or administrative proceedings in which you are or were a party under any environmental law. You are required to disclose the name of the governmental unit that was a party in the proceeding and the docket number of the proceeding. The name of the court or other tribunal must also be stated. In reporting the status or disposition of the case, include all settlements and orders by any court or other tribunal.

Question 18: Nature, Location, and Name of Business

a. You must list the names and addresses of all businesses in which you were an officer, director, partner (other than a limited partner) of a partnership, or managing executive of a corporation, partnership, or sole proprietorship within the six years prior to the filing of your petition. If you were self-employed in a trade, profession, or other activity, either full- or part-time during the six years before commencement of your case, you are also required to list that information. In addition, you must list the name and address of any business in which you owned five percent or more of the voting or equity securities within the same six years.

b. Identify any business listed in response to subdivision a., that is "single asset real estate" as defined in 11 U.S.C. §101.

Partnership and corporate debtors must list the names and addresses of all businesses in which the debtor was a partner or owned five percent or more of the voting or equity securities within the six years before commencement of the case.

All of the above types of debtors should state the name, address, last four digits of the taxpayer identification number, and nature of any business listed in question 10(a) that is "single asset real estate" as defined in 11 U.S.C. §101 (51B).

Questions 19 Through 25

These are to be completed by every debtor that is a corporation or partnership, and by any individual or joint debtor who is or has been "in business," as defined on the first page of the form. You should complete questions 19 through 25 only if you are or have been in business within the six years prior to commencement of your case. Care should be taken to provide information for the years specified in each question. Additional sheets may be attached, if necessary.

If you do not meet the definition of "in business," proceed directly to the last page of the form and the section labeled "Signatures of Debtors." Instructions for this section appear later in this chapter of the book.

Question 19: Books, Records, and Financial Statements

a. You must list all bookkeepers and accountants who kept or supervised the keeping of your books of account and records, within the two years prior to filing your bankruptcy case. In the space provided, state the names, addresses, and dates of services rendered.

b. You must list all firms or individuals who have audited your books of account and records, or prepared a financial statement on your behalf, within the two years prior to filing your bankruptcy case. In the space provided, state the names, addresses, and dates of services rendered.

c. List all firms or individuals who were in possession of your books of account and records at the time of the commencement of this case. State in the space provided the names and addresses of the firms or individuals.

d. List all financial institutions, creditors, and other parties, including mercantile and trade agencies, to whom you issued a financial statement within the two years prior to commencement of your case. State the name and address of the entity and the date the financial statement was issued.

Question 20: Inventories

a. State the dates of the last two inventories taken of your property, the name of the person who supervised the taking of each inventory, and the dollar amount and basis of each inventory. You are asked to specify the cost, market or other basis.

b. List the name and address of the person having possession of your records for the two inventories reported in question 20(a).

Question 21 : Current Partners, Officers, Directors, and Shareholders

a. If you are a partnership debtor, you must list the nature and percentage of the partnership interest of each partner, including general partners and limited partners.

b. If you are a corporate debtor, you must list all officers, directors, and stockholders the corporation has, who directly or indirectly own, control, or hold five percent or more of the voting securities of the corporation.

Question 22: Former Partners, Officers, Directors, and Shareholders

a. If you are a partnership debtor, you must list each partner, including general partners and limited partners, who withdrew from the partnership within one year prior to the commencement of your case.

b. If you are a corporate debtor, you must list all officers or directors whose relationship with the corporation terminated within one year prior to the commencement of your case.

Question 23: Withdrawals from a Partnership or Distributions by a Corporation

If you are a partnership or corporate debtor, you must disclose all withdrawals or distributions credited or given to an insider, including compensation (in any form), bonuses, loans, stock redemptions, options exercised, and any other benefit during the year prior to commencement of your case. List the name and address of each recipient, their relationship to you, the date and purpose of the withdrawal, and the amount of money or a description and value of any applicable property.

Question 24: Tax Consolidation Group

If you are a corporation that is or has been, at any time within the six years prior to commencement of your case, a member of a consolidated group for tax purposes, you are required to report the name and federal taxpayer identification number of the parent corporation of that group.

Question 25: Pension Funds

If you are or have been an employer and are not filing as an individual, you must provide the name and federal taxpayer identification number of any pension fund to which you have been responsible for contributing at any time within the six years prior to commencement of your case.

Signature of Debtor

You must sign and date the Statement of Financial Affairs. In a joint case, both spouses must sign. By signing the Statement of Financial Affairs, you are declaring, under the penalty of perjury, that the information in the form is true and correct.

Signature of Individual Signing on Behalf of a Partnership or Corporation

This is a section for a partnership or corporate debtor. Individuals and joint debtors should leave this space blank. The individual authorized by the debtor entity to file the petition should sign the Statement of Financial Affairs on behalf of the debtor and include the individual's name and title, as well as the date, on the lines provided. The authorized agent of a debtor corporation or partnership should indicate the agent's position or relationship to the debtor. By signing the petition, the authorized individual is asserting that the information in the Statement of Financial Affairs is true and correct.

Continuation Sheets

Count the number of continuation sheets and place that number in the space provided on the last page. Continuation sheets must be attached to the Official Form.

Certification and Signature of Non-Attorney Bankruptcy Petition Preparer

The Statement of Financial Affairs is a document for filing, which may be prepared by a bankruptcy petition preparer as defined in 11 U.S.C. §110. Therefore, a signature line is provided.

Individual Debtor's Statement of Intention

Any debts secured by property of the estate must be reported here. Most prisoners do not have debts secured by property. You will note that the example petition is a case involving unsecured debts. As such, no example will be provided for the Chapter 7 Individual Debtor's Statement of Intention form. However, that form's parts A and B are provided in the back of this book.

Statement of Social Security Number(s)

You are required to provide your full Social Security Number. If filing jointly, you and your spouse may sign and file the same form.

Example Statement of Financial Affairs

B 7 (Official Form 7) (04/10)

UNITED STATES BANKRUPTCY COURT

In re: Zachary Adrian Smith , Case No. _____
             Debtor   (if known)

STATEMENT OF FINANCIAL AFFAIRS

This statement is to be completed by every debtor. Spouses filing a joint petition may file a single statement on which the information for both spouses is combined. If the case is filed under chapter 12 or chapter 13, a married debtor must furnish information for both spouses whether or not a joint petition is filed, unless the spouses are separated and a joint petition is not filed. An individual debtor engaged in business as a sole proprietor, partner, family farmer, or self-employed professional, should provide the information requested on this statement concerning all such activities as well as the individual's personal affairs. To indicate payments, transfers and the like to minor children, state the child's initials and the name and address of the child's parent or guardian, such as "A.B., a minor child, by John Doe, guardian." Do not disclose the child's name. See, 11 U.S.C. §112 and Fed. R. Bankr. P. 1007(m).

Questions 1 - 18 are to be completed by all debtors. Debtors that are or have been in business, as defined below, also must complete Questions 19 - 25. **If the answer to an applicable question is "None," mark the box labeled "None."** If additional space is needed for the answer to any question, use and attach a separate sheet properly identified with the case name, case number (if known), and the number of the question.

DEFINITIONS

"In business." A debtor is "in business" for the purpose of this form if the debtor is a corporation or partnership. An individual debtor is "in business" for the purpose of this form if the debtor is or has been, within six years immediately preceding the filing of this bankruptcy case, any of the following: an officer, director, managing executive, or owner of 5 percent or more of the voting or equity securities of a corporation; a partner, other than a limited partner, of a partnership; a sole proprietor or self-employed full-time or part-time. An individual debtor also may be "in business" for the purpose of this form if the debtor engages in a trade, business, or other activity, other than as an employee, to supplement income from the debtor's primary employment.

"Insider." The term "insider" includes but is not limited to: relatives of the debtor; general partners of the debtor and their relatives; corporations of which the debtor is an officer, director, or person in control; officers, directors, and any owner of 5 percent or more of the voting or equity securities of a corporate debtor and their relatives; affiliates of the debtor and insiders of such affiliates; any managing agent of the debtor. 11 U.S.C. § 101.

---

1. **Income from employment or operation of business**

None
☑   State the gross amount of income the debtor has received from employment, trade, or profession, or from operation of the debtor's business, including part-time activities either as an employee or in independent trade or business, from the beginning of this calendar year to the date this case was commenced. State also the gross amounts received during the **two years** immediately preceding this calendar year. (A debtor that maintains, or has maintained, financial records on the basis of a fiscal rather than a calendar year may report fiscal year income. Identify the beginning and ending dates of the debtor's fiscal year.) If a joint petition is filed, state income for each spouse separately. (Married debtors filing under chapter 12 or chapter 13 must state income of both spouses whether or not a joint petition is filed, unless the spouses are separated and a joint petition is not filed.)

AMOUNT   SOURCE

Example Statement of Financial Affairs (cont.)

2

2. Income other than from employment or operation of business

None
☒

State the amount of income received by the debtor other than from employment, trade, profession, operation of the debtor's business during the **two years** immediately preceding the commencement of this case. Give particulars. If a joint petition is filed, state income for each spouse separately. (Married debtors filing under chapter 12 or chapter 13 must state income for each spouse whether or not a joint petition is filed, unless the spouses are separated and a joint petition is not filed.)

AMOUNT	SOURCE
$8.50	Missouri Department of Corrections

3. Payments to creditors

Complete a. or b., as appropriate, and c.

None
☒

a. *Individual or joint debtor(s) with primarily consumer debts:* List all payments on loans, installment purchases of goods or services, and other debts to any creditor made within **90 days** immediately preceding the commencement of this case unless the aggregate value of all property that constitutes or is affected by such transfer is less than $600. Indicate with an asterisk (*) any payments that were made to a creditor on account of a domestic support obligation or as part of an alternative repayment schedule under a plan by an approved nonprofit budgeting and credit counseling agency. (Married debtors filing under chapter 12 or chapter 13 must include payments by either or both spouses whether or not a joint petition is filed, unless the spouses are separated and a joint petition is not filed.)

NAME AND ADDRESS OF CREDITOR	DATES OF PAYMENTS	AMOUNT PAID	AMOUNT STILL OWING

None
☒

b. *Debtor whose debts are not primarily consumer debts:* List each payment or other transfer to any creditor made within **90 days** immediately preceding the commencement of the case unless the aggregate value of all property that constitutes or is affected by such transfer is less than $5,850*. If the debtor is an individual, indicate with an asterisk (*) any payments that were made to a creditor on account of a domestic support obligation or as part of an alternative repayment schedule under a plan by an approved nonprofit budgeting and credit counseling agency. (Married debtors filing under chapter 12 or chapter 13 must include payments and other transfers by either or both spouses whether or not a joint petition is filed, unless the spouses are separated and a joint petition is not filed.)

NAME AND ADDRESS OF CREDITOR	DATES OF PAYMENTS/ TRANSFERS	AMOUNT PAID OR VALUE OF TRANSFERS	AMOUNT STILL OWING

*Amount subject to adjustment on 4/01/13, and every three years thereafter with respect to cases commenced on or after the date of adjustment.

Example Statement of Financial Affairs (cont.)

3

None

☑ c. *All debtors:* List all payments made within **one year** immediately preceding the commencement of this case to or for the benefit of creditors who are or were insiders. (Married debtors filing under chapter 12 or chapter 13 must include payments by either or both spouses whether or not a joint petition is filed, unless the spouses are separated and a joint petition is not filed.)

NAME AND ADDRESS OF CREDITOR AND RELATIONSHIP TO DEBTOR	DATE OF PAYMENT	AMOUNT PAID	AMOUNT STILL OWING

4. Suits and administrative proceedings, executions, garnishments and attachments

None

☐ a. List all suits and administrative proceedings to which the debtor is or was a party within **one year** immediately preceding the filing of this bankruptcy case. (Married debtors filing under chapter 12 or chapter 13 must include information concerning either or both spouses whether or not a joint petition is filed, unless the spouses are separated and a joint petition is not filed.)

CAPTION OF SUIT AND CASE NUMBER	NATURE OF PROCEEDING	COURT OR AGENCY AND LOCATION	STATUS OR DISPOSITION
State ex rel. Koster V. Smith, Case No. 07AC-CCC0010901	MIRA	Cole County Circuit Court	Pending

None

☐ b. Describe all property that has been attached, garnished or seized under any legal or equitable process within **one year** immediately preceding the commencement of this case. (Married debtors filing under chapter 12 or chapter 13 must include information concerning property of either or both spouses whether or not a joint petition is filed, unless the spouses are separated and a joint petition is not filed.)

NAME AND ADDRESS OF PERSON FOR WHOSE BENEFIT PROPERTY WAS SEIZED	DATE OF SEIZURE	DESCRIPTION AND VALUE OF PROPERTY
MIRA judgment issued, and 90% of any money deposited into offender account taken and sent to the Attorney General's Office.		

5. Repossessions, foreclosures and returns

None

☑ List all property that has been repossessed by a creditor, sold at a foreclosure sale, transferred through a deed in lieu of foreclosure or returned to the seller, within **one year** immediately preceding the commencement of this case. (Married debtors filing under chapter 12 or chapter 13 must include information concerning property of either or both spouses whether or not a joint petition is filed, unless the spouses are separated and a joint petition is not filed.)

NAME AND ADDRESS OF CREDITOR OR SELLER	DATE OF REPOSSESSION, FORECLOSURE SALE, TRANSFER OR RETURN	DESCRIPTION AND VALUE OF PROPERTY

Example Statement of Financial Affairs (cont.)

4

6. **Assignments and receiverships**

None ☒

a. Describe any assignment of property for the benefit of creditors made within **120 days** immediately preceding the commencement of this case. (Married debtors filing under chapter 12 or chapter 13 must include any assignment by either or both spouses whether or not a joint petition is filed, unless the spouses are separated and a joint petition is not filed.)

NAME AND ADDRESS OF ASSIGNEE	DATE OF ASSIGNMENT	TERMS OF ASSIGNMENT OR SETTLEMENT

None ☑

b. List all property which has been in the hands of a custodian, receiver, or court-appointed official within **one year** immediately preceding the commencement of this case. (Married debtors filing under chapter 12 or chapter 13 must include information concerning property of either or both spouses whether or not a joint petition is filed, unless the spouses are separated and a joint petition is not filed.)

NAME AND ADDRESS OF CUSTODIAN	NAME AND LOCATION OF COURT CASE TITLE & NUMBER	DATE OF ORDER	DESCRIPTION AND VALUE Of PROPERTY

7. **Gifts**

None ☑

List all gifts or charitable contributions made within **one year** immediately preceding the commencement of this case except ordinary and usual gifts to family members aggregating less than $200 in value per individual family member and charitable contributions aggregating less than $100 per recipient. (Married debtors filing under chapter 12 or chapter 13 must include gifts or contributions by either or both spouses whether or not a joint petition is filed, unless the spouses are separated and a joint petition is not filed.)

NAME AND ADDRESS OF PERSON OR ORGANIZATION	RELATIONSHIP TO DEBTOR, IF ANY	DATE OF GIFT	DESCRIPTION AND VALUE OF GIFT

8. **Losses**

None ☑

List all losses from fire, theft, other casualty or gambling within **one year** immediately preceding the commencement of this case **or since the commencement of this case**. (Married debtors filing under chapter 12 or chapter 13 must include losses by either or both spouses whether or not a joint petition is filed, unless the spouses are separated and a joint petition is not filed.)

DESCRIPTION AND VALUE OF PROPERTY	DESCRIPTION OF CIRCUMSTANCES AND, IF LOSS WAS COVERED IN WHOLE OR IN PART BY INSURANCE, GIVE PARTICULARS	DATE OF LOSS

Example Statement of Financial Affairs (cont.)

5

9. Payments related to debt counseling or bankruptcy

None ☑

List all payments made or property transferred by or on behalf of the debtor to any persons, including attorneys, for consultation concerning debt consolidation, relief under the bankruptcy law or preparation of a petition in bankruptcy within **one year** immediately preceding the commencement of this case.

NAME AND ADDRESS OF PAYEE	DATE OF PAYMENT, NAME OF PAYER IF OTHER THAN DEBTOR	AMOUNT OF MONEY OR DESCRIPTION AND VALUE OF PROPERTY

10. Other transfers

None ☑

a. List all other property, other than property transferred in the ordinary course of the business or financial affairs of the debtor, transferred either absolutely or as security within **two years** immediately preceding the commencement of this case. (Married debtors filing under chapter 12 or chapter 13 must include transfers by either or both spouses whether or not a joint petition is filed, unless the spouses are separated and a joint petition is not filed.)

NAME AND ADDRESS OF TRANSFEREE, RELATIONSHIP TO DEBTOR	DATE	DESCRIBE PROPERTY TRANSFERRED AND VALUE RECEIVED

None ☑

b. List all property transferred by the debtor within **ten years** immediately preceding the commencement of this case to a self-settled trust or similar device of which the debtor is a beneficiary.

NAME OF TRUST OR OTHER DEVICE	DATE(S) OF TRANSFER(S)	AMOUNT OF MONEY OR DESCRIPTION AND VALUE OF PROPERTY OR DEBTOR'S INTEREST IN PROPERTY

11. Closed financial accounts

None ☑

List all financial accounts and instruments held in the name of the debtor or for the benefit of the debtor which were closed, sold, or otherwise transferred within **one year** immediately preceding the commencement of this case. Include checking, savings, or other financial accounts, certificates of deposit, or other instruments; shares and share accounts held in banks, credit unions, pension funds, cooperatives, associations, brokerage houses and other financial institutions. (Married debtors filing under chapter 12 or chapter 13 must include information concerning accounts or instruments held by or for either or both spouses whether or not a joint petition is filed, unless the spouses are separated and a joint petition is not filed.)

NAME AND ADDRESS OF INSTITUTION	TYPE OF ACCOUNT, LAST FOUR DIGITS OF ACCOUNT NUMBER, AND AMOUNT OF FINAL BALANCE	AMOUNT AND DATE OF SALE OR CLOSING

Example Statement of Financial Affairs (cont.)

6

12. Safe deposit boxes

None
☒

List each safe deposit or other box or depository in which the debtor has or had securities, cash, or other valuables within **one year** immediately preceding the commencement of this case. (Married debtors filing under chapter 12 or chapter 13 must include boxes or depositories of either or both spouses whether or not a joint petition is filed, unless the spouses are separated and a joint petition is not filed.)

NAME AND ADDRESS OF BANK OR OTHER DEPOSITORY	NAMES AND ADDRESSES OF THOSE WITH ACCESS TO BOX OR DEPOSITORY	DESCRIPTION OF CONTENTS	DATE OF TRANSFER OR SURRENDER, IF ANY

13. Setoffs

None
☒

List all setoffs made by any creditor, including a bank, against a debt or deposit of the debtor within **90 days** preceding the commencement of this case. (Married debtors filing under chapter 12 or chapter 13 must include information concerning either or both spouses whether or not a joint petition is filed, unless the spouses are separated and a joint petition is not filed.)

NAME AND ADDRESS OF CREDITOR	DATE OF SETOFF	AMOUNT OF SETOFF

14. Property held for another person

None
☑

List all property owned by another person that the debtor holds or controls.

NAME AND ADDRESS OF OWNER	DESCRIPTION AND VALUE OF PROPERTY	LOCATION OF PROPERTY

15. Prior address of debtor

None
☒

If debtor has moved within **three years** immediately preceding the commencement of this case, list all premises which the debtor occupied during that period and vacated prior to the commencement of this case. If a joint petition is filed, report also any separate address of either spouse.

ADDRESS	NAME USED	DATES OF OCCUPANCY

Example Statement of Financial Affairs (cont.)

7

16. Spouses and Former Spouses

None ☑ If the debtor resides or resided in a community property state, commonwealth, or territory (including Alaska, Arizona, California, Idaho, Louisiana, Nevada, New Mexico, Puerto Rico, Texas, Washington, or Wisconsin) within **eight years** immediately preceding the commencement of the case, identify the name of the debtor's spouse and of any former spouse who resides or resided with the debtor in the community property state.

NAME

---

17. Environmental Information.

For the purpose of this question, the following definitions apply:

"Environmental Law" means any federal, state, or local statute or regulation regulating pollution, contamination, releases of hazardous or toxic substances, wastes or material into the air, land, soil, surface water, groundwater, or other medium, including, but not limited to, statutes or regulations regulating the cleanup of these substances, wastes, or material.

"Site" means any location, facility, or property as defined under any Environmental Law, whether or not presently or formerly owned or operated by the debtor, including, but not limited to, disposal sites.

"Hazardous Material" means anything defined as a hazardous waste, hazardous substance, toxic substance, hazardous material, pollutant, or contaminant or similar term under an Environmental Law.

None ☒ a. List the name and address of every site for which the debtor has received notice in writing by a governmental unit that it may be liable or potentially liable under or in violation of an Environmental Law. Indicate the governmental unit, the date of the notice, and, if known, the Environmental Law:

SITE NAME AND ADDRESS	NAME AND ADDRESS OF GOVERNMENTAL UNIT	DATE OF NOTICE	ENVIRONMENTAL LAW

None ☒ b. List the name and address of every site for which the debtor provided notice to a governmental unit of a release of Hazardous Material. Indicate the governmental unit to which the notice was sent and the date of the notice.

SITE NAME AND ADDRESS	NAME AND ADDRESS OF GOVERNMENTAL UNIT	DATE OF NOTICE	ENVIRONMENTAL LAW

None ☒ c. List all judicial or administrative proceedings, including settlements or orders, under any Environmental Law with respect to which the debtor is or was a party. Indicate the name and address of the governmental unit that is or was a party to the proceeding, and the docket number.

NAME AND ADDRESS OF GOVERNMENTAL UNIT	DOCKET NUMBER	STATUS OR DISPOSITION

---

18. Nature, location and name of business

None ☒ a. *If the debtor is an individual*, list the names, addresses, taxpayer-identification numbers, nature of the businesses, and beginning and ending dates of all businesses in which the debtor was an officer, director, partner, or managing

Example Statement of Financial Affairs (cont.)

8

executive of a corporation, partner in a partnership, sole proprietor, or was self-employed in a trade, profession, or other activity either full- or part-time within **six years** immediately preceding the commencement of this case, or in which the debtor owned 5 percent or more of the voting or equity securities within **six years** immediately preceding the commencement of this case.

If the debtor is a partnership, list the names, addresses, taxpayer-identification numbers, nature of the businesses, and beginning and ending dates of all businesses in which the debtor was a partner or owned 5 percent or more of the voting or equity securities, within **six years** immediately preceding the commencement of this case.

If the debtor is a corporation, list the names, addresses, taxpayer-identification numbers, nature of the businesses, and beginning and ending dates of all businesses in which the debtor was a partner or owned 5 percent or more of the voting or equity securities within **six years** immediately preceding the commencement of this case.

NAME	LAST FOUR DIGITS OF SOCIAL-SECURITY OR OTHER INDIVIDUAL TAXPAYER-I.D. NO. (ITIN)/ COMPLETE EIN	ADDRESS	NATURE OF BUSINESS	BEGINNING AND ENDING DATES

None
☒

b. Identify any business listed in response to subdivision a., above, that is "single asset real estate" as defined in 11 U.S.C. § 101.

NAME	ADDRESS

The following questions are to be completed by every debtor that is a corporation or partnership and by any individual debtor who is or has been, within **six years** immediately preceding the commencement of this case, any of the following: an officer, director, managing executive, or owner of more than 5 percent of the voting or equity securities of a corporation; a partner, other than a limited partner, of a partnership, a sole proprietor, or self-employed in a trade, profession, or other activity, either full- or part-time.

(An individual or joint debtor should complete this portion of the statement only if the debtor is or has been in business, as defined above, within six years immediately preceding the commencement of this case. A debtor who has not been in business within those six years should go directly to the signature page.)

---

19. Books, records and financial statements

None
☐

a. List all bookkeepers and accountants who within **two years** immediately preceding the filing of this bankruptcy case kept or supervised the keeping of books of account and records of the debtor.

NAME AND ADDRESS	DATES SERVICES RENDERED

None
☐

b. List all firms or individuals who within **two years** immediately preceding the filing of this bankruptcy case have audited the books of account and records, or prepared a financial statement of the debtor.

NAME	ADDRESS	DATES SERVICES RENDERED

Example Statement of Financial Affairs (cont.)

9

None ☐

c. List all firms or individuals who at the time of the commencement of this case were in possession of the books of account and records of the debtor. If any of the books of account and records are not available, explain.

NAME   ADDRESS

None ☐

d. List all financial institutions, creditors and other parties, including mercantile and trade agencies, to whom a financial statement was issued by the debtor within **two years** immediately preceding the commencement of this case.

NAME AND ADDRESS   DATE ISSUED

---

20. Inventories

None ☐

a. List the dates of the last two inventories taken of your property, the name of the person who supervised the taking of each inventory, and the dollar amount and basis of each inventory.

		DOLLAR AMOUNT OF INVENTORY
DATE OF INVENTORY	INVENTORY SUPERVISOR	(Specify cost, market or other basis)

None ☐

b. List the name and address of the person having possession of the records of each of the inventories reported in a., above.

	NAME AND ADDRESSES OF CUSTODIAN
DATE OF INVENTORY	OF INVENTORY RECORDS

---

21. Current Partners, Officers, Directors and Shareholders

None ☐

a. If the debtor is a partnership, list the nature and percentage of partnership interest of each member of the partnership.

NAME AND ADDRESS	NATURE OF INTEREST	PERCENTAGE OF INTEREST

None ☐

b.   If the debtor is a corporation, list all officers and directors of the corporation, and each stockholder who directly or indirectly owns, controls, or holds 5 percent or more of the voting or equity securities of the corporation.

NAME AND ADDRESS	TITLE	NATURE AND PERCENTAGE OF STOCK OWNERSHIP

Example Statement of Financial Affairs (cont.)

10

22. Former partners, officers, directors and shareholders

None ☐
a. If the debtor is a partnership, list each member who withdrew from the partnership within **one year** immediately preceding the commencement of this case.

NAME	ADDRESS	DATE OF WITHDRAWAL

None ☐
b. If the debtor is a corporation, list all officers or directors whose relationship with the corporation terminated within **one year** immediately preceding the commencement of this case.

NAME AND ADDRESS	TITLE	DATE OF TERMINATION

23. Withdrawals from a partnership or distributions by a corporation

None ☐
If the debtor is a partnership or corporation, list all withdrawals or distributions credited or given to an insider, including compensation in any form, bonuses, loans, stock redemptions, options exercised and any other perquisite during **one year** immediately preceding the commencement of this case.

NAME & ADDRESS OF RECIPIENT, RELATIONSHIP TO DEBTOR	DATE AND PURPOSE OF WITHDRAWAL	AMOUNT OF MONEY OR DESCRIPTION AND VALUE OF PROPERTY

24. Tax Consolidation Group.

None ☐
If the debtor is a corporation, list the name and federal taxpayer-identification number of the parent corporation of any consolidated group for tax purposes of which the debtor has been a member at any time within **six years** immediately preceding the commencement of the case.

NAME OF PARENT CORPORATION	TAXPAYER-IDENTIFICATION NUMBER (EIN)

25. Pension Funds.

None ☐
If the debtor is not an individual, list the name and federal taxpayer-identification number of any pension fund to which the debtor, as an employer, has been responsible for contributing at any time within **six years** immediately preceding the commencement of the case.

NAME OF PENSION FUND	TAXPAYER-IDENTIFICATION NUMBER (EIN)

* * * * * *

Example Statement of Financial Affairs (cont.)

11

[If completed by an individual or individual and spouse]

I declare under penalty of perjury that I have read the answers contained in the foregoing statement of financial affairs and any attachments thereto and that they are true and correct.

Date XX–XX–XX _____   Signature of Debtor *Z.A. Smith* _____

Date _____   Signature of Joint Debtor (if any) _____

_____

[If completed on behalf of a partnership or corporation]

I declare under penalty of perjury that I have read the answers contained in the foregoing statement of financial affairs and any attachments thereto and that they are true and correct to the best of my knowledge, information and belief.

Date _____   Signature _____

Print Name and Title _____

[An individual signing on behalf of a partnership or corporation must indicate position or relationship to debtor.]

___continuation sheets attached

Penalty for making a false statement: Fine of up to $500,000 or imprisonment for up to 5 years, or both. 18 U.S.C. §§ 152 and 3571

DECLARATION AND SIGNATURE OF NON-ATTORNEY BANKRUPTCY PETITION PREPARER (See 11 U.S.C. § 110)

I declare under penalty of perjury that: (1) I am a bankruptcy petition preparer as defined in 11 U.S.C. § 110; (2) I prepared this document for compensation and have provided the debtor with a copy of this document and the notices and information required under 11 U.S.C. §§ 110(b), 110(h), and 342(b); and, (3) if rules or guidelines have been promulgated pursuant to 11 U.S.C. § 110(h) setting a maximum fee for services chargeable by bankruptcy petition preparers, I have given the debtor notice of the maximum amount before preparing any document for filing for a debtor or accepting any fee from the debtor, as required by that section.

_____   _____
Printed or Typed Name and Title, if any, of Bankruptcy Petition Preparer   Social-Security No. (Required by 11 U.S.C. § 110.)

If the bankruptcy petition preparer is not an individual, state the name, title (if any), address, and social-security number of the officer, principal, responsible person, or partner who signs this document.

_____
Address

_____   _____
Signature of Bankruptcy Petition Preparer   Date

Names and Social-Security numbers of all other individuals who prepared or assisted in preparing this document unless the bankruptcy petition preparer is not an individual:

If more than one person prepared this document, attach additional signed sheets conforming to the appropriate Official Form for each person

A bankruptcy petition preparer's failure to comply with the provisions of title 11 and the Federal Rules of Bankruptcy Procedure may result in fines or imprisonment or both. 18 U.S.C. § 156.

Example Statement of Social Security Number(s)

B 21 (Official Form 21) (12/07)

UNITED STATES BANKRUPTCY COURT

In re Zachary Adrian Smith   ,   )
　　　　[Set forth here all names including married, maiden,   )
　　　　and trade names used by debtor within last 8 years]   )
　　　　　　　　　　　　　　　　　　　　　　　　　　　　)
　　　　　　　　　　　　　　Debtor　　　　　　　　　) Case No. _____
Address Crossroads Corr. Center　　　　　　　　)
　　　　 1115 E. Pence Road　　　　　　　　　　　) Chapter __7_____
　　　　 Cameron, Missouri 64429　　　　　　　　)
Last four digits of Social-Security or Individual Taxpayer-　)
Identification (ITIN) No(s)..(if any):　　　　　　　　)
XXX-XX-XXXX　　　　　　　　　　　　　　　　)
Employer Tax-Identification (EIN) No(s).(if any):　　　)
　　　　　　　　　　　　　　　　　　　　　　　　　　　　)

STATEMENT OF SOCIAL-SECURITY NUMBER(S)
(or other Individual Taxpayer-Identification Number(s) (ITIN(s)))

1.Name of Debtor (Last, First, Middle):_____ Smith, Zachary Adrian
(Check the appropriate box and, if applicable, provide the required information.)

　　☒ Debtor has a Social-Security Number and it is: XXX-XX-XXXX
　　　　(If more than one, state all.)
　　☐ Debtor does not have a Social-Security Number but has an Individual Taxpayer-Identification
　　　　Number (ITIN), and it is: _____
　　　　(If more than one, state all.)
　　☐ Debtor does not have either a Social-Security Number or an Individual Taxpayer-Identification
　　　　Number (ITIN).

2.Name of Joint Debtor (Last, First, Middle):_____
(Check the appropriate box and, if applicable, provide the required information.)

　　☐ Joint Debtor has a Social-Security Number and it is: _____
　　　　(If more than one, state all.)
　　☐ Joint Debtor does not have a Social-Security Number but has an Individual Taxpayer-Identification
　　　　Number (ITIN) and it is: _____
　　　　(If more than one, state all.)
　　☐ Joint Debtor does not have either a Social-Security Number or an Individual Taxpayer-Identification
　　　　Number (ITIN).

I declare under penalty of perjury that the foregoing is true and correct.

X　 *ZA. Smith*　　　　　　　XX-XX-XX
　　　　Signature of Debtor　　　　　　　　　Date
X　 _____
　　　　Signature of Joint Debtor　　　　　　　Date

_____

* *Joint debtors must provide information for both spouses.*

*Penalty for making a false statement: Fine of up to $250,000 or up to 5 years imprisonment or both. 18
U.S.C. §§ 152 and 3571.*

111

<7> POSTPETITION PERSONAL FINANCIAL MANAGEMENT COURSE; MEETING OF THE CREDITORS; AND DISCHARGE

Postpetition Personal Financial Management

Before you receive a discharge, you must complete a postpetition instructional course concerning personal financial management.

As discussed in Chapter 2 of this book, you may use the same agency that provided you with prepetition credit counseling. The agency will send you a workbook. Once you have read the book, you will be instructed to contact the agency by phone to complete your course. When you call to complete your course, you will be asked approximately twenty-five multiple choice and true/false questions. After which, you'll be told whether you passed or failed. If you passed, you may be then asked to fill out and mail back a survey to receive your certificate.

Once you receive your certificate, you must fill out the Debtor's Certification of Completion of Postpetition Instructional Course Concerning Personal Financial Management form, attach your certificate, then file both items with the court clerk. You must do this within 45 days of the first date set for the meeting of creditors, under 341 of the Bankruptcy Code.

Notice of Commencement of Bankruptcy Case, Meeting of Creditors, and Fixing of Dates

Official Form 9 is used to notify creditors, equity security holders, and other interested parties of the filing of your bankruptcy case. It provides the time, date, and location of the meeting of creditors, the time for filing various documents in the case, instructions for filing proofs of claim, and other information concerning your case.

Generally the clerk will complete this form and mail (or transmit electronically) a copy to your creditors and other entities whose names and addresses appear on the mailing list or matrix you file with your petition.

Waiver of Personal Appearance at Meeting of Creditors

Pursuant to §243 of the Bankruptcy Code, the debtor shall appear and submit to examination under oath at the meeting of creditors under section 341(a). Because of this requirement, the

United States trustee will only agree to a waiver of your personal appearance at a meeting of creditors in limited circumstances.

You must first make an effort to appear by phone to be examined by the trustee and any creditors who wish to examine you.

Upon receiving your notice of meeting of creditors, contact your caseworker or equivalent prison staff to explain your situation, and make arrangements to take your postpetition personal financial management course and to be present at the meeting of creditors via telephone. Then write to your assigned trustee, explain that you are incarcerated, and ask to waive your personal appearance and appear via telephone. Be sure to give the trustee contact information for your institution so that arrangements can be made for you to have access to a telephone at the time set for the meeting of creditors. See example letter at the end of this chapter.

Meeting of Creditors

The meeting of creditors is relatively a formal proceeding. The trustee will ask you a number of questions concerning your financial situation, while under oath. The creditors most likely will not attend. The meeting usually takes less than an hour.

Discharge

As discussed in the first chapter of this book, the court usually grants a discharge promptly after the time expires for filing a complaint objecting to discharge or for filing a motion to dismiss your case for substantial abuse (which is 60 days following the first date set for the meeting of creditors). Typically a discharge occurs about four months after the date the petition is filed with the clerk of the bankruptcy court.

Once the court grants a discharge in your case, the court clerk will send a copy to you and your creditors.

Conclusion

Good luck with your fresh start. Feel free to share the information contained in this book with your fellow prisoners so they too can secure the financial freedom we all have a right to.

Example Notice of Ch 7 Bankruptcy Case, Meeting of Creditors, and Deadlines

FORM B9A (Chapter 7 Individual or Joint Debtor No Asset Case) (11/10)	Case Number **10–50921–jwv7**

UNITED STATES BANKRUPTCY COURT
WESTERN DISTRICT of MISSOURI

Notice of Chapter 7 Bankruptcy Case, Meeting of Creditors, & Deadlines

A chapter 7 bankruptcy case concerning the debtor(s) listed below was filed on 9/14/10 . You may be a creditor of the debtor. **This notice lists important deadlines.** You may want to consult an attorney to protect your rights.
All documents filed in the case may be inspected at the bankruptcy clerk's office at the address listed below. NOTE: The staff of the bankruptcy clerk's office cannot give legal advice.

See Reverse Side For Important Explanations

Debtor(s) (name(s) used by the debtor(s) in the last 8 years, including married, maiden, trade, and address):
Zachary Adrain Smith
Crossroads Correctional Center
1115 E. Pence Road
Cameron, MO 64429

Case Number: 10–50921–jwv7	Social Security/Taxpayer ID/Employer ID/Other Nos.:
Attorney for Debtor(s) (name and address): Zachary Adrain Smith Crossroads Correctional Center 1115 E. Pence Road Cameron, MO 64429 Telephone number:	Bankruptcy Trustee (name and address): Bruce E. Strauss Merrick Baker Strauss 1044 Main Street, 4th Floor Kansas City, MO 64105 Telephone number: 816–221–8855

Meeting of Creditors

Date: **January 7, 2011**   Time: **08:30 AM**
Location: **2nd Floor, 8th and Edmond Street, St. Joseph, MO 64502**

Presumption of Abuse under 11 U.S.C. § 707(b)
See "Presumption of Abuse" on reverse side.

Insufficient information has been filed to date to permit the clerk to make any determination concerning the presumption of abuse. If more complete information, when filed, shows that the presumption has arisen, creditors will be notified.

Deadlines:

Papers must be *received* by the bankruptcy clerk's office by the following deadlines:
Deadline to File a Complaint Objecting to Discharge of the Debtor or to Determine Dischargeability of Certain Debts: 3/8/11

Deadline to Object to Exemptions:

30 days after the conclusion of the meeting of creditors or within 30 days of any amendment to the list
or supplemental schedules, unless as otherwise provided under Bankruptcy Rule 1019(2)(B) for converted cases.

Creditors May Not Take Certain Actions:

In most instances, the filing of the bankruptcy case automatically stays certain collection and other actions against the debtor and the debtor's property. Under certain circumstances, the stay may be limited to 30 days or not exist at all, although the debtor can request the court to extend or impose a stay. If you attempt to collect a debt or take other action in violation of the Bankruptcy Code, you may be penalized. Consult a lawyer to determine your rights in this case.

Please Do Not File a Proof of Claim Unless You Receive a Notice To Do So.

Foreign Creditors

A creditor to whom this notice is sent at a foreign address should read the information under "Do Not File a Proof of Claim at This Time" on the reverse side.

Bankruptcy Clerk's Office: www.mow.uscourts.gov 400 E. 9th Street, Room 1510 Kansas City, MO 64106 Telephone Number: 816–512–1800 VCIS Number toll free: 888–205–2527	**For the Court:** Court Executive: Ann Thompson
Hours Open: Monday – Friday 9:00 AM – 4:30 PM	Date: 11/29/10

The trustee may give notice at the meeting of his intent to abandon property unless objections are filed within 15 days.
Creditors with a security interest in the property must provide evidence of perfection to the trustee prior to this meeting.
Pursuant to 11 USC § 727 (a)(12), creditors and parties in interest seeking to delay or postpone debtor(s)' discharge on grounds that 11 USC § 522 (q)(1) may be applicable to debtor(s) or that a proceeding is pending in which the debtor(s) may be found guilty of a felony as described in 11 USC § 522 (q)(1)(A) or may be liable for a debt as described in 11 USC § 522 (q)(1)(B) must file a motion to delay or postpone such discharge prior to the last day to object to the discharge, as set out above.
If hearing location is Kansas City, please call (816) 512–1800 menu item #6 for information regarding handicapped access to the courthouse.

Example Notice of Ch 7 Bankruptcy Case, Meeting of Creditors, and Deadlines (cont.)

EXPLANATIONS

FORM B9A (11/10)

Filing of Chapter 7 Bankruptcy Case	A bankruptcy case under Chapter 7 of the Bankruptcy Code (title 11, United States Code) has been filed in this court by or against the debtor(s) listed on the front side, and an order for relief has been entered.
Legal Advice	The staff of the bankruptcy clerk's office cannot give legal advice. Consult a lawyer to determine your rights in this case.
Creditors Generally May Not Take Certain Actions	Prohibited collection actions are listed in Bankruptcy Code §362. Common examples of prohibited actions include contacting the debtor by telephone, mail or otherwise to demand repayment; taking actions to collect money or obtain property from the debtor; repossessing the debtor's property; starting or continuing lawsuits or foreclosures; and garnishing or deducting from the debtor's wages. Under certain circumstances, the stay may be limited to 30 days or not exist at all, although the debtor can request the court to extend or impose a stay.
Presumption of Abuse	If the presumption of abuse arises, creditors may have the right to file a motion to dismiss the case under § 707(b) of the Bankruptcy Code. The debtor may rebut the presumption by showing special circumstances.
Meeting of Creditors	A meeting of creditors is scheduled for the date, time and location listed on the front side. *The debtor (both spouses in a joint case) must be present at the meeting to be questioned under oath by the trustee and by creditors.* Creditors are welcome to attend, but are not required to do so. The meeting may be continued and concluded at a later date without further notice.
Do Not File a Proof of Claim at This Time	There does not appear to be any property available to the trustee to pay creditors. *You therefore should not file a proof of claim at this time.* If it later appears that assets are available to pay creditors, you will be sent another notice telling you that you may file a proof of claim, and telling you the deadline for filing your proof of claim. If this notice is mailed to a creditor at a foreign address, the creditor may file a motion requesting the court to extend the deadline.
Discharge of Debts	The debtor is seeking a discharge of most debts, which may include your debt. A discharge means that you may never try to collect the debt from the debtor. If you believe that the debtor is not entitled to receive a discharge under Bankruptcy Code §727(a) *or* that a debt owed to you is not dischargeable under Bankruptcy Code §523(a)(2), (4), or (6), you must start a lawsuit by filing a complaint in the bankruptcy clerk's office by the "Deadline to File a Complaint Objecting to Discharge of the Debtor or to Determine Dischargeability of Certain Debts" listed on the front side. The bankruptcy clerk's office must receive the complaint and any required filing fee by that Deadline.
Exempt Property	The debtor is permitted by law to keep certain property as exempt. Exempt property will not be sold and distributed to creditors. The debtor must file a list of all property claimed as exempt. You may inspect that list at the bankruptcy clerk's office. If you believe that an exemption claimed by the debtor is not authorized by law, you may file an objection to that exemption. The bankruptcy clerk's office must receive the objections by the "Deadline to Object to Exemptions" listed on the front side.
Bankruptcy Clerk's Office	Any paper that you file in this bankruptcy case should be filed at the bankruptcy clerk's office at the address listed on the front side. You may inspect all papers filed, including the list of the debtor's property and debts and the list of the property claimed as exempt, at the bankruptcy clerk's office.
Foreign Creditors	Consult a lawyer familiar with United States bankruptcy law if you have any questions regarding your rights in this case.

— Refer to Other Side for Important Deadlines and Notices —

Example Waiver Letter to U.S. Trustee

November 29, 2010

U.S. Trustee
Room 3440
400 E. 9th Street
Kansas City, MO 64106

RE: Zachary Adrian Smith, Case No. 10-50921-jwv7

Dear U.S. Trustee:

I'm writing to you in regard to the above mentioned bankruptcy case. I am incarcerated, serving a sentence of life without the possibility of probation or parole. There is no way I can attend a meeting of the creditors. However, I desperately need a discharge of a $100,000 judgment. The creditors take 90% of any money deposited into my prison account.

I've written to the assigned trustee, Bruce E. Strauss, but he has not responded to my letter or taken my call even though it was prepaid.

I have taken the pre and post credit counseling courses.

Under the circumstances, I request to be permitted to attend the meeting of creditors via telephonically or by written interrogatories. Arrangements for my appearance via telephonically can be made by calling (816)632-2727 and setting up the date and time for the meeting of creditors with prison staff.

In light of the circumstances, I ask you to waive my personal appearance and allow me to attend the meeting by one of the methods stated above. Thank you for your time and assistance in this matter. I'll be looking forward to some kind of reply. Take care.

Respectfully,

Z.A.Smith

Zachary Smith, #521163
Crossroads Corr. Center
1115 E. Pence Road
Cameron, MO 64429

Example Letter from Trustee

U.S. Department of Justice

United States Trustee
Region 13
Arkansas, Missouri and Nebraska

United States Courthouse	
400 East 9 th St., Rm 3440	TEL: (816) 512-1940
Kansas City, Missouri 64106	FAX: (816) 512-1967

December 8, 2010

Zachary Adrain Smith, #521163
Crossroads Corr. Center
1115 E. Pence Road
Cameron, MO64429

Re: **Request for Waiver of Personal Appearance at Creditors' Meeting-
Zachary Adrain Smith, Case no. 10-50921 - 341 date: 1-7-11**

Dear Mr. Smith:

We have your request for waiver of personal appearance at the statutory creditors' meeting.

As you know, Section 343 of the Bankruptcy Code provides that the debtor "shall appear and submit to examination under oath at the meeting of creditors under section 341(a). . . ." Because of this requirement, our office will agree to a waiver of personal appearance only in limited circumstances.

In view of the requirements of the Bankruptcy Code, our office will consider a personal waiver only after you have made an effort to appear by phone to be examined by the trustee and any creditors who wish to examine you.

Accordingly, please note that your 341 will be continued from January 7, 2011 in St. Joseph to January 20, 2011 at 11:30 a.m. to be held telephonically from the U.S. Courthouse in Kansas City. Trustee Bruce Strauss will call you on that date and time at the phone number of 816-632-2727 as set out in your Request for Waiver. Because you are seeking an exception to the requirement of a personal appearance, it will be your responsibility to make yourself available to ensure attendance for the call.

Please call me if you have any questions at 816-512-1958.

Very truly yours,

Barbara J. Marquez
Legal Clerk for U.S. Trustee Program
Region 13, Kansas City

/bjm
cc: Bruce E. Strauss, Chapter 7 Trustee
(Via email to bruces@merrickbakerstrauss.com)

Example Debtor's Certification

B 23 (Official Form 23) (12/08)

UNITED STATES BANKRUPTCY COURT

In re ___Zachary Adrian Smith___,   Case No. _____
Debtor

                                                      Chapter ___7___

DEBTOR'S CERTIFICATION OF COMPLETION OF POSTPETITION INSTRUCTIONAL COURSE CONCERNING PERSONAL FINANCIAL MANAGEMENT

Every individual debtor in a chapter 7, chapter 11 in which § 1141(d)(3) applies, or chapter 13 case must file this certification. If a joint petition is filed, each spouse must complete and file a separate certification. Complete one of the following statements and file by the deadline stated below:

☒ I, ___Zachary Adrian Smith___, the debtor in the above-styled case, hereby
          (Printed Name of Debtor)
certify that on ___11-22-01___ *(Date)*, I completed an instructional course in personal financial management

provided by ___Institute of Financial Literacy, Inc.,___, an approved personal financial
              (Name of Provider)
management provider.

   Certificate No. *(if any)*: ___00252-MOE-DE-013086510___.

☐ I, _____, the debtor in the above-styled case, hereby
          (Printed Name of Debtor)
certify that no personal financial management course is required because of *[Check the appropriate box.]*:

   ☐ Incapacity or disability, as defined in 11 U.S.C. § 109(h);

   ☐ Active military duty in a military combat zone; or

   ☐ Residence in a district in which the United States trustee *(or bankruptcy administrator)* has determined that the approved instructional courses are not adequate at this time to serve the additional individuals who would otherwise be required to complete such courses.

Signature of Debtor: ___Z.A.Smith___

Date: ___XX-XX-XX___

Instructions: Use this form only to certify whether you completed a course in personal financial management. (Fed. R. Bankr. P. 1007(b)(7).) Do NOT use this form to file the certificate given to you by your prepetition credit counseling provider and do NOT include with the petition when filing your case.

Filing Deadlines: In a chapter 7 case, file within 45 days of the first date set for the meeting of creditors under § 341 of the Bankruptcy Code. In a chapter 11 or 13 case, file no later than the last payment made by the debtor as required by the plan or the filing of a motion for a discharge under § 1141(d)(5)(B) or § 1328(b) of the Code. (See Fed. R. Bankr. P. 1007(c).)

Example Certificate of Debtor Education

Certificate Number: 00252-MOE-DE-013086510

Bankruptcy Case Number: 10-50921

00252-MOE-DE-013086510

CERTIFICATE OF DEBTOR EDUCATION

I CERTIFY that on November 22, 2010, at 2:33 o'clock PM EST, Zachary A. Smith completed a course on personal financial management given by internet and telephone by Institute for Financial Literacy, Inc., a provider approved pursuant to 11 U.S.C. § 111 to provide an instructional course concerning personal financial management in the Eastern District of Missouri.

Date: November 22, 2010   By: /s/Oscar Corral-Lopez

                                           Name: Oscar Corral-Lopez

                                           Title: Credit Counselor

Example Discharge of Debtor

B18 (Official Form 18) (12/07)

United States Bankruptcy Court

Western District of Missouri
Case No. <u>10-50921-jwv7</u>
Chapter 7

In re Debtor(s) (name(s) used by the debtor(s) in the last 8 years, including married, maiden, trade, and address):
Zachary Adrian Smith
Crossroads Correctional Center
1115 E. Pence Road
Cameron, MO 64429

Social Security / Individual Taxpayer ID No.:
xxx-xx-9119

Employer Tax ID / Other nos.:

DISCHARGE OF DEBTOR

It appearing that the debtor is entitled to a discharge,

IT IS ORDERED:

The debtor is granted a discharge under section 727 of title 11, United States Code, (the Bankruptcy Code).

BY THE COURT

Dated: <u>3/11/11</u>

<u>Jerry W. Venters</u>
United States Bankruptcy Judge

SEE THE BACK OF THIS ORDER FOR IMPORTANT INFORMATION.

Example Discharge of Debtor (cont.)

B18 (Official Form 18) (12/07) – Cont.

EXPLANATION OF BANKRUPTCY DISCHARGE
IN A CHAPTER 7 CASE

This court order grants a discharge to the person named as the debtor. It is not a dismissal of the case and it does not determine how much money, if any, the trustee will pay to creditors.

Collection of Discharged Debts Prohibited

The discharge prohibits any attempt to collect from the debtor a debt that has been discharged. For example, a creditor is not permitted to contact a debtor by mail, phone, or otherwise, to file or continue a lawsuit, to attach wages or other property, or to take any other action to collect a discharged debt from the debtor. *[In a case involving community property:* There are also special rules that protect certain community property owned by the debtor's spouse, even if that spouse did not file a bankruptcy case.] A creditor who violates this order can be required to pay damages and attorney's fees to the debtor.

However, a creditor may have the right to enforce a valid lien, such as a mortgage or security interest, against the debtor's property after the bankruptcy, if that lien was not avoided or eliminated in the bankruptcy case. Also, a debtor may voluntarily pay any debt that has been discharged.

Debts That are Discharged

The chapter 7 discharge order eliminates a debtor's legal obligation to pay a debt that is discharged. Most, but not all, types of debts are discharged if the debt existed on the date the bankruptcy case was filed. (If this case was begun under a different chapter of the Bankruptcy Code and converted to chapter 7, the discharge applies to debts owed when the bankruptcy case was converted.)

Debts That are Not Discharged

Some of the common types of debts which are not discharged in a chapter 7 bankruptcy case are:

a. Debts for most taxes;

b. Debts incurred to pay nondischargeable taxes;

c. Debts that are domestic support obligations;

d. Debts for most student loans;

e. Debts for most fines, penalties, forfeitures, or criminal restitution obligations;

f. Debts for personal injuries or death caused by the debtor's operation of a motor vehicle, vessel, or aircraft while intoxicated;

g. Some debts which were not properly listed by the debtor;

h. Debts that the bankruptcy court specifically has decided or will decide in this bankruptcy case are not discharged;

i. Debts for which the debtor has given up the discharge protections by signing a reaffirmation agreement in compliance with the Bankruptcy Code requirements for reaffirmation of debts; and

j. Debts owed to certain pension, profit sharing, stock bonus, other retirement plans, or to the Thrift Savings Plan for federal employees for certain types of loans from these plans.

This information is only a general summary of the bankruptcy discharge. There are exceptions to these general rules. Because the law is complicated, you may want to consult an attorney to determine the exact effect of the discharge in this case.

$

BANKRUPTCY FORMS

The forms contained on the following pages may be copied and/or removed, filled out, and filed with the appropriate bankruptcy court. These forms were obtained from the *U.S. Courts* website (listed below) and are being provided as a convenience. At the time of publication, these were the most current versions, however, updates are made periodically and some forms may now look differently than the examples contained in this book. (For instance, if you are in the state of MISSOURI, please flip to page 253). The author and publisher bear no responsibility for the accuracy, legality, or validity of these forms. The most current versions can be obtained online at the following web address:

http://www.uscourts.gov/FormsAndFees/Forms/BankruptcyForms.aspx

UNITED STATES BANKRUPTCY COURT	**VOLUNTARY PETITION**

Name of Debtor (if individual, enter Last, First, Middle):	Name of Joint Debtor (Spouse) (Last, First, Middle):
All Other Names used by the Debtor in the last 8 years (include married, maiden, and trade names):	All Other Names used by the Joint Debtor in the last 8 years (include married, maiden, and trade names):
Last four digits of Soc. Sec. or Individual-Taxpayer I.D. (ITIN)/Complete EIN (if more than one, state all):	Last four digits of Soc. Sec. or Individual-Taxpayer I.D. (ITIN)/Complete EIN (if more than one, state all):
Street Address of Debtor (No. and Street, City, and State): ZIP CODE	Street Address of Joint Debtor (No. and Street, City, and State): ZIP CODE
County of Residence or of the Principal Place of Business:	County of Residence or of the Principal Place of Business:
Mailing Address of Debtor (if different from street address): ZIP CODE	Mailing Address of Joint Debtor (if different from street address): ZIP CODE
Location of Principal Assets of Business Debtor (if different from street address above): ZIP CODE	

Type of Debtor (Form of Organization) (Check **one** box.)	**Nature of Business** (Check **one** box.)	**Chapter of Bankruptcy Code Under Which the Petition is Filed** (Check **one** box.)
☐ Individual (includes Joint Debtors) *See Exhibit D on page 2 of this form.* ☐ Corporation (includes LLC and LLP) ☐ Partnership ☐ Other (If debtor is not one of the above entities, check this box and state type of entity below.)	☐ Health Care Business ☐ Single Asset Real Estate as defined in 11 U.S.C. § 101(51B) ☐ Railroad ☐ Stockbroker ☐ Commodity Broker ☐ Clearing Bank ☐ Other	☐ Chapter 7 ☐ Chapter 15 Petition for Recognition of a Foreign Main Proceeding ☐ Chapter 9 ☐ Chapter 11 ☐ Chapter 12 ☐ Chapter 15 Petition for Recognition of a Foreign Nonmain Proceeding ☐ Chapter 13

Chapter 15 Debtors Country of debtor's center of main interests: Each country in which a foreign proceeding by, regarding, or against debtor is pending:	**Tax-Exempt Entity** (Check box, if applicable.) ☐ Debtor is a tax-exempt organization under title 26 of the United States Code (the Internal Revenue Code).	**Nature of Debts** (Check **one** box.) ☐ Debts are primarily consumer debts, defined in 11 U.S.C. § 101(8) as "incurred by an individual primarily for a personal, family, or household purpose." ☐ Debts are primarily business debts.

Filing Fee (Check one box.)	**Chapter 11 Debtors**
☐ Full Filing Fee attached. ☐ Filing Fee to be paid in installments (applicable to individuals only). Must attach signed application for the court's consideration certifying that the debtor is unable to pay fee except in installments. Rule 1006(b). See Official Form 3A. ☐ Filing Fee waiver requested (applicable to chapter 7 individuals only). Must attach signed application for the court's consideration. See Official Form 3B.	**Check one box:** ☐ Debtor is a small business debtor as defined in 11 U.S.C. § 101(51D). ☐ Debtor is not a small business debtor as defined in 11 U.S.C. § 101(51D). **Check if:** ☐ Debtor's aggregate noncontingent liquidated debts (excluding debts owed to insiders or affiliates) are less than $2,490,925 (*amount subject to adjustment on 4/01/16 and every three years thereafter*). - **Check all applicable boxes:** ☐ A plan is being filed with this petition. ☐ Acceptances of the plan were solicited prepetition from one or more classes of creditors, in accordance with 11 U.S.C. § 1126(b).

Statistical/Administrative Information

☐ Debtor estimates that funds will be available for distribution to unsecured creditors.
☐ Debtor estimates that, after any exempt property is excluded and administrative expenses paid, there will be no funds available for distribution to unsecured creditors.

THIS SPACE IS FOR COURT USE ONLY

Estimated Number of Creditors

☐ 1-49	☐ 50-99	☐ 100-199	☐ 200-999	☐ 1,000-5,000	☐ 5,001-10,000	☐ 10,001-25,000	☐ 25,001-50,000	☐ 50,001-100,000	☐ Over 100,000

Estimated Assets

☐ $0 to $50,000	☐ $50,001 to $100,000	☐ $100,001 to $500,000	☐ $500,001 to $1 million	☐ $1,000,001 to $10 million	☐ $10,000,001 to $50 million	☐ $50,000,001 to $100 million	☐ $100,000,001 to $500 million	☐ $500,000,001 to $1 billion	☐ More than $1 billion

Estimated Liabilities

☐ $0 to $50,000	☐ $50,001 to $100,000	☐ $100,001 to $500,000	☐ $500,001 to $1 million	☐ $1,000,001 to $10 million	☐ $10,000,001 to $50 million	☐ $50,000,001 to $100 million	☐ $100,000,001 to $500 million	☐ $500,000,001 to $1 billion	☐ More than $1 billion

Voluntary Petition *(This page must be completed and filed in every case.)*	Name of Debtor(s):

All Prior Bankruptcy Cases Filed Within Last 8 Years (If more than two, attach additional sheet.)

Location Where Filed:	Case Number:	Date Filed:
Location Where Filed:	Case Number:	Date Filed:

Pending Bankruptcy Case Filed by any Spouse, Partner, or Affiliate of this Debtor (If more than one, attach additional sheet.)

Name of Debtor:	Case Number:	Date Filed:
District:	Relationship:	Judge:

Exhibit A (To be completed if debtor is required to file periodic reports (e.g., forms 10K and 10Q) with the Securities and Exchange Commission pursuant to Section 13 or 15(d) of the Securities Exchange Act of 1934 and is requesting relief under chapter 11.) ☐ Exhibit A is attached and made a part of this petition.	**Exhibit B** (To be completed if debtor is an individual whose debts are primarily consumer debts.) I, the attorney for the petitioner named in the foregoing petition, declare that I have informed the petitioner that [he or she] may proceed under chapter 7, 11, 12, or 13 of title 11, United States Code, and have explained the relief available under each such chapter. I further certify that I have delivered to the debtor the notice required by 11 U.S.C. § 342(b). X _____ Signature of Attorney for Debtor(s) (Date)

Exhibit C

Does the debtor own or have possession of any property that poses or is alleged to pose a threat of imminent and identifiable harm to public health or safety?

☐ Yes, and Exhibit C is attached and made a part of this petition.

☐ No.

Exhibit D

(To be completed by every individual debtor. If a joint petition is filed, each spouse must complete and attach a separate Exhibit D.)

☐ Exhibit D, completed and signed by the debtor, is attached and made a part of this petition.

If this is a joint petition:

☐ Exhibit D, also completed and signed by the joint debtor, is attached and made a part of this petition.

Information Regarding the Debtor - Venue
(Check any applicable box.)

☐ Debtor has been domiciled or has had a residence, principal place of business, or principal assets in this District for 180 days immediately preceding the date of this petition or for a longer part of such 180 days than in any other District.

☐ There is a bankruptcy case concerning debtor's affiliate, general partner, or partnership pending in this District.

☐ Debtor is a debtor in a foreign proceeding and has its principal place of business or principal assets in the United States in this District, or has no principal place of business or assets in the United States but is a defendant in an action or proceeding [in a federal or state court] in this District, or the interests of the parties will be served in regard to the relief sought in this District.

Certification by a Debtor Who Resides as a Tenant of Residential Property
(Check all applicable boxes.)

☐ Landlord has a judgment against the debtor for possession of debtor's residence. (If box checked, complete the following.)

_____
(Name of landlord that obtained judgment)

_____
(Address of landlord)

☐ Debtor claims that under applicable nonbankruptcy law, there are circumstances under which the debtor would be permitted to cure the entire monetary default that gave rise to the judgment for possession, after the judgment for possession was entered, and

☐ Debtor has included with this petition the deposit with the court of any rent that would become due during the 30-day period after the filing of the petition.

☐ Debtor certifies that he/she has served the Landlord with this certification. (11 U.S.C. § 362(l)).

Voluntary Petition *(This page must be completed and filed in every case.)*	Name of Debtor(s):

Signatures

Signature(s) of Debtor(s) (Individual/Joint)	**Signature of a Foreign Representative**

I declare under penalty of perjury that the information provided in this petition is true and correct.
 	
 [If petitioner is an individual whose debts are primarily consumer debts and has chosen to file under chapter 7] I am aware that I may proceed under chapter 7, 11, 12 or 13 of title 11, United States Code, understand the relief available under each such chapter, and choose to proceed under chapter 7.
 	
 [If no attorney represents me and no bankruptcy petition preparer signs the petition] I have obtained and read the notice required by 11 U.S.C. § 342(b).
 	
 I request relief in accordance with the chapter of title 11, United States Code, specified in this petition.
 	
 X _____
     Signature of Debtor
 	
 X _____
     Signature of Joint Debtor
 	
     Telephone Number (if not represented by attorney)
 	
     Date
	I declare under penalty of perjury that the information provided in this petition is true and correct, that I am the foreign representative of a debtor in a foreign proceeding, and that I am authorized to file this petition.
	
	 (Check only **one** box.)
	
	 ☐ I request relief in accordance with chapter 15 of title 11, United States Code. Certified copies of the documents required by 11 U.S.C. § 1515 are attached.
	
	 ☐ Pursuant to 11 U.S.C. § 1511, I request relief in accordance with the chapter of title 11 specified in this petition. A certified copy of the order granting recognition of the foreign main proceeding is attached.
	
	 X _____
	     (Signature of Foreign Representative)
	
	     (Printed Name of Foreign Representative)
	
	     Date

Signature of Attorney*	**Signature of Non-Attorney Bankruptcy Petition Preparer**

X _____
     Signature of Attorney for Debtor(s)
 	
     Printed Name of Attorney for Debtor(s)
 	
     Firm Name
 	
     Address
 	
     Telephone Number
 	
     Date
 	
 *In a case in which § 707(b)(4)(D) applies, this signature also constitutes a certification that the attorney has no knowledge after an inquiry that the information in the schedules is incorrect.
	I declare under penalty of perjury that: (1) I am a bankruptcy petition preparer as defined in 11 U.S.C. § 110; (2) I prepared this document for compensation and have provided the debtor with a copy of this document and the notices and information required under 11 U.S.C. §§ 110(b), 110(h), and 342(b); and, (3) if rules or guidelines have been promulgated pursuant to 11 U.S.C. § 110(h) setting a maximum fee for services chargeable by bankruptcy petition preparers, I have given the debtor notice of the maximum amount before preparing any document for filing for a debtor or accepting any fee from the debtor, as required in that section. Official Form 19 is attached.
	
	     Printed Name and title, if any, of Bankruptcy Petition Preparer
	
	     Social-Security number (If the bankruptcy petition preparer is not an individual, state the Social-Security number of the officer, principal, responsible person or partner of the bankruptcy petition preparer.) (Required by 11 U.S.C. § 110.)

Signature of Debtor (Corporation/Partnership)	Address X _____ Signature

I declare under penalty of perjury that the information provided in this petition is true and correct, and that I have been authorized to file this petition on behalf of the debtor.
 	
 The debtor requests the relief in accordance with the chapter of title 11, United States Code, specified in this petition.
 	
 X _____
     Signature of Authorized Individual
 	
     Printed Name of Authorized Individual
 	
     Title of Authorized Individual
 	
     Date
	Date
	
	 Signature of bankruptcy petition preparer or officer, principal, responsible person, or partner whose Social-Security number is provided above.
	
	 Names and Social-Security numbers of all other individuals who prepared or assisted in preparing this document unless the bankruptcy petition preparer is not an individual.
	
	 If more than one person prepared this document, attach additional sheets conforming to the appropriate official form for each person.
	
	 A bankruptcy petition preparer's failure to comply with the provisions of title 11 and the Federal Rules of Bankruptcy Procedure may result in fines or imprisonment or both. 11 U.S.C. § 110; 18 U.S.C. § 156.

B 1C (Official Form 1, Exhibit C) (9/01)

[If, to the best of the debtor's knowledge, the debtor owns or has possession of property that poses or is alleged to pose a threat of imminent and identifiable harm to the public health or safety, attach this Exhibit "C" to the petition.]

UNITED STATES BANKRUPTCY COURT

In re _____ ,) Case No. _____

Debtor)

)

) Chapter _____

EXHIBIT "C" TO VOLUNTARY PETITION

    1. Identify and briefly describe all real or personal property owned by or in possession of the debtor that, to the best of the debtor's knowledge, poses or is alleged to pose a threat of imminent and identifiable harm to the public health or safety (attach additional sheets if necessary):

    2. With respect to each parcel of real property or item of personal property identified in question 1, describe the nature and location of the dangerous condition, whether environmental or otherwise, that poses or is alleged to pose a threat of imminent and identifiable harm to the public health or safety (attach additional sheets if necessary):

B 1D (Official Form 1, Exhibit D) (12/09)

UNITED STATES BANKRUPTCY COURT

In re_____   Case No._____
            Debtor   (if known)

EXHIBIT D - INDIVIDUAL DEBTOR'S STATEMENT OF COMPLIANCE WITH CREDIT COUNSELING REQUIREMENT

Warning: You must be able to check truthfully one of the five statements regarding credit counseling listed below. If you cannot do so, you are not eligible to file a bankruptcy case, and the court can dismiss any case you do file. If that happens, you will lose whatever filing fee you paid, and your creditors will be able to resume collection activities against you. If your case is dismissed and you file another bankruptcy case later, you may be required to pay a second filing fee and you may have to take extra steps to stop creditors' collection activities.

Every individual debtor must file this Exhibit D. If a joint petition is filed, each spouse must complete and file a separate Exhibit D. Check one of the five statements below and attach any documents as directed.

❐ 1. Within the 180 days **before the filing of my bankruptcy case**, I received a briefing from a credit counseling agency approved by the United States trustee or bankruptcy administrator that outlined the opportunities for available credit counseling and assisted me in performing a related budget analysis, and I have a certificate from the agency describing the services provided to me. *Attach a copy of the certificate and a copy of any debt repayment plan developed through the agency.*

❐ 2. Within the 180 days **before the filing of my bankruptcy case**, I received a briefing from a credit counseling agency approved by the United States trustee or bankruptcy administrator that outlined the opportunities for available credit counseling and assisted me in performing a related budget analysis, but I do not have a certificate from the agency describing the services provided to me. *You must file a copy of a certificate from the agency describing the services provided to you and a copy of any debt repayment plan developed through the agency no later than 14 days after your bankruptcy case is filed.*

❒ 3. I certify that I requested credit counseling services from an approved agency but was unable to obtain the services during the seven days from the time I made my request, and the following exigent circumstances merit a temporary waiver of the credit counseling requirement so I can file my bankruptcy case now. *[Summarize exigent circumstances here.]*

If your certification is satisfactory to the court, you must still obtain the credit counseling briefing within the first 30 days after you file your bankruptcy petition and promptly file a certificate from the agency that provided the counseling, together with a copy of any debt management plan developed through the agency. Failure to fulfill these requirements may result in dismissal of your case. Any extension of the 30-day deadline can be granted only for cause and is limited to a maximum of 15 days. Your case may also be dismissed if the court is not satisfied with your reasons for filing your bankruptcy case without first receiving a credit counseling briefing.

❒ 4. I am not required to receive a credit counseling briefing because of: *[Check the applicable statement.] [Must be accompanied by a motion for determination by the court.]*

❒ Incapacity. (Defined in 11 U.S.C. § 109(h)(4) as impaired by reason of mental illness or mental deficiency so as to be incapable of realizing and making rational decisions with respect to financial responsibilities.);
❒ Disability. (Defined in 11 U.S.C. § 109(h)(4) as physically impaired to the extent of being unable, after reasonable effort, to participate in a credit counseling briefing in person, by telephone, or through the Internet.);
❒ Active military duty in a military combat zone.

❒ 5. The United States trustee or bankruptcy administrator has determined that the credit counseling requirement of 11 U.S.C. § 109(h) does not apply in this district.

I certify under penalty of perjury that the information provided above is true and correct.

Signature of Debtor: _____

Date: _____

DECLARATION UNDER PENALTY OF PERJURY
ON BEHALF OF A CORPORATION OR PARTNERSHIP

I, [the president *or* other officer *or* an authorized agent of the corporation] [*or* a member *or* an authorized agent of the partnership] named as the debtor in this case, declare under penalty of perjury that I have read the foregoing [list *or* schedule *or* amendment *or* other document (describe)] and that it is true and correct to the best of my information and belief.

Date _____

Signature _____

_____
(Print Name and Title)

Fill in this information to identify your case:

Debtor 1 _____
　　　　　　　First Name　　　　　　Middle Name　　　　　Last Name

Debtor 2 _____
(Spouse, if filing) First Name　　　　Middle Name　　　　　Last Name

United States Bankruptcy Court for the: _____ District of _____
　　　　　　　　　　　　　　　　　　　　　　　　　　　　　　　　(State)

Case number _____
(If known)

☐ Check if this is an
amended filing

Official Form B 3A

Application for Individuals to Pay the Filing Fee in Installments　　06/14

Be as complete and accurate as possible. If two married people are filing together, both are equally responsible for supplying correct information.

Part 1:　Specify Your Proposed Payment Timetable

1. **Which chapter of the Bankruptcy Code are you choosing to file under?**

   ☐ Chapter 7 .... *Fee:*　**$335**
   ☐ Chapter 11 .... *Fee:*　**$1,717**
   ☐ Chapter 12 .... *Fee:*　**$275**
   ☐ Chapter 13 .... *Fee:*　**$310**

2. **You may apply to pay the filing fee in up to four installments. Fill in the amounts you propose to pay and the dates you plan to pay them. Be sure all dates are business days. Then add the payments you propose to pay.**

   You must propose to pay the entire fee no later than 120 days after you file this bankruptcy case. If the court approves your application, the court will set your final payment timetable.

   You propose to pay...

   $_____　☐ With the filing of the petition
   　　　　　　　　☐ On or before this date .... MM / DD / YYYY

   $_____　On or before this date .... MM / DD / YYYY

   $_____　On or before this date .... MM / DD / YYYY

   + $_____　On or before this date .... MM / DD / YYYY

   Total　$_____　◀ Your total must equal the entire fee for the chapter you checked in line 1.

Part 2:　Sign Below

By signing here, you state that you are unable to pay the full filing fee at once, that you want to pay the fee in installments, and that you understand that:

▓　You must pay your entire filing fee before you make any more payments or transfer any more property to an attorney, bankruptcy petition preparer, or anyone else for services in connection with your bankruptcy case.

▓　You must pay the entire fee no later than 120 days after you first file for bankruptcy, unless the court later extends your deadline. Your debts will not be discharged until your entire fee is paid.

▓　If you do not make any payment when it is due, your bankruptcy case may be dismissed, and your rights in other bankruptcy proceedings may be affected.

✗ _____　✗ _____　✗ _____
　Signature of Debtor 1　　　　　　　　　Signature of Debtor 2　　　　　　　　Your attorney's name and signature, if you used one

Date _____　　　　　　　Date _____　　　　　　Date _____
　　MM / DD / YYYY　　　　　　　　　　　MM / DD / YYYY　　　　　　　　　MM / DD / YYYY

Order Approving Payment of Filing Fee in Installments

After considering the *Application for Individuals to Pay the Filing Fee in Installments* (Official Form B 3A), the court orders that:

[ ] The debtor(s) may pay the filing fee in installments on the terms proposed in the application.

[ ] The debtor(s) must pay the filing fee according to the following terms:

You must pay…	On or before this date…
$_____	_____ Month / day / year
$_____	_____ Month / day / year
$_____	_____ Month / day / year
+ $_____	_____ Month / day / year
Total $_____	

Until the filing fee is paid in full, the debtor(s) must not make any additional payment or transfer any additional property to an attorney or to anyone else for services in connection with this case.

_____   **By the court:**   _____
Month / day / year   United States Bankruptcy Judge

Fill in this information to identify your case:

Debtor 1 _____
        First Name   Middle Name   Last Name

Debtor 2 _____
(Spouse, if filing) First Name   Middle Name   Last Name

United States Bankruptcy Court for the: _____ District of _____
                                                      (State)

Case number _____
(If known)

☐ Check if this is an amended filing

Official Form B 3B

Application to Have the Chapter 7 Filing Fee Waived

06/14

Be as complete and accurate as possible. If two married people are filing together, both are equally responsible for supplying correct information. If more space is needed, attach a separate sheet to this form. On the top of any additional pages, write your name and case number (if known).

Part 1:   Tell the Court About Your Family and Your Family's Income

1. What is the size of your family?

Your family includes you, your spouse, and any dependents listed on *Schedule J: Current Expenditures of Individual Debtor(s)* (Official Form 6J).

Check all that apply:

☐ You

☐ Your spouse

☐ Your dependents _____
                      How many dependents?

_____
Total number of people

2. Fill in your family's average monthly income.

Include your spouse's income if your spouse is living with you, even if your spouse is not filing.

Do not include your spouse's income if you are separated and your spouse is not filing with you.

Add your income and your spouse's income. Include the value (if known) of any non-cash governmental assistance that you receive, such as food stamps (benefits under the Supplemental Nutrition Assistance Program) or housing subsidies.

If you have already filled out *Schedule I: Your Income*, see line 10 of that schedule.

Subtract any non-cash governmental assistance that you included above.

Your family's average monthly net income

That person's average monthly net income (take-home pay)

You .... $_____

Your spouse ... + $_____

Subtotal............ $_____

                 − $_____

Total................ $_____

3. Do you receive non-cash governmental assistance?

☐ No
☐ Yes. Describe...........

Type of assistance

4. Do you expect your family's average monthly net income to increase or decrease by more than 10% during the next 6 months?

☐ No
☐ Yes. Explain. ....

5. Tell the court why you are unable to pay the filing fee in installments within 120 days. If you have some additional circumstances that cause you to not be able to pay your filing fee in installments, explain them.

Debtor 1 _____   Case number (if known) _____
            First Name   Middle Name   Last Name

6. **Estimate your average monthly expenses.**

   Include amounts paid by any government assistance that you reported on line 2. $ _____

   If you have already filled out *Schedule J, Your Expenses,* copy line 22 from that form.

---

7. **Do these expenses cover anyone who is not included in your family as reported in line 1?**

   ☐ No
   ☐ Yes. Identify who .... [   ]

---

8. **Does anyone other than you regularly pay any of these expenses?**

   If you have already filled out *Schedule I: Your Income,* copy the total from line 11.

   ☐ No
   ☐ Yes. How much do you regularly receive as contributions? $_____ monthly

---

9. **Do you expect your average monthly expenses to increase or decrease by more than 10% during the next 6 months?**

   ☐ No
   ☐ Yes. Explain .... [   ]

If you have already filled out *Schedule A: Real Property (Official Form B 6A)* and *Schedule B: Personal Property (Official Form B 6B),* attach copies to this application and go to Part 4.

10. **How much cash do you have?**

    Examples: Money you have in your wallet, in your home, and on hand when you file this application

    Cash: $ _____

11. **Bank accounts and other deposits of money?**

    Examples: Checking, savings, money market, or other financial accounts; certificates of deposit; shares in banks, credit unions, brokerage houses, and other similar institutions. If you have more than one account with the same institution, list each. Do not include 401(k) and IRA accounts.

	Institution name:	Amount:
Checking account:	_____	$_____
Savings account:	_____	$_____
Other financial accounts:	_____	$_____
Other financial accounts:	_____	$_____

12. **Your home?** (if you own it outright or are purchasing it)

    Examples: House, condominium, manufactured home, or mobile home

    Number   Street _____   Current value: $_____

    City _____ State ___ ZIP Code ___   Amount you owe on mortgage and liens: $_____

13. **Other real estate?**

    Number   Street _____   Current value: $_____

    City _____ State ___ ZIP Code ___   Amount you owe on mortgage and liens: $_____

14. **The vehicles you own?**

    Examples: Cars, vans, trucks, sports utility vehicles, motorcycles, tractors, boats

    Make: _____
    Model: _____   Current value: $_____
    Year: _____
    Mileage _____   Amount you owe on liens: $_____

    Make: _____
    Model: _____   Current value: $_____
    Year: _____
    Mileage _____   Amount you owe on liens: $_____

Debtor 1 _____ Case number (if known) _____
         First Name   Middle Name   Last Name

15. Other assets?

Do not include household items and clothing.

Describe the other assets:

[   ]

Current value: $_____

Amount you owe on liens: $_____

16. Money or property due you?

Examples: Tax refunds, past due or lump sum alimony, spousal support, child support, maintenance, divorce or property settlements, Social Security benefits, Workers' compensation, personal injury recovery

Who owes you the money or property?

_____

_____

How much is owed?

$_____

$_____

Do you believe you will likely receive payment in the next 180 days?

❏ No
❏ Yes. Explain:

[   ]

Part 4: Answer These Additional Questions

17. Have you paid anyone for services for this case, including filling out this application, the bankruptcy filing package, or the schedules?

❏ No
❏ Yes. **Whom did you pay?** *Check all that apply:*
   ❏ An attorney
   ❏ A bankruptcy petition preparer, paralegal, or typing service
   ❏ Someone else _____

How much did you pay?
$_____

18. Have you promised to pay or do you expect to pay someone for services for your bankruptcy case?

❏ No
❏ Yes. **Whom do you expect to pay?** *Check all that apply:*
   ❏ An attorney
   ❏ A bankruptcy petition preparer, paralegal, or typing service
   ❏ Someone else _____

How much do you expect to pay?
$_____

19. Has anyone paid someone on your behalf for services for this case?

❏ No
❏ Yes. **Who was paid on your behalf?** *Check all that apply:*
   ❏ An attorney
   ❏ A bankruptcy petition preparer, paralegal, or typing service
   ❏ Someone else _____

Who paid? *Check all that apply:*
   ❏ Parent
   ❏ Brother or sister
   ❏ Friend
   ❏ Pastor or clergy
   ❏ Someone else _____

How much did someone else pay?
$_____

20. Have you filed for bankruptcy within the last 8 years?

❏ No
❏ Yes. District _____ When _____ Case number _____
                              MM/ DD/ YYYY
        District _____ When _____ Case number _____
                              MM/ DD/ YYYY
        District _____ When _____ Case number _____
                              MM/ DD/ YYYY

Part 5: Sign Below

By signing here under penalty of perjury, I declare that I cannot afford to pay the filing fee either in full or in installments. I also declare that the information I provided in this application is true and correct.

✗ _____   ✗ _____
Signature of Debtor 1   Signature of Debtor 2

Date _____   Date _____
     MM / DD / YYYY   MM / DD / YYYY

Fill in this information to identify the case:

Debtor 1 _____
          First Name   Middle Name   Last Name

Debtor 2 _____
(Spouse, if filing) First Name   Middle Name   Last Name

United States Bankruptcy Court for the: _____ District of _____
                                                                 (State)

Case number _____
(If known)

Order on the Application to Have the Chapter 7 Filing Fee Waived

After considering the debtor's *Application to Have the Chapter 7 Filing Fee Waived* (Official Form B 3B), the court orders that the application is:

[ ] **Granted.** However, the court may order the debtor to pay the fee in the future if developments in administering the bankruptcy case show that the waiver was unwarranted.

[ ] **Denied.** The debtor must pay the $335 filing fee according to the following terms:

You must pay…	On or before this date…
$_____	_____ Month / day / year
$_____	_____ Month / day / year
$_____	_____ Month / day / year
+ $_____	_____ Month / day / year

Total

If the debtor would like to propose a different payment timetable, the debtor must file a motion promptly with a payment proposal. The debtor may use *Application for Individuals to Pay the Filing Fee in Installments* (Official Form B 3A) for this purpose. The court will consider it.

The debtor must pay the entire filing fee before making any more payments or transferring any more property to an attorney, bankruptcy petition preparer, or anyone else in connection with the bankruptcy case. The debtor must also pay the entire filing fee to receive a discharge. If the debtor does not make any payment when it is due, the bankruptcy case may be dismissed and the debtor's rights in future bankruptcy cases may be affected.

[ ] **Scheduled for hearing.**

A hearing to consider the debtor's application will be held

on _____ at _____ AM / PM at _____.
    Month / day / year   Address of courthouse

If the debtor does not appear at this hearing, the court may deny the application.

_____   **By the court:** _____
Month / day / year   United States Bankruptcy Judge

UNITED STATES BANKRUPTCY COURT

In re _____,   Case No. _____
            Debtor

                                                   Chapter _____

SUMMARY OF SCHEDULES

Indicate as to each schedule whether that schedule is attached and state the number of pages in each. Report the totals from Schedules A, B, D, E, F, I, and J in the boxes provided. Add the amounts from Schedules A and B to determine the total amount of the debtor's assets. Add the amounts of all claims from Schedules D, E, and F to determine the total amount of the debtor's liabilities. Individual debtors also must complete the "Statistical Summary of Certain Liabilities and Related Data" if they file a case under chapter 7, 11, or 13.

NAME OF SCHEDULE	ATTACHED (YES/NO)	NO. OF SHEETS	ASSETS	LIABILITIES	OTHER
A - Real Property			$		
B - Personal Property			$		
C - Property Claimed as Exempt					
D - Creditors Holding Secured Claims				$	
E - Creditors Holding Unsecured Priority Claims (Total of Claims on Schedule E)				$	
F - Creditors Holding Unsecured Nonpriority Claims				$	
G - Executory Contracts and Unexpired Leases					
H - Codebtors					
I - Current Income of Individual Debtor(s)					$
J - Current Expenditures of Individual Debtors(s)					$
TOTAL			$	$	

UNITED STATES BANKRUPTCY COURT

— —

In re _____,   Case No. _____
          Debtor

                                                         Chapter _____

STATISTICAL SUMMARY OF CERTAIN LIABILITIES AND RELATED DATA (28 U.S.C. § 159)

If you are an individual debtor whose debts are primarily consumer debts, as defined in § 101(8) of the Bankruptcy Code (11 U.S.C. § 101(8)), filing a case under chapter 7, 11 or 13, you must report all information requested below.

☐ Check this box if you are an individual debtor whose debts are NOT primarily consumer debts. You are not required to report any information here.

This information is for statistical purposes only under 28 U.S.C. § 159.

Summarize the following types of liabilities, as reported in the Schedules, and total them.

Type of Liability	Amount
Domestic Support Obligations (from Schedule E)	$
Taxes and Certain Other Debts Owed to Governmental Units (from Schedule E)	$
Claims for Death or Personal Injury While Debtor Was Intoxicated (from Schedule E) (whether disputed or undisputed)	$
Student Loan Obligations (from Schedule F)	$
Domestic Support, Separation Agreement, and Divorce Decree Obligations Not Reported on Schedule E	$
Obligations to Pension or Profit-Sharing, and Other Similar Obligations (from Schedule F)	$
TOTAL	$

State the following:

Average Income (from Schedule I, Line 12)	$
Average Expenses (from Schedule J, Line 22)	$
Current Monthly Income (from Form 22A Line 12; **OR**, Form 22B Line 11; **OR**, Form 22C Line 20)	$

State the following:

1. Total from Schedule D, "UNSECURED PORTION, IF ANY" column		$
2. Total from Schedule E, "AMOUNT ENTITLED TO PRIORITY" column.	$	
3. Total from Schedule E, "AMOUNT NOT ENTITLED TO PRIORITY, IF ANY" column		$
4. Total from Schedule F		$
5. Total of non-priority unsecured debt (sum of 1, 3, and 4)		$

In re _____,   Case No. _____
                    Debtor   **(If known)**

SCHEDULE A - REAL PROPERTY

Except as directed below, list all real property in which the debtor has any legal, equitable, or future interest, including all property owned as a co-tenant, community property, or in which the debtor has a life estate. Include any property in which the debtor holds rights and powers exercisable for the debtor's own benefit. If the debtor is married, state whether the husband, wife, both, or the marital community own the property by placing an "H," "W," "J," or "C" in the column labeled "Husband, Wife, Joint, or Community." If the debtor holds no interest in real property, write "None" under "Description and Location of Property."

Do not include interests in executory contracts and unexpired leases on this schedule. List them in Schedule G - Executory Contracts and Unexpired Leases.

If an entity claims to have a lien or hold a secured interest in any property, state the amount of the secured claim. See Schedule D. If no entity claims to hold a secured interest in the property, write "None" in the column labeled "Amount of Secured Claim."

If the debtor is an individual or if a joint petition is filed, state the amount of any exemption claimed in the property only in Schedule C - Property Claimed as Exempt.

DESCRIPTION AND LOCATION OF PROPERTY	NATURE OF DEBTOR'S INTEREST IN PROPERTY	HUSBAND, WIFE, JOINT, OR COMMUNITY	CURRENT VALUE OF DEBTOR'S INTEREST IN PROPERTY, WITHOUT DEDUCTING ANY SECURED CLAIM OR EXEMPTION	AMOUNT OF SECURED CLAIM

Total ▶

(Report also on Summary of Schedules.)

In re _____,   Case No. _____
                    Debtor   **(If known)**

SCHEDULE B - PERSONAL PROPERTY

Except as directed below, list all personal property of the debtor of whatever kind. If the debtor has no property in one or more of the categories, place an "x" in the appropriate position in the column labeled "None." If additional space is needed in any category, attach a separate sheet properly identified with the case name, case number, and the number of the category. If the debtor is married, state whether the husband, wife, both, or the marital community own the property by placing an "H," "W," "J," or "C" in the column labeled "Husband, Wife, Joint, or Community." If the debtor is an individual or a joint petition is filed, state the amount of any exemptions claimed only in Schedule C - Property Claimed as Exempt.

Do not list interests in executory contracts and unexpired leases on this schedule. List them in Schedule G - Executory Contracts and Unexpired Leases.

If the property is being held for the debtor by someone else, state that person's name and address under "Description and Location of Property." If the property is being held for a minor child, simply state the child's initials and the name and address of the child's parent or guardian, such as "A.B., a minor child, by John Doe, guardian." Do not disclose the child's name. See, 11 U.S.C. §112 and Fed. R. Bankr. P. 1007(m).

TYPE OF PROPERTY	N O N E	DESCRIPTION AND LOCATION OF PROPERTY	HUSBAND, WIFE, JOINT, OR COMMUNITY	CURRENT VALUE OF DEBTOR'S INTEREST IN PROPERTY, WITH- OUT DEDUCTING ANY SECURED CLAIM OR EXEMPTION
1. Cash on hand.				
2. Checking, savings or other financial accounts, certificates of deposit or shares in banks, savings and loan, thrift, building and loan, and homestead associations, or credit unions, brokerage houses, or cooperatives.				
3. Security deposits with public utilities, telephone companies, landlords, and others.				
4. Household goods and furnishings, including audio, video, and computer equipment.				
5. Books; pictures and other art objects; antiques; stamp, coin, record, tape, compact disc, and other collections or collectibles.				
6. Wearing apparel.				
7. Furs and jewelry.				
8. Firearms and sports, photographic, and other hobby equipment.				
9. Interests in insurance policies. Name insurance company of each policy and itemize surrender or refund value of each.				
10. Annuities. Itemize and name each issuer.				
11. Interests in an education IRA as defined in 26 U.S.C. § 530(b)(1) or under a qualified State tuition plan as defined in 26 U.S.C. § 529(b)(1). Give particulars. (File separately the record(s) of any such interest(s). 11 U.S.C. § 521(c).)				

In re _____,   Case No. _____
                    Debtor   **(If known)**

SCHEDULE B - PERSONAL PROPERTY
(Continuation Sheet)

TYPE OF PROPERTY	N O N E	DESCRIPTION AND LOCATION OF PROPERTY	HUSBAND, WIFE, JOINT, OR COMMUNITY	CURRENT VALUE OF DEBTOR'S INTEREST IN PROPERTY, WITH-OUT DEDUCTING ANY SECURED CLAIM OR EXEMPTION
12. Interests in IRA, ERISA, Keogh, or other pension or profit sharing plans. Give particulars.				
13. Stock and interests in incorporated and unincorporated businesses. Itemize.				
14. Interests in partnerships or joint ventures. Itemize.				
15. Government and corporate bonds and other negotiable and non-negotiable instruments.				
16. Accounts receivable.				
17. Alimony, maintenance, support, and property settlements to which the debtor is or may be entitled. Give particulars.				
18. Other liquidated debts owed to debtor including tax refunds. Give particulars.				
19. Equitable or future interests, life estates, and rights or powers exercisable for the benefit of the debtor other than those listed in Schedule A – Real Property.				
20. Contingent and noncontingent interests in estate of a decedent, death benefit plan, life insurance policy, or trust.				
21. Other contingent and unliquidated claims of every nature, including tax refunds, counterclaims of the debtor, and rights to setoff claims. Give estimated value of each.				

In re _____,   Case No. _____
                    Debtor   **(If known)**

SCHEDULE B - PERSONAL PROPERTY
(Continuation Sheet)

TYPE OF PROPERTY	N O N E	DESCRIPTION AND LOCATION OF PROPERTY	HUSBAND, WIFE, JOINT, OR COMMUNITY	CURRENT VALUE OF DEBTOR'S INTEREST IN PROPERTY, WITH-OUT DEDUCTING ANY SECURED CLAIM OR EXEMPTION
22. Patents, copyrights, and other intellectual property. Give particulars.				
23. Licenses, franchises, and other general intangibles. Give particulars.				
24. Customer lists or other compilations containing personally identifiable information (as defined in 11 U.S.C. § 101(41A)) provided to the debtor by individuals in connection with obtaining a product or service from the debtor primarily for personal, family, or household purposes.				
25. Automobiles, trucks, trailers, and other vehicles and accessories.				
26. Boats, motors, and accessories.				
27. Aircraft and accessories.				
28. Office equipment, furnishings, and supplies.				
29. Machinery, fixtures, equipment, and supplies used in business.				
30. Inventory.				
31. Animals.				
32. Crops - growing or harvested. Give particulars.				
33. Farming equipment and implements.				
34. Farm supplies, chemicals, and feed.				
35. Other personal property of any kind not already listed. Itemize.				

_____continuation sheets attached   Total▶ $ _____

(Include amounts from any continuation sheets attached. Report total also on Summary of Schedules.)

In re _____,   Case No. _____
                        Debtor   *(If known)*

SCHEDULE C - PROPERTY CLAIMED AS EXEMPT

Debtor claims the exemptions to which debtor is entitled under:
(Check one box)
☐ 11 U.S.C. § 522(b)(2)
☐ 11 U.S.C. § 522(b)(3)

☐ Check if debtor claims a homestead exemption that exceeds
$155,675.*

DESCRIPTION OF PROPERTY	SPECIFY LAW PROVIDING EACH EXEMPTION	VALUE OF CLAIMED EXEMPTION	CURRENT VALUE OF PROPERTY WITHOUT DEDUCTING EXEMPTION

* *Amount subject to adjustment on 4/01/16, and every three years thereafter with respect to cases commenced on or after the date of adjustment.*

In re _____,   Case No. _____
            Debtor   **(If known)**

SCHEDULE D - CREDITORS HOLDING SECURED CLAIMS

State the name, mailing address, including zip code, and last four digits of any account number of all entities holding claims secured by property of the debtor as of the date of filing of the petition. The complete account number of any account the debtor has with the creditor is useful to the trustee and the creditor and may be provided if the debtor chooses to do so. List creditors holding all types of secured interests such as judgment liens, garnishments, statutory liens, mortgages, deeds of trust, and other security interests.

List creditors in alphabetical order to the extent practicable. If a minor child is the creditor, state the child's initials and the name and address of the child's parent or guardian, such as "A.B., a minor child, by John Doe, guardian." Do not disclose the child's name. See, 11 U.S.C. §112 and Fed. R. Bankr. P. 1007(m). If all secured creditors will not fit on this page, use the continuation sheet provided.

If any entity other than a spouse in a joint case may be jointly liable on a claim, place an "X" in the column labeled "Codebtor," include the entity on the appropriate schedule of creditors, and complete Schedule H – Codebtors. If a joint petition is filed, state whether the husband, wife, both of them, or the marital community may be liable on each claim by placing an "H," "W," "J," or "C" in the column labeled "Husband, Wife, Joint, or Community."

If the claim is contingent, place an "X" in the column labeled "Contingent." If the claim is unliquidated, place an "X" in the column labeled "Unliquidated." If the claim is disputed, place an "X" in the column labeled "Disputed." (You may need to place an "X" in more than one of these three columns.)

Total the columns labeled "Amount of Claim Without Deducting Value of Collateral" and "Unsecured Portion, if Any" in the boxes labeled "Total(s)" on the last sheet of the completed schedule. Report the total from the column labeled "Amount of Claim Without Deducting Value of Collateral" also on the Summary of Schedules and, if the debtor is an individual with primarily consumer debts, report the total from the column labeled "Unsecured Portion, if Any" on the Statistical Summary of Certain Liabilities and Related Data.

☐   Check this box if debtor has no creditors holding secured claims to report on this Schedule D.

CREDITOR'S NAME AND MAILING ADDRESS INCLUDING ZIP CODE AND AN ACCOUNT NUMBER *(See Instructions Above.)*	CODEBTOR	HUSBAND, WIFE, JOINT, OR COMMUNITY	DATE CLAIM WAS INCURRED, NATURE OF LIEN, AND DESCRIPTION AND VALUE OF PROPERTY SUBJECT TO LIEN	CONTINGENT	UNLIQUIDATED	DISPUTED	AMOUNT OF CLAIM WITHOUT DEDUCTING VALUE OF COLLATERAL	UNSECURED PORTION, IF ANY
ACCOUNT NO.								
			VALUE $					
ACCOUNT NO.								
			VALUE $					
ACCOUNT NO.								
			VALUE $					
_____ continuation sheets attached			Subtotal ▶ (Total of this page)				$	$
			Total ▶ (Use only on last page)				$	$
							(Report also on Summary of Schedules.)	(If applicable, report also on Statistical Summary of Certain Liabilities and Related Data.)

In re _____ ,   Case No. _____
                        Debtor   **(if known)**

SCHEDULE D - CREDITORS HOLDING SECURED CLAIMS
(Continuation Sheet)

CREDITOR'S NAME AND MAILING ADDRESS INCLUDING ZIP CODE AND AN ACCOUNT NUMBER (*See Instructions Above.*)	CODEBTOR	HUSBAND, WIFE, JOINT, OR COMMUNITY	DATE CLAIM WAS INCURRED, NATURE OF LIEN , AND DESCRIPTION AND VALUE OF PROPERTY SUBJECT TO LIEN	CONTINGENT	UNLIQUIDATED	DISPUTED	AMOUNT OF CLAIM WITHOUT DEDUCTING VALUE OF COLLATERAL	UNSECURED PORTION, IF ANY
ACCOUNT NO.								
			VALUE $					
ACCOUNT NO.								
			VALUE $					
ACCOUNT NO.								
			VALUE $					
ACCOUNT NO.								
			VALUE $					
ACCOUNT NO.								
			VALUE $					
Sheet no._____of_____continuation sheets attached to Schedule of Creditors Holding Secured Claims			Subtotal (s)▶ (Total(s) of this page)				$	$
			Total(s) ▶ (Use only on last page)				$	$
							(Report also on Summary of Schedules.)	(If applicable, report also on Statistical Summary of Certain Liabilities and Related Data.)

In re _____,   Case No._____
                 Debtor   *(if known)*

SCHEDULE E - CREDITORS HOLDING UNSECURED PRIORITY CLAIMS

A complete list of claims entitled to priority, listed separately by type of priority, is to be set forth on the sheets provided. Only holders of unsecured claims entitled to priority should be listed in this schedule. In the boxes provided on the attached sheets, state the name, mailing address, including zip code, and last four digits of the account number, if any, of all entities holding priority claims against the debtor or the property of the debtor, as of the date of the filing of the petition. Use a separate continuation sheet for each type of priority and label each with the type of priority.

The complete account number of any account the debtor has with the creditor is useful to the trustee and the creditor and may be provided if the debtor chooses to do so. If a minor child is a creditor, state the child's initials and the name and address of the child's parent or guardian, such as "A.B., a minor child, by John Doe, guardian." Do not disclose the child's name. See, 11 U.S.C. §112 and Fed. R. Bankr. P. 1007(m).

If any entity other than a spouse in a joint case may be jointly liable on a claim, place an "X" in the column labeled "Codebtor," include the entity on the appropriate schedule of creditors, and complete Schedule H-Codebtors. If a joint petition is filed, state whether the husband, wife, both of them, or the marital community may be liable on each claim by placing an "H," "W," "J," or "C" in the column labeled "Husband, Wife, Joint, or Community."   If the claim is contingent, place an "X" in the column labeled "Contingent." If the claim is unliquidated, place an "X" in the column labeled "Unliquidated." If the claim is disputed, place an "X" in the column labeled "Disputed." (You may need to place an "X" in more than one of these three columns.)

Report the total of claims listed on each sheet in the box labeled "Subtotals" on each sheet. Report the total of all claims listed on this Schedule E in the box labeled "Total" on the last sheet of the completed schedule. Report this total also on the Summary of Schedules.

Report the total of amounts entitled to priority listed on each sheet in the box labeled "Subtotals" on each sheet. Report the total of all amounts entitled to priority listed on this Schedule E in the box labeled "Totals" on the last sheet of the completed schedule. Individual debtors with primarily consumer debts report this total also on the Statistical Summary of Certain Liabilities and Related Data.

Report the total of amounts not entitled to priority listed on each sheet in the box labeled "Subtotals" on each sheet. Report the total of all amounts not entitled to priority listed on this Schedule E in the box labeled "Totals" on the last sheet of the completed schedule. Individual debtors with primarily consumer debts report this total also on the Statistical Summary of Certain Liabilities and Related Data.

☐ Check this box if debtor has no creditors holding unsecured priority claims to report on this Schedule E.

TYPES OF PRIORITY CLAIMS (Check the appropriate box(es) below if claims in that category are listed on the attached sheets.)

☐ **Domestic Support Obligations**

Claims for domestic support that are owed to or recoverable by a spouse, former spouse, or child of the debtor, or the parent, legal guardian, or responsible relative of such a child, or a governmental unit to whom such a domestic support claim has been assigned to the extent provided in 11 U.S.C. § 507(a)(1).

☐ **Extensions of credit in an involuntary case**

Claims arising in the ordinary course of the debtor's business or financial affairs after the commencement of the case but before the earlier of the appointment of a trustee or the order for relief. 11 U.S.C. § 507(a)(3).

☐ **Wages, salaries, and commissions**

Wages, salaries, and commissions, including vacation, severance, and sick leave pay owing to employees and commissions owing to qualifying independent sales representatives up to $12,475* per person earned within 180 days immediately preceding the filing of the original petition, or the cessation of business, whichever occurred first, to the extent provided in 11 U.S.C. § 507(a)(4).

☐ **Contributions to employee benefit plans**

Money owed to employee benefit plans for services rendered within 180 days immediately preceding the filing of the original petition, or the cessation of business, whichever occurred first, to the extent provided in 11 U.S.C. § 507(a)(5).

_____

* Amount subject to adjustment on 4/01/16, and every three years thereafter with respect to cases commenced on or after the date of adjustment.

In re _____ ,   **Case No.**_____
              Debtor   *(if known)*

☐ **Certain farmers and fishermen**

   Claims of certain farmers and fishermen, up to $6,150* per farmer or fisherman, against the debtor, as provided in 11 U.S.C. § 507(a)(6).

☐ **Deposits by individuals**

   Claims of individuals up to $2,775* for deposits for the purchase, lease, or rental of property or services for personal, family, or household use, that were not delivered or provided. 11 U.S.C. § 507(a)(7).

☐ **Taxes and Certain Other Debts Owed to Governmental Units**

   Taxes, customs duties, and penalties owing to federal, state, and local governmental units as set forth in 11 U.S.C. § 507(a)(8).

☐ **Commitments to Maintain the Capital of an Insured Depository Institution**

   Claims based on commitments to the FDIC, RTC, Director of the Office of Thrift Supervision, Comptroller of the Currency, or Board of Governors of the Federal Reserve System, or their predecessors or successors, to maintain the capital of an insured depository institution. 11 U.S.C. § 507 (a)(9).

☐ **Claims for Death or Personal Injury While Debtor Was Intoxicated**

   Claims for death or personal injury resulting from the operation of a motor vehicle or vessel while the debtor was intoxicated from using alcohol, a drug, or another substance. 11 U.S.C. § 507(a)(10).

* Amounts are subject to adjustment on 4/01/16, and every three years thereafter with respect to cases commenced on or after the date of adjustment.

_____ continuation sheets attached

In re _____,   **Case No.** _____
　　　　　　　　　Debtor　　　　　　　　　　　　　　　　　　　　　　　*(if known)*

SCHEDULE E - CREDITORS HOLDING UNSECURED PRIORITY CLAIMS

(Continuation Sheet)

Type of Priority for Claims Listed on This Sheet

CREDITOR'S NAME, MAILING ADDRESS INCLUDING ZIP CODE, AND ACCOUNT NUMBER *(See instructions above.)*	CODEBTOR	HUSBAND, WIFE, JOINT, OR COMMUNITY	DATE CLAIM WAS INCURRED AND CONSIDERATION FOR CLAIM	CONTINGENT	UNLIQUIDATED	DISPUTED	AMOUNT OF CLAIM	AMOUNT ENTITLED TO PRIORITY	AMOUNT NOT ENTITLED TO PRIORITY, IF ANY
Account No.									
Account No.									
Account No.									
Account No.									

Sheet no. ___ of ___ continuation sheets attached to Schedule of Creditors Holding Priority Claims

Subtotals▶ (Totals of this page) ... $ ... $

Total▶ (Use only on last page of the completed Schedule E. Report also on the Summary of Schedules.) ... $

Totals▶ (Use only on last page of the completed Schedule E. If applicable, report also on the Statistical Summary of Certain Liabilities and Related Data.) ... $ ... $

In re _____,   Case No. _____
                    Debtor   **(if known)**

SCHEDULE F - CREDITORS HOLDING UNSECURED NONPRIORITY CLAIMS

State the name, mailing address, including zip code, and last four digits of any account number, of all entities holding unsecured claims without priority against the debtor or the property of the debtor, as of the date of filing of the petition. The complete account number of any account the debtor has with the creditor is useful to the trustee and the creditor and may be provided if the debtor chooses to do so. If a minor child is a creditor, state the child's initials and the name and address of the child's parent or guardian, such as "A.B., a minor child, by John Doe, guardian." Do not disclose the child's name. See, 11 U.S.C. §112 and Fed. R. Bankr. P. 1007(m). Do not include claims listed in Schedules D and E. If all creditors will not fit on this page, use the continuation sheet provided.

If any entity other than a spouse in a joint case may be jointly liable on a claim, place an "X" in the column labeled "Codebtor," include the entity on the appropriate schedule of creditors, and complete Schedule H - Codebtors. If a joint petition is filed, state whether the husband, wife, both of them, or the marital community may be liable on each claim by placing an "H," "W," "J," or "C" in the column labeled "Husband, Wife, Joint, or Community."

If the claim is contingent, place an "X" in the column labeled "Contingent." If the claim is unliquidated, place an "X" in the column labeled "Unliquidated." If the claim is disputed, place an "X" in the column labeled "Disputed." (You may need to place an "X" in more than one of these three columns.)

Report the total of all claims listed on this schedule in the box labeled "Total" on the last sheet of the completed schedule. Report this total also on the Summary of Schedules and, if the debtor is an individual with primarily consumer debts, report this total also on the Statistical Summary of Certain Liabilities and Related Data..

☐ Check this box if debtor has no creditors holding unsecured claims to report on this Schedule F.

CREDITOR'S NAME, MAILING ADDRESS INCLUDING ZIP CODE, AND ACCOUNT NUMBER *(See instructions above.)*	CODEBTOR	HUSBAND, WIFE, JOINT, OR COMMUNITY	DATE CLAIM WAS INCURRED AND CONSIDERATION FOR CLAIM. IF CLAIM IS SUBJECT TO SETOFF, SO STATE.	CONTINGENT	UNLIQUIDATED	DISPUTED	AMOUNT OF CLAIM
ACCOUNT NO.							
ACCOUNT NO.							
ACCOUNT NO.							
ACCOUNT NO.							
				Subtotal►			$

_____continuation sheets attached

Total► $

(Use only on last page of the completed Schedule F.)
(Report also on Summary of Schedules and, if applicable, on the Statistical Summary of Certain Liabilities and Related Data.)

In re _____ ,   Case No. _____
               Debtor   **(if known)**

SCHEDULE F - CREDITORS HOLDING UNSECURED NONPRIORITY CLAIMS
(Continuation Sheet)

CREDITOR'S NAME, MAILING ADDRESS INCLUDING ZIP CODE, AND ACCOUNT NUMBER (See instructions above.)	CODEBTOR	HUSBAND, WIFE, JOINT, OR COMMUNITY	DATE CLAIM WAS INCURRED AND CONSIDERATION FOR CLAIM. IF CLAIM IS SUBJECT TO SETOFF, SO STATE.	CONTINGENT	UNLIQUIDATED	DISPUTED	AMOUNT OF CLAIM
ACCOUNT NO.							
ACCOUNT NO.							
ACCOUNT NO.							
ACCOUNT NO.							
ACCOUNT NO.							

Sheet no._____ of_____ continuation sheets attached
to Schedule of Creditors Holding Unsecured
Nonpriority Claims

Subtotal➤ $

Total➤ $
(Use only on last page of the completed Schedule F.)
(Report also on Summary of Schedules and, if applicable on the Statistical
Summary of Certain Liabilities and Related Data.)

In re _____ ,   Case No._____
                    Debtor   **(if known)**

SCHEDULE G - EXECUTORY CONTRACTS AND UNEXPIRED LEASES

      Describe all executory contracts of any nature and all unexpired leases of real or personal property. Include any timeshare interests. State nature of debtor's interest in contract, i.e., "Purchaser," "Agent," etc. State whether debtor is the lessor or lessee of a lease. Provide the names and complete mailing addresses of all other parties to each lease or contract described. If a minor child is a party to one of the leases or contracts, state the child's initials and the name and address of the child's parent or guardian, such as "A.B., a minor child, by John Doe, guardian." Do not disclose the child's name. See, 11 U.S.C. §112 and Fed. R. Bankr. P. 1007(m).

☐ Check this box if debtor has no executory contracts or unexpired leases.

NAME AND MAILING ADDRESS, INCLUDING ZIP CODE, OF OTHER PARTIES TO LEASE OR CONTRACT.	DESCRIPTION OF CONTRACT OR LEASE AND NATURE OF DEBTOR'S INTEREST. STATE WHETHER LEASE IS FOR NONRESIDENTIAL REAL PROPERTY. STATE CONTRACT NUMBER OF ANY GOVERNMENT CONTRACT.

B 6H (Official Form 6H) (12/07)

In re _____ ,   **Case No.** _____
                    Debtor   **(if known)**

SCHEDULE H - CODEBTORS

Provide the information requested concerning any person or entity, other than a spouse in a joint case, that is also liable on any debts listed by the debtor in the schedules of creditors. Include all guarantors and co-signers. If the debtor resides or resided in a community property state, commonwealth, or territory (including Alaska, Arizona, California, Idaho, Louisiana, Nevada, New Mexico, Puerto Rico, Texas, Washington, or Wisconsin) within the eight-year period immediately preceding the commencement of the case, identify the name of the debtor's spouse and of any former spouse who resides or resided with the debtor in the community property state, commonwealth, or territory. Include all names used by the nondebtor spouse during the eight years immediately preceding the commencement of this case. If a minor child is a codebtor or a creditor, state the child's initials and the name and address of the child's parent or guardian, such as "A.B., a minor child, by John Doe, guardian." Do not disclose the child's name. See, 11 U.S.C. §112 and Fed. R. Bankr. P. 1007(m).

☐ Check this box if debtor has no codebtors.

NAME AND ADDRESS OF CODEBTOR	NAME AND ADDRESS OF CREDITOR

Debtor 1 _____
       First Name   Middle Name   Last Name

Debtor 2 _____
(Spouse, if filing) First Name   Middle Name   Last Name

United States Bankruptcy Court for the: _____ District of _____

Case number _____
(If known)

Check if this is:

☐ An amended filing

☐ A supplement showing post-petition chapter 13 income as of the following date:

_____
MM / DD / YYYY

Official Form B 6I

Schedule I: Your Income

12/13

Be as complete and accurate as possible. If two married people are filing together (Debtor 1 and Debtor 2), both are equally responsible for supplying correct information. If you are married and not filing jointly, and your spouse is living with you, include information about your spouse. If you are separated and your spouse is not filing with you, do not include information about your spouse. If more space is needed, attach a separate sheet to this form. On the top of any additional pages, write your name and case number (if known). Answer every question.

Part 1: Describe Employment

1. **Fill in your employment information.**

   If you have more than one job, attach a separate page with information about additional employers.

   Include part-time, seasonal, or self-employed work.

   Occupation may Include student or homemaker, if it applies.

	Debtor 1	Debtor 2 or non-filing spouse
Employment status	☐ Employed ☐ Not employed	☐ Employed ☐ Not employed
Occupation	_____	_____
Employer's name	_____	_____
Employer's address	_____	_____
	Number Street	Number Street
	_____	_____
	_____	_____
	City State ZIP Code	City State ZIP Code
How long employed there?	_____	_____

Part 2: Give Details About Monthly Income

Estimate monthly income as of the date you file this form. If you have nothing to report for any line, write $0 in the space. Include your non-filing spouse unless you are separated.

If you or your non-filing spouse have more than one employer, combine the information for all employers for that person on the lines below. If you need more space, attach a separate sheet to this form.

		For Debtor 1	For Debtor 2 or non-filing spouse
2.	**List monthly gross wages, salary, and commissions** (before all payroll deductions). If not paid monthly, calculate what the monthly wage would be.	2. $_____	$_____
3.	**Estimate and list monthly overtime pay.**	3. + $_____	+ $_____
4.	**Calculate gross income.** Add line 2 + line 3.	4. $_____	$_____

		For Debtor 1	For Debtor 2 or non-filing spouse
Copy line 4 here .... ➔ 4.		$_____	$_____

5. **List all payroll deductions:**

		For Debtor 1	For Debtor 2 or non-filing spouse
5a. **Tax, Medicare, and Social Security deductions**	5a.	$_____	$_____
5b. **Mandatory contributions for retirement plans**	5b.	$_____	$_____
5c. **Voluntary contributions for retirement plans**	5c.	$_____	$_____
5d. **Required repayments of retirement fund loans**	5d.	$_____	$_____
5e. **Insurance**	5e.	$_____	$_____
5f. **Domestic support obligations**	5f.	$_____	$_____
5g. **Union dues**	5g.	$_____	$_____
5h. **Other deductions.** Specify: _____	5h.	+ $_____	+ $_____

6. **Add the payroll deductions.** Add lines 5a + 5b + 5c + 5d + 5e +5f + 5g +5h.   6. $_____ $_____

7. **Calculate total monthly take-home pay.** Subtract line 6 from line 4.   7. $_____ $_____

8. **List all other income regularly received:**

8a. **Net income from rental property and from operating a business, profession, or farm**

Attach a statement for each property and business showing gross receipts, ordinary and necessary business expenses, and the total monthly net income.   8a. $_____ $_____

8b. **Interest and dividends**   8b. $_____ $_____

8c. **Family support payments that you, a non-filing spouse, or a dependent regularly receive**

Include alimony, spousal support, child support, maintenance, divorce settlement, and property settlement.   8c. $_____ $_____

8d. **Unemployment compensation**   8d. $_____ $_____

8e. **Social Security**   8e. $_____ $_____

8f. **Other government assistance that you regularly receive**

Include cash assistance and the value (if known) of any non-cash assistance that you receive, such as food stamps (benefits under the Supplemental Nutrition Assistance Program) or housing subsidies.
Specify: _____   8f. $_____ $_____

8g. **Pension or retirement income**   8g. $_____ $_____

8h. **Other monthly income.** Specify: _____   8h.   + $_____   + $_____

9. **Add all other income.** Add lines 8a + 8b + 8c + 8d + 8e + 8f +8g + 8h.   9. $_____ $_____

10. **Calculate monthly income.** Add line 7 + line 9.
Add the entries in line 10 for Debtor 1 and Debtor 2 or non-filing spouse.   10. $_____ **+** $_____ **=** $_____

11. **State all other regular contributions to the expenses that you list in *Schedule J*.**

Include contributions from an unmarried partner, members of your household, your dependents, your roommates, and other friends or relatives.

Do not include any amounts already included in lines 2-10 or amounts that are not available to pay expenses listed in *Schedule J.*

Specify: _____   11. **+** $_____

12. **Add the amount in the last column of line 10 to the amount in line 11.** The result is the combined monthly income.
Write that amount on the *Summary of Schedules* and *Statistical Summary of Certain Liabilities and Related Data,* if it applies   12. $_____
                                                      Combined monthly income

13. **Do you expect an increase or decrease within the year after you file this form?**

☐ No.

☐ Yes. Explain: _____

Fill in this information to identify your case:

Debtor 1 _____
           First Name   Middle Name   Last Name

Debtor 2 _____
(Spouse, if filing) First Name   Middle Name   Last Name

United States Bankruptcy Court for the: _____ District of _____

Case number _____
(If known)

Check if this is:

☐ An amended filing

☐ A supplement showing post-petition chapter 13 expenses as of the following date:

_____
MM / DD / YYYY

☐ A separate filing for Debtor 2 because Debtor 2 maintains a separate household

Official Form B 6J

Schedule J: Your Expenses

12/13

Be as complete and accurate as possible. If two married people are filing together, both are equally responsible for supplying correct information. If more space is needed, attach another sheet to this form. On the top of any additional pages, write your name and case number (if known). Answer every question.

Part 1: Describe Your Household

1. **Is this a joint case?**

   ☐ No. Go to line 2.

   ☐ Yes. **Does Debtor 2 live in a separate household?**

          ☐ No

          ☐ Yes. Debtor 2 must file a separate Schedule J.

2. **Do you have dependents?**

   Do not list Debtor 1 and Debtor 2.

   Do not state the dependents' names.

   ☐ No

   ☐ Yes. Fill out this information for each dependent..........................

Dependent's relationship to Debtor 1 or Debtor 2	Dependent's age	Does dependent live with you?
_____	_____	☐ No ☐ Yes
_____	_____	☐ No ☐ Yes
_____	_____	☐ No ☐ Yes
_____	_____	☐ No ☐ Yes
_____	_____	☐ No ☐ Yes

3. **Do your expenses include expenses of people other than yourself and your dependents?**

   ☐ No

   ☐ Yes

Part 2: Estimate Your Ongoing Monthly Expenses

Estimate your expenses as of your bankruptcy filing date unless you are using this form as a supplement in a Chapter 13 case to report expenses as of a date after the bankruptcy is filed. If this is a supplemental *Schedule J*, check the box at the top of the form and fill in the applicable date.

Include expenses paid for with non-cash government assistance if you know the value of such assistance and have included it on *Schedule I: Your Income* (Official Form B 6I.)

Your expenses

4. **The rental or home ownership expenses for your residence.** Include first mortgage payments and any rent for the ground or lot.

                                                 4. $_____

If not included in line 4:

4a. Real estate taxes   4a. $_____

4b. Property, homeowner's, or renter's insurance   4b. $_____

4c. Home maintenance, repair, and upkeep expenses 4c. $_____

4d. Homeowner's association or condominium dues 4d. $_____

Official Form B 6J   **Schedule J: Your Expenses**   page 1

Your expenses

5. **Additional mortgage payments for your residence**, such as home equity loans   5. $_____

6. **Utilities:**

   6a. Electricity, heat, natural gas   6a. $_____

   6b. Water, sewer, garbage collection   6b. $_____

   6c. Telephone, cell phone, Internet, satellite, and cable services   6c. $_____

   6d. Other. Specify: _____   6d. $_____

7. **Food and housekeeping supplies**   7. $_____

8. **Childcare and children's education costs**   8. $_____

9. **Clothing, laundry, and dry cleaning**   9. $_____

10. **Personal care products and services**   10. $_____

11. **Medical and dental expenses**   11. $_____

12. **Transportation.** Include gas, maintenance, bus or train fare.
Do not include car payments.   12. $_____

13. **Entertainment, clubs, recreation, newspapers, magazines, and books**   13. $_____

14. **Charitable contributions and religious donations**   14. $_____

15. **Insurance.**
Do not include insurance deducted from your pay or included in lines 4 or 20.

   15a. Life insurance   15a. $_____

   15b. Health insurance   15b. $_____

   15c. Vehicle insurance   15c. $_____

   15d. Other insurance. Specify:_____   15d. $_____

16. **Taxes.** Do not include taxes deducted from your pay or included in lines 4 or 20.
Specify: _____   16. $_____

17. **Installment or lease payments:**

   17a. Car payments for Vehicle 1   17a. $_____

   17b. Car payments for Vehicle 2   17b. $_____

   17c. Other. Specify:_____   17c. $_____

   17d. Other. Specify:_____   17d. $_____

18. **Your payments of alimony, maintenance, and support that you did not report as deducted
from your pay on line 5, *Schedule I, Your Income* (Official Form B 6I).**   18. $_____

19. **Other payments you make to support others who do not live with you.**
Specify:_____   19. $_____

20. **Other real property expenses not included in lines 4 or 5 of this form or on *Schedule I: Your Income*.**

   20a. Mortgages on other property   20a. $_____

   20b. Real estate taxes   20b. $_____

   20c. Property, homeowner's, or renter's insurance   20c. $_____

   20d. Maintenance, repair, and upkeep expenses   20d. $_____

   20e. Homeowner's association or condominium dues   20e. $_____

21. **Other**. Specify: _____   21. **+** $_____

22. **Your monthly expenses.** Add lines 4 through 21.
    The result is your monthly expenses.   22. $_____

23. **Calculate your monthly net income.**

    23a. Copy line 12 *(your combined monthly income)* from *Schedule I.*   23a. $_____

    23b. Copy your monthly expenses from line 22 above.   23b. **−** $_____

    23c. Subtract your monthly expenses from your monthly income.
          The result is your *monthly net income*.   23c. $_____

24. **Do you expect an increase or decrease in your expenses within the year after you file this form?**

    For example, do you expect to finish paying for your car loan within the year or do you expect your
    mortgage payment to increase or decrease because of a modification to the terms of your mortgage?

    ☐ No.
    ☐ Yes.   Explain here:

In re _____ ,   Case No. _____
                 Debtor   **(if known)**

DECLARATION CONCERNING DEBTOR'S SCHEDULES

DECLARATION UNDER PENALTY OF PERJURY BY INDIVIDUAL DEBTOR

I declare under penalty of perjury that I have read the foregoing summary and schedules, consisting of _____ sheets, and that they are true and correct to the best of my knowledge, information, and belief.

Date _____   Signature: _____
                                                        Debtor

Date _____   Signature: _____
                                               (Joint Debtor, if any)

[If joint case, both spouses must sign.]

DECLARATION AND SIGNATURE OF NON-ATTORNEY BANKRUPTCY PETITION PREPARER (See 11 U.S.C. § 110)

I declare under penalty of perjury that: (1) I am a bankruptcy petition preparer as defined in 11 U.S.C. § 110; (2) I prepared this document for compensation and have provided the debtor with a copy of this document and the notices and information required under 11 U.S.C. §§ 110(b), 110(h) and 342(b); and, (3) if rules or guidelines have been promulgated pursuant to 11 U.S.C. § 110(h) setting a maximum fee for services chargeable by bankruptcy petition preparers, I have given the debtor notice of the maximum amount before preparing any document for filing for a debtor or accepting any fee from the debtor, as required by that section.

_____   _____
Printed or Typed Name and Title, if any,   Social Security No.
of Bankruptcy Petition Preparer   *(Required by 11 U.S.C. § 110.)*

If the bankruptcy petition preparer is not an individual, state the name, title (if any), address, and social security number of the officer, principal, responsible person, or partner who signs this document.

_____
_____
_____
Address

X _____   _____
  Signature of Bankruptcy Petition Preparer   Date

Names and Social Security numbers of all other individuals who prepared or assisted in preparing this document, unless the bankruptcy petition preparer is not an individual:

If more than one person prepared this document, attach additional signed sheets conforming to the appropriate Official Form for each person.

A bankruptcy petition preparer's failure to comply with the provisions of title 11 and the Federal Rules of Bankruptcy Procedure may result in fines or imprisonment or both. 11 U.S.C. § 110; 18 U.S.C. § 156.

DECLARATION UNDER PENALTY OF PERJURY ON BEHALF OF A CORPORATION OR PARTNERSHIP

I, the _____ [the president or other officer or an authorized agent of the corporation or a member or an authorized agent of the partnership] of the _____ [corporation or partnership] named as debtor in this case, declare under penalty of perjury that I have read the foregoing summary and schedules, consisting of _____ sheets (*Total shown on summary page plus 1*), and that they are true and correct to the best of my knowledge, information, and belief.

Date _____

                            Signature: _____

                                    _____
                                    [Print or type name of individual signing on behalf of debtor.]

[An individual signing on behalf of a partnership or corporation must indicate position or relationship to debtor.]

Penalty for making a false statement or concealing property: Fine of up to $500,000 or imprisonment for up to 5 years or both. 18 U.S.C. §§ 152 and 3571.

UNITED STATES BANKRUPTCY COURT

In re:_____,   Case No. _____
                  Debtor   (if known)

STATEMENT OF FINANCIAL AFFAIRS

This statement is to be completed by every debtor. Spouses filing a joint petition may file a single statement on which the information for both spouses is combined. If the case is filed under chapter 12 or chapter 13, a married debtor must furnish information for both spouses whether or not a joint petition is filed, unless the spouses are separated and a joint petition is not filed. An individual debtor engaged in business as a sole proprietor, partner, family farmer, or self-employed professional, should provide the information requested on this statement concerning all such activities as well as the individual's personal affairs. To indicate payments, transfers and the like to minor children, state the child's initials and the name and address of the child's parent or guardian, such as "A.B., a minor child, by John Doe, guardian." Do not disclose the child's name. See, 11 U.S.C. §112 and Fed. R. Bankr. P. 1007(m).

Questions 1 - 18 are to be completed by all debtors. Debtors that are or have been in business, as defined below, also must complete Questions 19 - 25. **If the answer to an applicable question is "None," mark the box labeled "None."** If additional space is needed for the answer to any question, use and attach a separate sheet properly identified with the case name, case number (if known), and the number of the question.

DEFINITIONS

"In business." A debtor is "in business" for the purpose of this form if the debtor is a corporation or partnership. An individual debtor is "in business" for the purpose of this form if the debtor is or has been, within six years immediately preceding the filing of this bankruptcy case, any of the following: an officer, director, managing executive, or owner of 5 percent or more of the voting or equity securities of a corporation; a partner, other than a limited partner, of a partnership; a sole proprietor or self-employed full-time or part-time. An individual debtor also may be "in business" for the purpose of this form if the debtor engages in a trade, business, or other activity, other than as an employee, to supplement income from the debtor's primary employment.

"Insider." The term "insider" includes but is not limited to: relatives of the debtor; general partners of the debtor and their relatives; corporations of which the debtor is an officer, director, or person in control; officers, directors, and any persons in control of a corporate debtor and their relatives; affiliates of the debtor and insiders of such affiliates; and any managing agent of the debtor. 11 U.S.C. § 101(2), (31).

---

1. **Income from employment or operation of business**

None
☐

State the gross amount of income the debtor has received from employment, trade, or profession, or from operation of the debtor's business, including part-time activities either as an employee or in independent trade or business, from the beginning of this calendar year to the date this case was commenced. State also the gross amounts received during the **two years** immediately preceding this calendar year. (A debtor that maintains, or has maintained, financial records on the basis of a fiscal rather than a calendar year may report fiscal year income. Identify the beginning and ending dates of the debtor's fiscal year.) If a joint petition is filed, state income for each spouse separately. (Married debtors filing under chapter 12 or chapter 13 must state income of both spouses whether or not a joint petition is filed, unless the spouses are separated and a joint petition is not filed.)

AMOUNT   SOURCE

2. Income other than from employment or operation of business

None ☐ State the amount of income received by the debtor other than from employment, trade, profession, operation of the debtor's business during the **two years** immediately preceding the commencement of this case. Give particulars. If a joint petition is filed, state income for each spouse separately. (Married debtors filing under chapter 12 or chapter 13 must state income for each spouse whether or not a joint petition is filed, unless the spouses are separated and a joint petition is not filed.)

AMOUNT   SOURCE

---

3. Payments to creditors

Complete a. or b., as appropriate, and c.

None ☐ a. *Individual or joint debtor(s) with primarily consumer debts:* List all payments on loans, installment purchases of goods or services, and other debts to any creditor made within **90 days** immediately preceding the commencement of this case unless the aggregate value of all property that constitutes or is affected by such transfer is less than $600. Indicate with an asterisk (*) any payments that were made to a creditor on account of a domestic support obligation or as part of an alternative repayment schedule under a plan by an approved nonprofit budgeting and credit counseling agency. (Married debtors filing under chapter 12 or chapter 13 must include payments by either or both spouses whether or not a joint petition is filed, unless the spouses are separated and a joint petition is not filed.)

NAME AND ADDRESS OF CREDITOR	DATES OF PAYMENTS	AMOUNT PAID	AMOUNT STILL OWING

None ☐ b. *Debtor whose debts are not primarily consumer debts: List each payment or other transfer to any creditor made within **90 days** immediately preceding the commencement of the case unless the aggregate value of all property that constitutes or is affected by such transfer is less than $6,225*. If the debtor is an individual, indicate with an asterisk (*) any payments that were made to a creditor on account of a domestic support obligation or as part of an alternative repayment schedule under a plan by an approved nonprofit budgeting and credit counseling agency. (Married debtors filing under chapter 12 or chapter 13 must include payments and other transfers by either or both spouses whether or not a joint petition is filed, unless the spouses are separated and a joint petition is not filed.)*

NAME AND ADDRESS OF CREDITOR	DATES OF PAYMENTS/ TRANSFERS	AMOUNT PAID OR VALUE OF TRANSFERS	AMOUNT STILL OWING

---

* *Amount subject to adjustment on 4/01/16, and every three years thereafter with respect to cases commenced on or after the date of adjustment.*

None

c. *All debtors:* List all payments made within **one year** immediately preceding the commencement of this case to or for the benefit of creditors who are or were insiders. (Married debtors filing under chapter 12 or chapter 13 must include payments by either or both spouses whether or not a joint petition is filed, unless the spouses are separated and a joint petition is not filed.)

NAME AND ADDRESS OF CREDITOR AND RELATIONSHIP TO DEBTOR	DATE OF PAYMENT	AMOUNT PAID	AMOUNT STILL OWING

---

4. Suits and administrative proceedings, executions, garnishments and attachments

None

a. List all suits and administrative proceedings to which the debtor is or was a party within **one year** immediately preceding the filing of this bankruptcy case. (Married debtors filing under chapter 12 or chapter 13 must include information concerning either or both spouses whether or not a joint petition is filed, unless the spouses are separated and a joint petition is not filed.)

CAPTION OF SUIT AND CASE NUMBER	NATURE OF PROCEEDING	COURT OR AGENCY AND LOCATION	STATUS OR DISPOSITION

None

b. Describe all property that has been attached, garnished or seized under any legal or equitable process within **one year** immediately preceding the commencement of this case. (Married debtors filing under chapter 12 or chapter 13 must include information concerning property of either or both spouses whether or not a joint petition is filed, unless the spouses are separated and a joint petition is not filed.)

NAME AND ADDRESS OF PERSON FOR WHOSE BENEFIT PROPERTY WAS SEIZED	DATE OF SEIZURE	DESCRIPTION AND VALUE OF PROPERTY

---

5.   Repossessions, foreclosures and returns

None

List all property that has been repossessed by a creditor, sold at a foreclosure sale, transferred through a deed in lieu of foreclosure or returned to the seller, within **one year** immediately preceding the commencement of this case. (Married debtors filing under chapter 12 or chapter 13 must include information concerning property of either or both spouses whether or not a joint petition is filed, unless the spouses are separated and a joint petition is not filed.)

NAME AND ADDRESS OF CREDITOR OR SELLER	DATE OF REPOSSESSION, FORECLOSURE SALE, TRANSFER OR RETURN	DESCRIPTION AND VALUE OF PROPERTY

---

6. Assignments and receiverships

None

a. Describe any assignment of property for the benefit of creditors made within **120 days** immediately preceding the commencement of this case. (Married debtors filing under chapter 12 or chapter 13 must include any assignment by either or both spouses whether or not a joint petition is filed, unless the spouses are separated and a joint petition is not filed.)

NAME AND ADDRESS OF ASSIGNEE	DATE OF ASSIGNMENT	TERMS OF ASSIGNMENT OR SETTLEMENT

None

b. List all property which has been in the hands of a custodian, receiver, or court-appointed official within **one year** immediately preceding the commencement of this case. (Married debtors filing under chapter 12 or chapter 13 must include information concerning property of either or both spouses whether or not a joint petition is filed, unless the spouses are separated and a joint petition is not filed.)

NAME AND ADDRESS OF CUSTODIAN	NAME AND LOCATION OF COURT CASE TITLE & NUMBER	DATE OF ORDER	DESCRIPTION AND VALUE Of PROPERTY

7. Gifts

None

List all gifts or charitable contributions made within **one year** immediately preceding the commencement of this case except ordinary and usual gifts to family members aggregating less than $200 in value per individual family member and charitable contributions aggregating less than $100 per recipient. (Married debtors filing under chapter 12 or chapter 13 must include gifts or contributions by either or both spouses whether or not a joint petition is filed, unless the spouses are separated and a joint petition is not filed.)

NAME AND ADDRESS OF PERSON OR ORGANIZATION	RELATIONSHIP TO DEBTOR, IF ANY	DATE OF GIFT	DESCRIPTION AND VALUE OF GIFT

8. Losses

None

List all losses from fire, theft, other casualty or gambling within **one year** immediately preceding the commencement of this case **or since the commencement of this case**. (Married debtors filing under chapter 12 or chapter 13 must include losses by either or both spouses whether or not a joint petition is filed, unless the spouses are separated and a joint petition is not filed.)

DESCRIPTION AND VALUE OF PROPERTY	DESCRIPTION OF CIRCUMSTANCES AND, IF LOSS WAS COVERED IN WHOLE OR IN PART BY INSURANCE, GIVE PARTICULARS	DATE OF LOSS

9.   Payments related to debt counseling or bankruptcy

None

List all payments made or property transferred by or on behalf of the debtor to any persons, including attorneys, for consultation concerning debt consolidation, relief under the bankruptcy law or preparation of a petition in bankruptcy within **one year** immediately preceding the commencement of this case.

NAME AND ADDRESS OF PAYEE	DATE OF PAYMENT, NAME OF PAYER IF OTHER THAN DEBTOR	AMOUNT OF MONEY OR DESCRIPTION AND VALUE OF PROPERTY

10. Other transfers

None

a.   List all other property, other than property transferred in the ordinary course of the business or financial affairs of the debtor, transferred either absolutely or as security within **two years** immediately preceding the commencement of this case. (Married debtors filing under chapter 12 or chapter 13 must include transfers by either or both spouses whether or not a joint petition is filed, unless the spouses are separated and a joint petition is not filed.)

NAME AND ADDRESS OF TRANSFEREE, RELATIONSHIP TO DEBTOR	DATE	DESCRIBE PROPERTY TRANSFERRED AND VALUE RECEIVED

None

b.   List all property transferred by the debtor within **ten years** immediately preceding the commencement of this case to a self-settled trust or similar device of which the debtor is a beneficiary.

NAME OF TRUST OR OTHER DEVICE	DATE(S) OF TRANSFER(S)	AMOUNT OF MONEY OR DESCRIPTION AND VALUE OF PROPERTY OR DEBTOR'S INTEREST IN PROPERTY

11. Closed financial accounts

None

List all financial accounts and instruments held in the name of the debtor or for the benefit of the debtor which were closed, sold, or otherwise transferred within **one year** immediately preceding the commencement of this case. Include checking, savings, or other financial accounts, certificates of deposit, or other instruments; shares and share accounts held in banks, credit unions, pension funds, cooperatives, associations, brokerage houses and other financial institutions. (Married debtors filing under chapter 12 or chapter 13 must include information concerning accounts or instruments held by or for either or both spouses whether or not a joint petition is filed, unless the spouses are separated and a joint petition is not filed.)

NAME AND ADDRESS OF INSTITUTION	TYPE OF ACCOUNT, LAST FOUR DIGITS OF ACCOUNT NUMBER, AND AMOUNT OF FINAL BALANCE	AMOUNT AND DATE OF SALE OR CLOSING

12. Safe deposit boxes

None ☐

List each safe deposit or other box or depository in which the debtor has or had securities, cash, or other valuables within **one year** immediately preceding the commencement of this case. (Married debtors filing under chapter 12 or chapter 13 must include boxes or depositories of either or both spouses whether or not a joint petition is filed, unless the spouses are separated and a joint petition is not filed.)

NAME AND ADDRESS OF BANK OR OTHER DEPOSITORY	NAMES AND ADDRESSES OF THOSE WITH ACCESS TO BOX OR DEPOSITORY	DESCRIPTION OF CONTENTS	DATE OF TRANSFER OR SURRENDER, IF ANY

---

13. Setoffs

None ☐

List all setoffs made by any creditor, including a bank, against a debt or deposit of the debtor within **90 days** preceding the commencement of this case. (Married debtors filing under chapter 12 or chapter 13 must include information concerning either or both spouses whether or not a joint petition is filed, unless the spouses are separated and a joint petition is not filed.)

NAME AND ADDRESS OF CREDITOR	DATE OF SETOFF	AMOUNT OF SETOFF

---

14. Property held for another person

None ☐

List all property owned by another person that the debtor holds or controls.

NAME AND ADDRESS OF OWNER	DESCRIPTION AND VALUE OF PROPERTY	LOCATION OF PROPERTY

---

15. Prior address of debtor

None ☐

If debtor has moved within **three years** immediately preceding the commencement of this case, list all premises which the debtor occupied during that period and vacated prior to the commencement of this case. If a joint petition is filed, report also any separate address of either spouse.

ADDRESS	NAME USED	DATES OF OCCUPANCY

---

16. Spouses and Former Spouses

None ☐

If the debtor resides or resided in a community property state, commonwealth, or territory (including Alaska, Arizona, California, Idaho, Louisiana, Nevada, New Mexico, Puerto Rico, Texas, Washington, or Wisconsin) within **eight years** immediately preceding the commencement of the case, identify the name of the debtor's spouse and of any former spouse who resides or resided with the debtor in the community property state.

NAME

---

17. Environmental Information.

For the purpose of this question, the following definitions apply:

"Environmental Law" means any federal, state, or local statute or regulation regulating pollution, contamination, releases of hazardous or toxic substances, wastes or material into the air, land, soil, surface water, groundwater, or other medium, including, but not limited to, statutes or regulations regulating the cleanup of these substances, wastes, or material.

"Site" means any location, facility, or property as defined under any Environmental Law, whether or not presently or formerly owned or operated by the debtor, including, but not limited to, disposal sites.

"Hazardous Material" means anything defined as a hazardous waste, hazardous substance, toxic substance, hazardous material, pollutant, or contaminant or similar term under an Environmental Law.

None ☐

a. List the name and address of every site for which the debtor has received notice in writing by a governmental unit that it may be liable or potentially liable under or in violation of an Environmental Law. Indicate the governmental unit, the date of the notice, and, if known, the Environmental Law:

SITE NAME AND ADDRESS	NAME AND ADDRESS OF GOVERNMENTAL UNIT	DATE OF NOTICE	ENVIRONMENTAL LAW

None ☐

b. List the name and address of every site for which the debtor provided notice to a governmental unit of a release of Hazardous Material. Indicate the governmental unit to which the notice was sent and the date of the notice.

SITE NAME AND ADDRESS	NAME AND ADDRESS OF GOVERNMENTAL UNIT	DATE OF NOTICE	ENVIRONMENTAL LAW

None ☐

c. List all judicial or administrative proceedings, including settlements or orders, under any Environmental Law with respect to which the debtor is or was a party. Indicate the name and address of the governmental unit that is or was a party to the proceeding, and the docket number.

NAME AND ADDRESS OF GOVERNMENTAL UNIT	DOCKET NUMBER	STATUS OR DISPOSITION

---

18 . Nature, location and name of business

None ☐

a. *If the debtor is an individual,* list the names, addresses, taxpayer-identification numbers, nature of the businesses, and beginning and ending dates of all businesses in which the debtor was an officer, director, partner, or managing executive of a corporation, partner in a partnership, sole proprietor, or was self-employed in a trade, profession, or

other activity either full- or part-time within **six years** immediately preceding the commencement of this case, or in which the debtor owned 5 percent or more of the voting or equity securities within **six years** immediately preceding the commencement of this case.

If the debtor is a partnership, list the names, addresses, taxpayer-identification numbers, nature of the businesses, and beginning and ending dates of all businesses in which the debtor was a partner or owned 5 percent or more of the voting or equity securities, within **six years** immediately preceding the commencement of this case.

If the debtor is a corporation, list the names, addresses, taxpayer-identification numbers, nature of the businesses, and beginning and ending dates of all businesses in which the debtor was a partner or owned 5 percent or more of the voting or equity securities within **six years** immediately preceding the commencement of this case.

NAME	LAST FOUR DIGITS OF SOCIAL-SECURITY OR OTHER INDIVIDUAL TAXPAYER-I.D. NO. (ITIN)/ COMPLETE EIN	ADDRESS	NATURE OF BUSINESS	BEGINNING AND ENDING DATES

None ☐

b. Identify any business listed in response to subdivision a., above, that is "single asset real estate" as defined in 11 U.S.C. § 101.

NAME	ADDRESS

The following questions are to be completed by every debtor that is a corporation or partnership and by any individual debtor who is or has been, within **six years** immediately preceding the commencement of this case, any of the following: an officer, director, managing executive, or owner of more than 5 percent of the voting or equity securities of a corporation; a partner, other than a limited partner, of a partnership, a sole proprietor, or self-employed in a trade, profession, or other activity, either full- or part-time.

*(An individual or joint debtor should complete this portion of the statement **only** if the debtor is or has been in business, as defined above, within six years immediately preceding the commencement of this case. A debtor who has not been in business within those six years should go directly to the signature page.)*

---

19. Books, records and financial statements

None ☐

a. List all bookkeepers and accountants who within **two years** immediately preceding the filing of this bankruptcy case kept or supervised the keeping of books of account and records of the debtor.

NAME AND ADDRESS	DATES SERVICES RENDERED

None ☐

b. List all firms or individuals who within **two years** immediately preceding the filing of this bankruptcy case have audited the books of account and records, or prepared a financial statement of the debtor.

NAME	ADDRESS	DATES SERVICES RENDERED

None ☐   c. List all firms or individuals who at the time of the commencement of this case were in possession of the books of account and records of the debtor. If any of the books of account and records are not available, explain.

NAME   ADDRESS

None ☐   d. List all financial institutions, creditors and other parties, including mercantile and trade agencies, to whom a financial statement was issued by the debtor within **two years** immediately preceding the commencement of this case.

NAME AND ADDRESS   DATE ISSUED

---

20. Inventories

None ☐   a. List the dates of the last two inventories taken of your property, the name of the person who supervised the taking of each inventory, and the dollar amount and basis of each inventory.

DATE OF INVENTORY   INVENTORY SUPERVISOR   DOLLAR AMOUNT
                                                         OF INVENTORY
                                                         (Specify cost, market or other basis)

None ☐   b. List the name and address of the person having possession of the records of each of the inventories reported in a., above.

DATE OF INVENTORY   NAME AND ADDRESSES
                                                           OF CUSTODIAN
                                                           OF INVENTORY RECORDS

---

21 . Current Partners, Officers, Directors and Shareholders

None ☐   a. If the debtor is a partnership, list the nature and percentage of partnership interest of each member of the partnership.

NAME AND ADDRESS   NATURE OF INTEREST   PERCENTAGE OF INTEREST

None ☐   b.   If the debtor is a corporation, list all officers and directors of the corporation, and each stockholder who directly or indirectly owns, controls, or holds 5 percent or more of the voting or equity securities of the corporation.

                                                 NATURE AND PERCENTAGE
NAME AND ADDRESS   TITLE   OF STOCK OWNERSHIP

---

22 . Former partners, officers, directors and shareholders

None

a.   If the debtor is a partnership, list each member who withdrew from the partnership within **one year** immediately preceding the commencement of this case.

NAME   ADDRESS   DATE OF WITHDRAWAL

None

b.   If the debtor is a corporation, list all officers or directors whose relationship with the corporation terminated within **one year** immediately preceding the commencement of this case.

NAME AND ADDRESS   TITLE   DATE OF TERMINATION

---

23 . Withdrawals from a partnership or distributions by a corporation

None

If the debtor is a partnership or corporation, list all withdrawals or distributions credited or given to an insider, including compensation in any form, bonuses, loans, stock redemptions, options exercised and any other perquisite during **one year** immediately preceding the commencement of this case.

NAME & ADDRESS   DATE AND PURPOSE   AMOUNT OF MONEY
OF RECIPIENT,   OF WITHDRAWAL   OR DESCRIPTION
RELATIONSHIP TO DEBTOR   AND VALUE OF PROPERTY

---

24. Tax Consolidation Group.

None

If the debtor is a corporation, list the name and federal taxpayer-identification number of the parent corporation of any consolidated group for tax purposes of which the debtor has been a member at any time within **six years** immediately preceding the commencement of the case.

NAME OF PARENT CORPORATION   TAXPAYER-IDENTIFICATION NUMBER (EIN)

---

25. Pension Funds.

None

If the debtor is not an individual, list the name and federal taxpayer-identification number of any pension fund to which the debtor, as an employer, has been responsible for contributing at any time within **six years** immediately preceding the commencement of the case.

NAME OF PENSION FUND   TAXPAYER-IDENTIFICATION NUMBER (EIN)

* * * * * *

[If completed by an individual or individual and spouse]

I declare under penalty of perjury that I have read the answers contained in the foregoing statement of financial affairs and any attachments thereto and that they are true and correct.

Date _____   Signature of Debtor _____

Date _____   Signature of Joint Debtor (if any) _____

[If completed on behalf of a partnership or corporation]

I declare under penalty of perjury that I have read the answers contained in the foregoing statement of financial affairs and any attachments thereto and that they are true and correct to the best of my knowledge, information and belief.

Date _____   Signature _____

                                Print Name and Title _____

[An individual signing on behalf of a partnership or corporation must indicate position or relationship to debtor.]

___continuation sheets attached

Penalty for making a false statement: Fine of up to $500,000 or imprisonment for up to 5 years, or both. 18 U.S.C. §§ 152 and 3571

DECLARATION AND SIGNATURE OF NON-ATTORNEY BANKRUPTCY PETITION PREPARER (See 11 U.S.C. § 110)

I declare under penalty of perjury that: (1) I am a bankruptcy petition preparer as defined in 11 U.S.C. § 110; (2) I prepared this document for compensation and have provided the debtor with a copy of this document and the notices and information required under 11 U.S.C. §§ 110(b), 110(h), and 342(b); and, (3) if rules or guidelines have been promulgated pursuant to 11 U.S.C. § 110(h) setting a maximum fee for services chargeable by bankruptcy petition preparers, I have given the debtor notice of the maximum amount before preparing any document for filing for a debtor or accepting any fee from the debtor, as required by that section.

_____   _____
Printed or Typed Name and Title, if any, of Bankruptcy Petition Preparer   Social-Security No. (Required by 11 U.S.C. § 110.)

If the bankruptcy petition preparer is not an individual, state the name, title (if any), address, and social-security number of the officer, principal, responsible person, or partner who signs this document.

_____
Address

_____   _____
Signature of Bankruptcy Petition Preparer   Date

Names and Social-Security numbers of all other individuals who prepared or assisted in preparing this document unless the bankruptcy petition preparer is not an individual:

If more than one person prepared this document, attach additional signed sheets conforming to the appropriate Official Form for each person

A bankruptcy petition preparer's failure to comply with the provisions of title 11 and the Federal Rules of Bankruptcy Procedure may result in fines or imprisonment or both. 18 U.S.C. § 156.

UNITED STATES BANKRUPTCY COURT

In re _____,   Case No. _____
            Debtor   Chapter 7

CHAPTER 7 INDIVIDUAL DEBTOR'S STATEMENT OF INTENTION

PART A – Debts secured by property of the estate. *(Part A must be fully completed for **EACH** debt which is secured by property of the estate. Attach additional pages if necessary.)*

Property No. 1	
Creditor's Name:	**Describe Property Securing Debt:**

Property will be *(check one)*:
   ❑ Surrendered   ❑ Retained

If retaining the property, I intend to *(check at least one)*:
   ❑ Redeem the property
   ❑ Reaffirm the debt
   ❑ Other. Explain _____ (for example, avoid lien
using 11 U.S.C. § 522(f)).

Property is *(check one)*:
   ❑ Claimed as exempt   ❑ Not claimed as exempt

Property No. 2 *(if necessary)*	
Creditor's Name:	**Describe Property Securing Debt:**

Property will be *(check one)*:
   ❑ Surrendered   ❑ Retained

If retaining the property, I intend to *(check at least one)*:
   ❑ Redeem the property
   ❑ Reaffirm the debt
   ❑ Other. Explain _____ (for example, avoid lien
using 11 U.S.C. § 522(f)).

Property is *(check one)*:
   ❑ Claimed as exempt   ❑ Not claimed as exempt

PART B – Personal property subject to unexpired leases. *(All three columns of Part B must be completed for each unexpired lease. Attach additional pages if necessary.)*

Property No. 1		
Lessor's Name:	**Describe Leased Property:**	Lease will be Assumed pursuant to 11 U.S.C. § 365(p)(2): ❏ YES ❏ NO

Property No. 2 *(if necessary)*		
Lessor's Name:	**Describe Leased Property:**	Lease will be Assumed pursuant to 11 U.S.C. § 365(p)(2): ❏ YES ❏ NO

Property No. 3 *(if necessary)*		
Lessor's Name:	**Describe Leased Property:**	Lease will be Assumed pursuant to 11 U.S.C. § 365(p)(2): ❏ YES ❏ NO

_____ continuation sheets attached *(if any)*

I declare under penalty of perjury that the above indicates my intention as to any property of my estate securing a debt and/or personal property subject to an unexpired lease.

Date: _____   _____
                                 Signature of Debtor

                                 _____
                                 Signature of Joint Debtor

CHAPTER 7 INDIVIDUAL DEBTOR'S STATEMENT OF INTENTION
(Continuation Sheet)

PART A - Continuation

Property No.	
Creditor's Name:	**Describe Property Securing Debt:**

Property will be *(check one)*:
    ❏ Surrendered   ❏ Retained

If retaining the property, I intend to *(check at least one)*:
    ❏ Redeem the property
    ❏ Reaffirm the debt
    ❏ Other. Explain _____ (for example, avoid lien using 11 U.S.C. § 522(f)).

Property is *(check one)*:
    ❏ Claimed as exempt   ❏ Not claimed as exempt

PART B - Continuation

Property No.		
Lessor's Name:	**Describe Leased Property:**	Lease will be Assumed pursuant to 11 U.S.C. § 365(p)(2): ❏ YES ❏ NO

Property No.		
Lessor's Name:	**Describe Leased Property:**	Lease will be Assumed pursuant to 11 U.S.C. § 365(p)(2): ❏ YES ❏ NO

In re _____
                Debtor(s)

Case Number: _____
                (If known)

According to the information required to be entered on this statement (check one box as directed in Part I, III, or VI of this statement):

☐ **The presumption arises.**
☐ **The presumption does not arise.**
☐ **The presumption is temporarily inapplicable.**

CHAPTER 7 STATEMENT OF CURRENT MONTHLY INCOME AND MEANS-TEST CALCULATION

In addition to Schedules I and J, this statement must be completed by every individual chapter 7 debtor. If none of the exclusions in Part I applies, joint debtors may complete one statement only. If any of the exclusions in Part I applies, joint debtors should complete separate statements if they believe this is required by § 707(b)(2)(C).

	Part I. MILITARY AND NON-CONSUMER DEBTORS
1A	**Disabled Veterans.** If you are a disabled veteran described in the Declaration in this Part IA, (1) check the box at the beginning of the Declaration, (2) check the box for "The presumption does not arise" at the top of this statement, and (3) complete the verification in Part VIII. Do not complete any of the remaining parts of this statement. ☐ **Declaration of Disabled Veteran.** By checking this box, I declare under penalty of perjury that I am a disabled veteran (as defined in 38 U.S.C. § 3741(1)) whose indebtedness occurred primarily during a period in which I was on active duty (as defined in 10 U.S.C. § 101(d)(1)) or while I was performing a homeland defense activity (as defined in 32 U.S.C. §901(1)).
1B	**Non-consumer Debtors.** If your debts are not primarily consumer debts, check the box below and complete the verification in Part VIII. Do not complete any of the remaining parts of this statement. ☐ **Declaration of non-consumer debts.** By checking this box, I declare that my debts are not primarily consumer debts.
1C	**Reservists and National Guard Members; active duty or homeland defense activity.** Members of a reserve component of the Armed Forces and members of the National Guard who were called to active duty (as defined in 10 U.S.C. § 101(d)(1)) after September 11, 2001, for a period of at least 90 days, or who have performed homeland defense activity (as defined in 32 U.S.C. § 901(1)) for a period of at least 90 days, are excluded from all forms of means testing during the time of active duty or homeland defense activity and for 540 days thereafter (the "exclusion period"). If you qualify for this temporary exclusion, (1) check the appropriate boxes and complete any required information in the Declaration of Reservists and National Guard Members below, (2) check the box for "The presumption is temporarily inapplicable" at the top of this statement, and (3) complete the verification in Part VIII. **During your exclusion period you are not required to complete the balance of this form, but you must complete the form no later than 14 days after the date on which your exclusion period ends, unless the time for filing a motion raising the means test presumption expires in your case before your exclusion period ends.** ☐ **Declaration of Reservists and National Guard Members.** By checking this box and making the appropriate entries below, I declare that I am eligible for a temporary exclusion from means testing because, as a member of a reserve component of the Armed Forces or the National Guard a. ☐ I was called to active duty after September 11, 2001, for a period of at least 90 days and 　　☐ I remain on active duty /or/ 　　☐ I was released from active duty on _____, which is less than 540 days before this bankruptcy case was filed; 　　OR b. ☐ I am performing homeland defense activity for a period of at least 90 days /or/ 　　☐ I performed homeland defense activity for a period of at least 90 days, terminating on _____, which is less than 540 days before this bankruptcy case was filed.

Part II. CALCULATION OF MONTHLY INCOME FOR § 707(b)(7) EXCLUSION

2	**Marital/filing status.** Check the box that applies and complete the balance of this part of this statement as directed. a. ☐ Unmarried. **Complete only Column A ("Debtor's Income") for Lines 3-11.** b. ☐ Married, not filing jointly, with declaration of separate households. By checking this box, debtor declares under penalty of perjury: "My spouse and I are legally separated under applicable non-bankruptcy law or my spouse and I are living apart other than for the purpose of evading the requirements of § 707(b)(2)(A) of the Bankruptcy Code." **Complete only Column A ("Debtor's Income") for Lines 3-11.** c. ☐ Married, not filing jointly, without the declaration of separate households set out in Line 2.b above. **Complete both Column A ("Debtor's Income") and Column B ("Spouse's Income") for Lines 3-11.** d. ☐ Married, filing jointly. **Complete both Column A ("Debtor's Income") and Column B ("Spouse's Income") for Lines 3-11.**

		Column A Debtor's Income	Column B Spouse's Income
	All figures must reflect average monthly income received from all sources, derived during the six calendar months prior to filing the bankruptcy case, ending on the last day of the month before the filing. If the amount of monthly income varied during the six months, you must divide the six-month total by six, and enter the result on the appropriate line.		
3	**Gross wages, salary, tips, bonuses, overtime, commissions.**	$	$
4	**Income from the operation of a business, profession or farm.** Subtract Line b from Line a and enter the difference in the appropriate column(s) of Line 4. If you operate more than one business, profession or farm, enter aggregate numbers and provide details on an attachment. Do not enter a number less than zero. **Do not include any part of the business expenses entered on Line b as a deduction in Part V.**		
	a. Gross receipts $		
	b. Ordinary and necessary business expenses $		
	c. Business income Subtract Line b from Line a	$	$
5	**Rent and other real property income.** Subtract Line b from Line a and enter the difference in the appropriate column(s) of Line 5. Do not enter a number less than zero. **Do not include any part of the operating expenses entered on Line b as a deduction in Part V.**		
	a. Gross receipts $		
	b. Ordinary and necessary operating expenses $		
	c. Rent and other real property income Subtract Line b from Line a	$	$
6	**Interest, dividends and royalties.**	$	$
7	**Pension and retirement income.**	$	$
8	**Any amounts paid by another person or entity, on a regular basis, for the household expenses of the debtor or the debtor's dependents, including child support paid for that purpose.** Do not include alimony or separate maintenance payments or amounts paid by your spouse if Column B is completed. Each regular payment should be reported in only one column; if a payment is listed in Column A, do not report that payment in Column B.	$	$
9	**Unemployment compensation.** Enter the amount in the appropriate column(s) of Line 9. However, if you contend that unemployment compensation received by you or your spouse was a benefit under the Social Security Act, do not list the amount of such compensation in Column A or B, but instead state the amount in the space below: Unemployment compensation claimed to be a benefit under the Social Security Act Debtor $ _____ Spouse $ _____	$	$

10	**Income from all other sources.** Specify source and amount. If necessary, list additional sources on a separate page. **Do not include alimony or separate maintenance payments paid by your spouse if Column B is completed, but include all other payments of alimony or separate maintenance.** Do not include any benefits received under the Social Security Act or payments received as a victim of a war crime, crime against humanity, or as a victim of international or domestic terrorism.		
	a.	$	
	b.	$	
	Total and enter on Line 10	$	$
11	**Subtotal of Current Monthly Income for § 707(b)(7).** Add Lines 3 thru 10 in Column A, and, if Column B is completed, add Lines 3 through 10 in Column B. Enter the total(s).	$	$
12	**Total Current Monthly Income for § 707(b)(7).** If Column B has been completed, add Line 11, Column A to Line 11, Column B, and enter the total. If Column B has not been completed, enter the amount from Line 11, Column A.	$	

Part III. APPLICATION OF § 707(b)(7) EXCLUSION

13	**Annualized Current Monthly Income for § 707(b)(7).** Multiply the amount from Line 12 by the number 12 and enter the result.	$
14	**Applicable median family income.** Enter the median family income for the applicable state and household size. (This information is available by family size at www.usdoj.gov/ust/ or from the clerk of the bankruptcy court.) a. Enter debtor's state of residence: _____ b. Enter debtor's household size: _____	$
15	**Application of Section 707(b)(7).** Check the applicable box and proceed as directed. ☐ **The amount on Line 13 is less than or equal to the amount on Line 14.** Check the box for "The presumption does not arise" at the top of page 1 of this statement, and complete Part VIII; do not complete Parts IV, V, VI or VII. ☐ **The amount on Line 13 is more than the amount on Line 14.** Complete the remaining parts of this statement.	

Complete Parts IV, V, VI, and VII of this statement only if required. (See Line 15.)

	Part IV. CALCULATION OF CURRENT MONTHLY INCOME FOR § 707(b)(2)	
16	**Enter the amount from Line 12.**	$
17	**Marital adjustment.** If you checked the box at Line 2.c, enter on Line 17 the total of any income listed in Line 11, Column B that was NOT paid on a regular basis for the household expenses of the debtor or the debtor's dependents. Specify in the lines below the basis for excluding the Column B income (such as payment of the spouse's tax liability or the spouse's support of persons other than the debtor or the debtor's dependents) and the amount of income devoted to each purpose. If necessary, list additional adjustments on a separate page. If you did not check box at Line 2.c, enter zero.	
	a. $	
	b. $	
	c. $	
	Total and enter on Line 17.	$
18	**Current monthly income for § 707(b)(2).** Subtract Line 17 from Line 16 and enter the result.	$

	Part V. CALCULATION OF DEDUCTIONS FROM INCOME	
	Subpart A: Deductions under Standards of the Internal Revenue Service (IRS)	
19A	**National Standards: food, clothing and other items.** Enter in Line 19A the "Total" amount from IRS National Standards for Food, Clothing and Other Items for the applicable number of persons. (This information is available at www.usdoj.gov/ust/ or from the clerk of the bankruptcy court.) The applicable number of persons is the number that would currently be allowed as exemptions on your federal income tax return, plus the number of any additional dependents whom you support.	$
19B	**National Standards: health care.** Enter in Line a1 below the amount from IRS National Standards for Out-of-Pocket Health Care for persons under 65 years of age, and in Line a2 the IRS National Standards for Out-of-Pocket Health Care for persons 65 years of age or older. (This information is available at www.usdoj.gov/ust/ or from the clerk of the bankruptcy court.) Enter in Line b1 the applicable number of persons who are under 65 years of age, and enter in Line b2 the applicable number of persons who are 65 years of age or older. (The applicable number of persons in each age category is the number in that category that would currently be allowed as exemptions on your federal income tax return, plus the number of any additional dependents whom you support.) Multiply Line a1 by Line b1 to obtain a total amount for persons under 65, and enter the result in Line c1. Multiply Line a2 by Line b2 to obtain a total amount for persons 65 and older, and enter the result in Line c2. Add Lines c1 and c2 to obtain a total health care amount, and enter the result in Line 19B.	

Persons under 65 years of age			**Persons 65 years of age or older**			
a1.	Allowance per person		a2.	Allowance per person		
b1.	Number of persons		b2.	Number of persons		
c1.	Subtotal		c2.	Subtotal		$

20A	**Local Standards: housing and utilities; non-mortgage expenses.** Enter the amount of the IRS Housing and Utilities Standards; non-mortgage expenses for the applicable county and family size. (This information is available at www.usdoj.gov/ust/ or from the clerk of the bankruptcy court). The applicable family size consists of the number that would currently be allowed as exemptions on your federal income tax return, plus the number of any additional dependents whom you support.	$
20B	**Local Standards: housing and utilities; mortgage/rent expense.** Enter, in Line a below, the amount of the IRS Housing and Utilities Standards; mortgage/rent expense for your county and family size (this information is available at www.usdoj.gov/ust/ or from the clerk of the bankruptcy court) (the applicable family size consists of the number that would currently be allowed as exemptions on your federal income tax return, plus the number of any additional dependents whom you support); enter on Line b the total of the Average Monthly Payments for any debts secured by your home, as stated in Line 42; subtract Line b from Line a and enter the result in Line 20B. **Do not enter an amount less than zero.**	

a.	IRS Housing and Utilities Standards; mortgage/rental expense	$	
b.	Average Monthly Payment for any debts secured by your home, if any, as stated in Line 42	$	
c.	Net mortgage/rental expense	Subtract Line b from Line a.	$

21	**Local Standards: housing and utilities; adjustment.** If you contend that the process set out in Lines 20A and 20B does not accurately compute the allowance to which you are entitled under the IRS Housing and Utilities Standards, enter any additional amount to which you contend you are entitled, and state the basis for your contention in the space below:	$

22A	**Local Standards: transportation; vehicle operation/public transportation expense.** You are entitled to an expense allowance in this category regardless of whether you pay the expenses of operating a vehicle and regardless of whether you use public transportation. Check the number of vehicles for which you pay the operating expenses or for which the operating expenses are included as a contribution to your household expenses in Line 8. ☐ 0 ☐ 1 ☐ 2 or more. If you checked 0, enter on Line 22A the "Public Transportation" amount from IRS Local Standards: Transportation. If you checked 1 or 2 or more, enter on Line 22A the "Operating Costs" amount from IRS Local Standards: Transportation for the applicable number of vehicles in the applicable Metropolitan Statistical Area or Census Region. (These amounts are available at www.usdoj.gov/ust/ or from the clerk of the bankruptcy court.)	$
22B	**Local Standards: transportation; additional public transportation expense.** If you pay the operating expenses for a vehicle and also use public transportation, and you contend that you are entitled to an additional deduction for your public transportation expenses, enter on Line 22B the "Public Transportation" amount from IRS Local Standards: Transportation. (This amount is available at www.usdoj.gov/ust/ or from the clerk of the bankruptcy court.)	$
23	**Local Standards: transportation ownership/lease expense; Vehicle 1.** Check the number of vehicles for which you claim an ownership/lease expense. (You may not claim an ownership/lease expense for more than two vehicles.) ☐ 1 ☐ 2 or more. Enter, in Line a below, the "Ownership Costs" for "One Car" from the IRS Local Standards: Transportation (available at www.usdoj.gov/ust/ or from the clerk of the bankruptcy court); enter in Line b the total of the Average Monthly Payments for any debts secured by Vehicle 1, as stated in Line 42; subtract Line b from Line a and enter the result in Line 23. **Do not enter an amount less than zero.**	
	a. IRS Transportation Standards, Ownership Costs — $	
	b. Average Monthly Payment for any debts secured by Vehicle 1, as stated in Line 42 — $	
	c. Net ownership/lease expense for Vehicle 1 — Subtract Line b from Line a.	$
24	**Local Standards: transportation ownership/lease expense; Vehicle 2.** Complete this Line only if you checked the "2 or more" Box in Line 23. Enter, in Line a below, the "Ownership Costs" for "One Car" from the IRS Local Standards: Transportation (available at www.usdoj.gov/ust/ or from the clerk of the bankruptcy court); enter in Line b the total of the Average Monthly Payments for any debts secured by Vehicle 2, as stated in Line 42; subtract Line b from Line a and enter the result in Line 24. **Do not enter an amount less than zero.**	
	a. IRS Transportation Standards, Ownership Costs — $	
	b. Average Monthly Payment for any debts secured by Vehicle 2, as stated in Line 42 — $	
	c. Net ownership/lease expense for Vehicle 2 — Subtract Line b from Line a.	$
25	**Other Necessary Expenses: taxes.** Enter the total average monthly expense that you actually incur for all federal, state and local taxes, other than real estate and sales taxes, such as income taxes, self-employment taxes, social-security taxes, and Medicare taxes. **Do not include real estate or sales taxes.**	$
26	**Other Necessary Expenses: involuntary deductions for employment.** Enter the total average monthly payroll deductions that are required for your employment, such as retirement contributions, union dues, and uniform costs. **Do not include discretionary amounts, such as voluntary 401(k) contributions.**	$
27	**Other Necessary Expenses: life insurance.** Enter total average monthly premiums that you actually pay for term life insurance for yourself. **Do not include premiums for insurance on your dependents, for whole life or for any other form of insurance.**	$
28	**Other Necessary Expenses: court-ordered payments.** Enter the total monthly amount that you are required to pay pursuant to the order of a court or administrative agency, such as spousal or child support payments. **Do not include payments on past due obligations included in Line 44.**	$

29	**Other Necessary Expenses: education for employment or for a physically or mentally challenged child.** Enter the total average monthly amount that you actually expend for education that is a condition of employment and for education that is required for a physically or mentally challenged dependent child for whom no public education providing similar services is available.	$
30	**Other Necessary Expenses: childcare.** Enter the total average monthly amount that you actually expend on childcare—such as baby-sitting, day care, nursery and preschool. **Do not include other educational payments.**	$
31	**Other Necessary Expenses: health care.** Enter the total average monthly amount that you actually expend on health care that is required for the health and welfare of yourself or your dependents, that is not reimbursed by insurance or paid by a health savings account, and that is in excess of the amount entered in Line 19B. **Do not include payments for health insurance or health savings accounts listed in Line 34.**	$
32	**Other Necessary Expenses: telecommunication services.** Enter the total average monthly amount that you actually pay for telecommunication services other than your basic home telephone and cell phone service— such as pagers, call waiting, caller id, special long distance, or internet service—to the extent necessary for your health and welfare or that of your dependents. **Do not include any amount previously deducted.**	$
33	**Total Expenses Allowed under IRS Standards.** Enter the total of Lines 19 through 32.	$

Subpart B: Additional Living Expense Deductions
Note: Do not include any expenses that you have listed in Lines 19-32

34	**Health Insurance, Disability Insurance, and Health Savings Account Expenses.** List the monthly expenses in the categories set out in lines a-c below that are reasonably necessary for yourself, your spouse, or your dependents.	
	<table><tr><td>a.</td><td>Health Insurance</td><td>$</td></tr><tr><td>b.</td><td>Disability Insurance</td><td>$</td></tr><tr><td>c.</td><td>Health Savings Account</td><td>$</td></tr></table> Total and enter on Line 34 **If you do not actually expend this total amount**, state your actual total average monthly expenditures in the space below: $ _____	$
35	**Continued contributions to the care of household or family members.** Enter the total average actual monthly expenses that you will continue to pay for the reasonable and necessary care and support of an elderly, chronically ill, or disabled member of your household or member of your immediate family who is unable to pay for such expenses.	$
36	**Protection against family violence.** Enter the total average reasonably necessary monthly expenses that you actually incurred to maintain the safety of your family under the Family Violence Prevention and Services Act or other applicable federal law. The nature of these expenses is required to be kept confidential by the court.	$
37	**Home energy costs.** Enter the total average monthly amount, in excess of the allowance specified by IRS Local Standards for Housing and Utilities, that you actually expend for home energy costs. **You must provide your case trustee with documentation of your actual expenses, and you must demonstrate that the additional amount claimed is reasonable and necessary.**	$
38	**Education expenses for dependent children less than 18.** Enter the total average monthly expenses that you actually incur, not to exceed $156.25* per child, for attendance at a private or public elementary or secondary school by your dependent children less than 18 years of age. **You must provide your case trustee with documentation of your actual expenses, and you must explain why the amount claimed is reasonable and necessary and not already accounted for in the IRS Standards.**	$

*Amount subject to adjustment on 4/01/16, and every three years thereafter with respect to cases commenced on or after the date of adjustment.

39	**Additional food and clothing expense.** Enter the total average monthly amount by which your food and clothing expenses exceed the combined allowances for food and clothing (apparel and services) in the IRS National Standards, not to exceed 5% of those combined allowances. (This information is available at www.usdoj.gov/ust/ or from the clerk of the bankruptcy court.) **You must demonstrate that the additional amount claimed is reasonable and necessary.**	$
40	**Continued charitable contributions.** Enter the amount that you will continue to contribute in the form of cash or financial instruments to a charitable organization as defined in 26 U.S.C. § 170(c)(1)-(2).	$
41	**Total Additional Expense Deductions under § 707(b).** Enter the total of Lines 34 through 40	$

Subpart C: Deductions for Debt Payment

42	**Future payments on secured claims.** For each of your debts that is secured by an interest in property that you own, list the name of the creditor, identify the property securing the debt, state the Average Monthly Payment, and check whether the payment includes taxes or insurance. The Average Monthly Payment is the total of all amounts scheduled as contractually due to each Secured Creditor in the 60 months following the filing of the bankruptcy case, divided by 60. If necessary, list additional entries on a separate page. Enter the total of the Average Monthly Payments on Line 42.	

	Name of Creditor	Property Securing the Debt	Average Monthly Payment	Does payment include taxes or insurance?	
a.			$	☐ yes ☐ no	
b.			$	☐ yes ☐ no	
c.			$	☐ yes ☐ no	
			Total: Add Lines a, b and c.		$

43	**Other payments on secured claims.** If any of debts listed in Line 42 are secured by your primary residence, a motor vehicle, or other property necessary for your support or the support of your dependents, you may include in your deduction 1/60th of any amount (the "cure amount") that you must pay the creditor in addition to the payments listed in Line 42, in order to maintain possession of the property. The cure amount would include any sums in default that must be paid in order to avoid repossession or foreclosure. List and total any such amounts in the following chart. If necessary, list additional entries on a separate page.	

	Name of Creditor	Property Securing the Debt	1/60th of the Cure Amount	
a.			$	
b.			$	
c.			$	
			Total: Add Lines a, b and c	$

44	**Payments on prepetition priority claims.** Enter the total amount, divided by 60, of all priority claims, such as priority tax, child support and alimony claims, for which you were liable at the time of your bankruptcy filing. **Do not include current obligations, such as those set out in Line 28.**	$

45	**Chapter 13 administrative expenses.** If you are eligible to file a case under chapter 13, complete the following chart, multiply the amount in line a by the amount in line b, and enter the resulting administrative expense.		
	a.	Projected average monthly chapter 13 plan payment.	$
	b.	Current multiplier for your district as determined under schedules issued by the Executive Office for United States Trustees. (This information is available at www.usdoj.gov/ust/ or from the clerk of the bankruptcy court.)	x
	c.	Average monthly administrative expense of chapter 13 case	Total: Multiply Lines a and b $

46	**Total Deductions for Debt Payment.** Enter the total of Lines 42 through 45.	$

Subpart D: Total Deductions from Income

47	**Total of all deductions allowed under § 707(b)(2).** Enter the total of Lines 33, 41, and 46.	$

Part VI. DETERMINATION OF § 707(b)(2) PRESUMPTION

48	**Enter the amount from Line 18 (Current monthly income for § 707(b)(2))**	$
49	**Enter the amount from Line 47 (Total of all deductions allowed under § 707(b)(2))**	$
50	**Monthly disposable income under § 707(b)(2).** Subtract Line 49 from Line 48 and enter the result	$
51	**60-month disposable income under § 707(b)(2).** Multiply the amount in Line 50 by the number 60 and enter the result.	$

52	**Initial presumption determination.** Check the applicable box and proceed as directed.
	☐ **The amount on Line 51 is less than $7,475*.** Check the box for "The presumption does not arise" at the top of page 1 of this statement, and complete the verification in Part VIII. Do not complete the remainder of Part VI.
	☐ **The amount set forth on Line 51 is more than $12,475*.** Check the box for "The presumption arises" at the top of page 1 of this statement, and complete the verification in Part VIII. You may also complete Part VII. Do not complete the remainder of Part VI.
	☐ **The amount on Line 51 is at least $7,475*, but not more than $12,475*.** Complete the remainder of Part VI (Lines 53 through 55).

53	**Enter the amount of your total non-priority unsecured debt**	$
54	**Threshold debt payment amount.** Multiply the amount in Line 53 by the number 0.25 and enter the result.	$

55	**Secondary presumption determination.** Check the applicable box and proceed as directed.
	☐ **The amount on Line 51 is less than the amount on Line 54.** Check the box for "The presumption does not arise" at the top of page 1 of this statement, and complete the verification in Part VIII.
	☐ **The amount on Line 51 is equal to or greater than the amount on Line 54.** Check the box for "The presumption arises" at the top of page 1 of this statement, and complete the verification in Part VIII. You may also complete Part VII.

Part VII: ADDITIONAL EXPENSE CLAIMS

56	**Other Expenses.** List and describe any monthly expenses, not otherwise stated in this form, that are required for the health and welfare of you and your family and that you contend should be an additional deduction from your current monthly income under § 707(b)(2)(A)(ii)(I). If necessary, list additional sources on a separate page. All figures should reflect your average monthly expense for each item. Total the expenses.		
		Expense Description	Monthly Amount
	a.		$
	b.		$
	c.		$
		Total: Add Lines a, b and c	$

**Amounts are subject to adjustment on 4/01/16, and every three years thereafter with respect to cases commenced on or after the date of adjustment.*

	Part VIII: VERIFICATION
57	I declare under penalty of perjury that the information provided in this statement is true and correct. *(If this is a joint case, both debtors must sign.)* Date: _____ Signature: _____ *(Debtor)* Date: _____ Signature: _____ *(Joint Debtor, if any)*

B 23 (Official Form 23) (12/13)

UNITED STATES BANKRUPTCY COURT

In re _____,
                    Debtor

Case No. _____

Chapter _____

DEBTOR'S CERTIFICATION OF COMPLETION OF POSTPETITION INSTRUCTIONAL COURSE CONCERNING PERSONAL FINANCIAL MANAGEMENT

This form should not be filed if an approved provider of a postpetition instructional course concerning personal financial management has already notified the court of the debtor's completion of the course. Otherwise, every individual debtor in a chapter 7 or a chapter 13 case or in a chapter 11 case in which § 1141(d)(3) applies must file this certification. If a joint petition is filed and this certification is required, each spouse must complete and file a separate certification. Complete one of the following statements and file by the deadline stated below:

☐ I, _____, the debtor in the above-styled case, hereby
            (Printed Name of Debtor)
certify that on _____ (Date), I completed an instructional course in personal financial management
provided by _____, an approved personal financial
                         (Name of Provider)
management provider.

Certificate No. (if any):_____.

☐ I, _____, the debtor in the above-styled case, hereby
            (Printed Name of Debtor)
certify that no personal financial management course is required because of *[Check the appropriate box.]*:
    ☐ Incapacity or disability, as defined in 11 U.S.C. § 109(h);
    ☐ Active military duty in a military combat zone; or
    ☐ Residence in a district in which the United States trustee (or bankruptcy administrator) has determined that
the approved instructional courses are not adequate at this time to serve the additional individuals who would otherwise
be required to complete such courses.

Signature of Debtor: _____

Date: _____

_____

Instructions: Use this form only to certify whether you completed a course in personal financial management and only if your course provider has not already notified the court of your completion of the course. (Fed. R. Bankr. P. 1007(b)(7).) Do NOT use this form to file the certificate given to you by your prepetition credit counseling provider and do NOT include with the petition when filing your case.

Filing Deadlines: In a chapter 7 case, file within 60 days of the first date set for the meeting of creditors under § 341 of the Bankruptcy Code. In a chapter 11 or 13 case, file no later than the last payment made by the debtor as required by the plan or the filing of a motion for a discharge under § 1141(d)(5)(B) or § 1328(b) of the Code. (See Fed. R. Bankr. P. 1007(c).)

B21 (Official Form 21) (12/12)

UNITED STATES BANKRUPTCY COURT

In re _____,)
    [Set forth here all names including married, maiden,)
    and trade names used by debtor within last 8 years])
                                      Debtor) Case No. _____
Address _____)
        _____) Chapter _____
)
Last four digits of Social-Security or Individual Taxpayer-)
Identification (ITIN) No(s).,(if any):)
_____)
Employer Tax-Identification (EIN) No(s).(if any):)
_____)

STATEMENT OF SOCIAL-SECURITY NUMBER(S)
(or other Individual Taxpayer-Identification Number(s) (ITIN(s)))

1.Name of Debtor (Last, First, Middle): _____
(Check the appropriate box and, if applicable, provide the required information.)

    ☐ Debtor has a Social-Security Number and it is: _____
        (If more than one, state all.)
    ☐ Debtor does not have a Social-Security Number but has an Individual Taxpayer-Identification
        Number (ITIN), and it is: _____
        (If more than one, state all.)
    ☐ Debtor does not have either a Social-Security Number or an Individual Taxpayer-Identification
        Number (ITIN).

2.Name of Joint Debtor (Last, First, Middle): _____
(Check the appropriate box and, if applicable, provide the required information.)

    ☐ Joint Debtor has a Social-Security Number and it is: _____
        (If more than one, state all.)
    ☐ Joint Debtor does not have a Social-Security Number but has an Individual Taxpayer-Identification Number
        (ITIN) and it is: _____
        (If more than one, state all.)
    ☐ Joint Debtor does not have either a Social-Security Number or an Individual Taxpayer-Identification
        Number (ITIN).

I declare under penalty of perjury that the foregoing is true and correct.

X _____   _____
        Signature of Debtor   Date

X _____   _____
        Signature of Joint Debtor   Date

Joint debtors must provide information for both spouses.
Penalty for making a false statement: Fine of up to $250,000 or up to 5 years imprisonment or both. 18 U.S.C. §§ 152 and 3571.

B9A (Official Form 9A) (Chapter 7 Individual or Joint Debtor No Asset Case) (12/12)

UNITED STATES BANKRUPTCY COURT_____ District of_____

<table>
<tr><td colspan="2" align="center">

Notice of
Chapter 7 Bankruptcy Case, Meeting of Creditors, & Deadlines

[A chapter 7 bankruptcy case concerning the debtor(s) listed below was filed on _____(date).]
or [A bankruptcy case concerning the debtor(s) listed below was originally filed under chapter_____on
_____(date) and was converted to a case under chapter 7 on_____(date).]

You may be a creditor of the debtor. **This notice lists important deadlines.** You may want to consult an attorney to protect your rights. All documents filed in the case may be inspected at the bankruptcy clerk's office at the address listed below. NOTE: The staff of the bankruptcy clerk's office cannot give legal advice.

Creditors -- Do not file this notice in connection with any proof of claim you submit to the court.
See Reverse Side for Important Explanations.
</td></tr>
<tr><td>

Debtor(s) (name(s) and address):

</td><td>

Case Number:

</td></tr>
<tr><td rowspan="2">

All other names used by the Debtor(s) in the last 8 years (include married, maiden, and trade names):

</td><td>

Last four digits of Social-Security or Individual Taxpayer-ID (ITIN) No(s)./Complete EIN:

</td></tr>
<tr><td rowspan="3">

Bankruptcy Trustee (name and address):

</td></tr>
<tr><td>

Attorney for Debtor(s) (name and address):

</td></tr>
<tr><td>

Telephone number:

</td></tr>
<tr><td colspan="2">

Telephone number:

</td></tr>
</table>

Meeting of Creditors
Date: / /   Time: ( ) A. M.   Location: ( ) P. M.

Presumption of Abuse under 11 U.S.C. § 707(b) *See "Presumption of Abuse" on the reverse side.*

Depending on the documents filed with the petition, one of the following statements will appear.
 	
     The presumption of abuse does not arise.
             Or
     The presumption of abuse arises.
             Or
     Insufficient information has been filed to date to permit the clerk to make any determination concerning the presumption of abuse. If more complete information, when filed, shows that the presumption has arisen, creditors will be notified.

Deadlines: Papers must be *received* by the bankruptcy clerk's office by the following deadlines: **Deadline to Object to Debtor's Discharge or to Challenge Dischargeability of Certain Debts:**

Deadline to Object to Exemptions: Thirty (30) days after the *conclusion* of the meeting of creditors.

Creditors May Not Take Certain Actions: In most instances, the filing of the bankruptcy case automatically stays certain collection and other actions against the debtor and the debtor's property. Under certain circumstances, the stay may be limited to 30 days or not exist at all, although the debtor can request the court to extend or impose a stay. If you attempt to collect a debt or take other action in violation of the Bankruptcy Code, you may be penalized. Consult a lawyer to determine your rights in this case.

Please Do Not File a Proof of Claim Unless You Receive a Notice To Do So.

Creditor with a Foreign Address: A creditor to whom this notice is sent at a foreign address should read the information under "Do Not File a Proof of Claim at This Time" on the reverse side.

<table>
<tr><td>

Address of the Bankruptcy Clerk's Office:

</td><td align="center">

For the Court:

</td></tr>
<tr><td rowspan="2">

Telephone number:

</td><td>

Clerk of the Bankruptcy Court:

</td></tr>
<tr><td>

</td></tr>
<tr><td>

Hours Open:

</td><td>

Date:

</td></tr>
</table>

EXPLANATIONS B9A (Official Form 9A) (12/12)

Filing of Chapter 7 Bankruptcy Case	A bankruptcy case under Chapter 7 of the Bankruptcy Code (title 11, United States Code) has been filed in this court by or against the debtor(s) listed on the front side, and an order for relief has been entered.
Legal Advice	The staff of the bankruptcy clerk's office cannot give legal advice. Consult a lawyer to determine your rights in this case.
Creditors Generally May Not Take Certain Actions	Prohibited collection actions are listed in Bankruptcy Code § 362. Common examples of prohibited actions include contacting the debtor by telephone, mail, or otherwise to demand repayment; taking actions to collect money or obtain property from the debtor; repossessing the debtor's property; starting or continuing lawsuits or foreclosures; and garnishing or deducting from the debtor's wages. Under certain circumstances, the stay may be limited to 30 days or not exist at all, although the debtor can request the court to extend or impose a stay.
Presumption of Abuse	If the presumption of abuse arises, creditors may have the right to file a motion to dismiss the case under § 707(b) of the Bankruptcy Code. The debtor may rebut the presumption by showing special circumstances.
Meeting of Creditors	A meeting of creditors is scheduled for the date, time, and location listed on the front side. *The debtor (both spouses in a joint case) must be present at the meeting to be questioned under oath by the trustee and by creditors.* Creditors are welcome to attend, but are not required to do so. The meeting may be continued and concluded at a later date specified in a notice filed with the court.
Do Not File a Proof of Claim at This Time	There does not appear to be any property available to the trustee to pay creditors. *You therefore should not file a proof of claim at this time.* If it later appears that assets are available to pay creditors, you will be sent another notice telling you that you may file a proof of claim, and telling you the deadline for filing your proof of claim. If this notice is mailed to a creditor at a foreign address, the creditor may file a motion requesting the court to extend the deadline. *Do not include this notice with any filing you make with the court.*
Discharge of Debts	The debtor is seeking a discharge of most debts, which may include your debt. A discharge means that you may never try to collect the debt from the debtor. If you believe that the debtor is not entitled to receive a discharge under Bankruptcy Code § 727(a) *or* that a debt owed to you is not dischargeable under Bankruptcy Code § 523(a)(2), (4), or (6), you must file a complaint -- or a motion if you assert the discharge should be denied under § 727(a)(8) or (a)(9) -- in the bankruptcy clerk's office by the "Deadline to Object to Debtor's Discharge or to Challenge the Dischargeability of Certain Debts" listed on the front of this form. The bankruptcy clerk's office must receive the complaint or motion and any required filing fee by that deadline.
Exempt Property	The debtor is permitted by law to keep certain property as exempt. Exempt property will not be sold and distributed to creditors. The debtor must file a list of all property claimed as exempt. You may inspect that list at the bankruptcy clerk's office. If you believe that an exemption claimed by the debtor is not authorized by law, you may file an objection to that exemption. The bankruptcy clerk's office must receive the objections by the "Deadline to Object to Exemptions" listed on the front side.
Bankruptcy Clerk's Office	Any paper that you file in this bankruptcy case should be filed at the bankruptcy clerk's office at the address listed on the front side. You may inspect all papers filed, including the list of the debtor's property and debts and the list of the property claimed as exempt, at the bankruptcy clerk's office.
Creditor with a Foreign Address	Consult a lawyer familiar with United States bankruptcy law if you have any questions regarding your rights in this case.

Refer To Other Side For Important Deadlines and Notices

UNITED STATES BANKRUPTCY COURT_____District of_____	

Notice of
Chapter 7 Bankruptcy Case, Meeting of Creditors, & Deadlines

[A chapter 7 bankruptcy case concerning the debtor(s) listed below was filed on _____(date).]
or [A bankruptcy case concerning the debtor(s) listed below was originally filed under chapter_____on
_____(date) and was converted to a case under chapter 7 on_____(date).]

You may be a creditor of the debtor. **This notice lists important deadlines.** You may want to consult an attorney to protect your rights. All documents filed in the case may be inspected at the bankruptcy clerk's office at the address listed below. NOTE: The staff of the bankruptcy clerk's office cannot give legal advice.

Creditors -- Do not file this notice in connection with any proof of claim you submit to the court.
See Reverse Side for Important Explanations.

Debtor(s) (name(s) and address):	Case Number:
	Last four digits of Social-Security or Individual Taxpayer-ID (ITIN) No(s)./Complete EIN:
All other names used by the Debtor(s) in the last 8 years (include married, maiden, and trade names):	Bankruptcy Trustee (name and address):
Attorney for Debtor(s) (name and address):	
Telephone number:	Telephone number:

Meeting of Creditors
Date: / /   Time: (   ) A. M.   Location:
                                 (   ) P. M.

Presumption of Abuse under 11 U.S.C. § 707(b)
See "Presumption of Abuse" on the reverse side.

Depending on the documents filed with the petition, one of the following statements will appear.
    The presumption of abuse does not arise.
        Or
The presumption of abuse arises.
        Or
Insufficient information has been filed to date to permit the clerk to make any determination concerning the presumption of abuse. If more complete information, when filed, shows that the presumption has arisen, creditors will be notified.

Deadlines:
Papers must be *received* by the bankruptcy clerk's office by the following deadlines:

Deadline to File a Proof of Claim:
For all creditors (except a governmental unit):   For a governmental unit:
Creditor with a Foreign Address:
A creditor to whom this notice is sent at a foreign address should read the information under "Claims" on the reverse side.

Deadline to Object to Debtor's Discharge or to Challenge Dischargeability of Certain Debts:

Deadline to Object to Exemptions:
Thirty (30) days after the *conclusion* of the meeting of creditors.

Creditors May Not Take Certain Actions:
In most instances, the filing of the bankruptcy case automatically stays certain collection and other actions against the debtor and the debtor's property. Under certain circumstances, the stay may be limited to 30 days or not exist at all, although the debtor can request the court to extend or impose a stay. If you attempt to collect a debt or take other action in violation of the Bankruptcy Code, you may be penalized. Consult a lawyer to determine your rights in this case.

Address of the Bankruptcy Clerk's Office:	For the Court:
	Clerk of the Bankruptcy Court:
Telephone number:	
Hours Open:	Date:

Filing of Chapter 7 Bankruptcy Case	A bankruptcy case under Chapter 7 of the Bankruptcy Code (title 11, United States Code) has been filed in this court by or against the debtor(s) listed on the front side, and an order for relief has been entered.
Legal Advice	The staff of the bankruptcy clerk's office cannot give legal advice. Consult a lawyer to determine your rights in this case.
Creditors Generally May Not Take Certain Actions	Prohibited collection actions are listed in Bankruptcy Code § 362. Common examples of prohibited actions include contacting the debtor by telephone, mail, or otherwise to demand repayment; taking actions to collect money or obtain property from the debtor; repossessing the debtor's property; starting or continuing lawsuits or foreclosures; and garnishing or deducting from the debtor's wages. Under certain circumstances, the stay may be limited to 30 days or not exist at all, although the debtor can request the court to extend or impose a stay.
Meeting of Creditors	A meeting of creditors is scheduled for the date, time, and location listed on the front side. *The debtor (both spouses in a joint case) must be present at the meeting to be questioned under oath by the trustee and by creditors.* Creditors are welcome to attend, but are not required to do so. The meeting may be continued and concluded at a later date specified in a notice filed with the court.
Claims	A Proof of Claim is a signed statement describing a creditor's claim. If a Proof of Claim form is not included with this notice, you can obtain one at any bankruptcy clerk's office. A secured creditor retains rights in its collateral regardless of whether that creditor files a Proof of Claim. If you do not file a Proof of Claim by the "Deadline to File a Proof of Claim" listed on the front side, you might not be paid any money on your claim from other assets in the bankruptcy case. To be paid, you must file a Proof of Claim even if your claim is listed in the schedules filed by the debtor. Filing a Proof of Claim submits the creditor to the jurisdiction of the bankruptcy court, with consequences a lawyer can explain. For example, a secured creditor who files a Proof of Claim may surrender important nonmonetary rights, including the right to a jury trial. **Filing Deadline for a Creditor with a Foreign Address:** The deadlines for filing claims set forth on the front of this notice apply to all creditors. If this notice has been mailed to a creditor at a foreign address, the creditor may file a motion requesting the court to extend the deadline. *Do not include this notice with any filing you make with the court.*
Discharge of Debts	The debtor is seeking a discharge of most debts, which may include your debt. A discharge means that you may never try to collect the debt from the debtor. If you believe that the debtor is not entitled to receive a discharge under Bankruptcy Code § 727(a) *or* that a debt owed to you is not dischargeable under Bankruptcy Code § 523(a)(2), (4), or (6), you must file a complaint -- or a motion if you assert the discharge should be denied under § 727(a)(8) or (a)(9) -- in the bankruptcy clerk's office by the "Deadline to Object to Debtor's Discharge or to Challenge the Dischargeability of Certain Debts" listed on the front of this form. The bankruptcy clerk's office must receive the complaint or motion and any required filing fee by that deadline.
Exempt Property	The debtor is permitted by law to keep certain property as exempt. Exempt property will not be sold and distributed to creditors. The debtor must file a list of all property claimed as exempt. You may inspect that list at the bankruptcy clerk's office. If you believe that an exemption claimed by the debtor is not authorized by law, you may file an objection to that exemption. The bankruptcy clerk's office must receive the objections by the "Deadline to Object to Exemptions" listed on the front side.
Presumption of Abuse	If the presumption of abuse arises, creditors may have the right to file a motion to dismiss the case under § 707(b) of the Bankruptcy Code. The debtor may rebut the presumption by showing special circumstances.
Bankruptcy Clerk's Office	Any paper that you file in this bankruptcy case should be filed at the bankruptcy clerk's office at the address listed on the front side. You may inspect all papers filed, including the list of the debtor's property and debts and the list of the property claimed as exempt, at the bankruptcy clerk's office.
Liquidation of the Debtor's Property and Payment of Creditors' Claims	The bankruptcy trustee listed on the front of this notice will collect and sell the debtor's property that is not exempt. If the trustee can collect enough money, creditors may be paid some or all of the debts owed to them, in the order specified by the Bankruptcy Code. To make sure you receive any share of that money, you must file a Proof of Claim, as described above.
Creditor with a Foreign Address	Consult a lawyer familiar with United States bankruptcy law if you have any questions regarding your rights in this case.

Refer To Other Side For Important Deadlines and Notices

$

UPDATED BANKRUPTCY FORMS

It has come to our attention that some states are no longer accepting the previous batch of forms. **This is especially true in MISSOURI.**

The forms contained on the following pages may be copied and/or removed, filled out, and filed with the appropriate bankruptcy court. These forms were obtained from the *U.S. Courts* website (listed below) and are being provided as a convenience. As of April 2018, these were the most current versions, however, updates are made periodically and some forms may now look differently than the examples contained in this book. The author and publisher bear no responsibility for the accuracy, legality, or validity of these forms. The most current versions can be obtained online at the following web address:

http://www.uscourts.gov/FormsAndFees/Forms/BankruptcyForms.aspx

United States Bankruptcy Court for the:

_____ District of _____

Case number (*If known*): _____

Chapter you are filing under:
- ☐ Chapter 7
- ☐ Chapter 11
- ☐ Chapter 12
- ☐ Chapter 13

☐ Check if this is an amended filing

Official Form 101

Voluntary Petition for Individuals Filing for Bankruptcy   12/17

The bankruptcy forms use *you* and *Debtor 1* to refer to a debtor filing alone. A married couple may file a bankruptcy case together—called a *joint case*—and in joint cases, these forms use *you* to ask for information from both debtors. For example, if a form asks, "Do you own a car," the answer would be *yes* if either debtor owns a car. When information is needed about the spouses separately, the form uses *Debtor 1* and *Debtor 2* to distinguish between them. In joint cases, one of the spouses must report information as *Debtor 1* and the other as *Debtor 2*. The same person must be *Debtor 1* in all of the forms.

Be as complete and accurate as possible. If two married people are filing together, both are equally responsible for supplying correct information. If more space is needed, attach a separate sheet to this form. On the top of any additional pages, write your name and case number (if known). Answer every question.

Part 1:   Identify Yourself

	About Debtor 1:	About Debtor 2 (Spouse Only in a Joint Case):
1. Your full name Write the name that is on your government-issued picture identification (for example, your driver's license or passport). Bring your picture identification to your meeting with the trustee.	First name Middle name Last name Suffix (Sr., Jr., II, III)	First name Middle name Last name Suffix (Sr., Jr., II, III)
2. All other names you have used in the last 8 years Include your married or maiden names.	First name Middle name Last name First name Middle name Last name	First name Middle name Last name First name Middle name Last name
3. Only the last 4 digits of your Social Security number or federal Individual Taxpayer Identification number (ITIN)	XXX – XX – ____ ____ ____ ____ OR 9 XX – XX – ____ ____ ____ ____	XXX – XX – ____ ____ ____ ____ OR 9 XX – XX – ____ ____ ____ ____

	About Debtor 1:	About Debtor 2 (Spouse Only in a Joint Case):
4. Any business names and Employer Identification Numbers (EIN) you have used in the last 8 years Include trade names and *doing business as* names	❏ I have not used any business names or EINs. _____ Business name _____ Business name ___ ___ - ___ ___ ___ ___ ___ ___ ___ EIN ___ ___ - ___ ___ ___ ___ ___ ___ ___ EIN	❏ I have not used any business names or EINs. _____ Business name _____ Business name ___ ___ - ___ ___ ___ ___ ___ ___ ___ EIN ___ ___ - ___ ___ ___ ___ ___ ___ ___ EIN
5. Where you live	 _____ Number Street _____ _____ City State ZIP Code _____ County **If your mailing address is different from the one above, fill it in here.** Note that the court will send any notices to you at this mailing address. _____ Number Street _____ P.O. Box _____ City State ZIP Code	**If Debtor 2 lives at a different address:** _____ Number Street _____ _____ City State ZIP Code _____ County **If Debtor 2's mailing address is different from yours, fill it in here.** Note that the court will send any notices to this mailing address. _____ Number Street _____ P.O. Box _____ City State ZIP Code
6. Why you are choosing *this district* to file for bankruptcy	*Check one:* ❏ Over the last 180 days before filing this petition, I have lived in this district longer than in any other district. ❏ I have another reason. Explain. (See 28 U.S.C. § 1408.) _____ _____ _____ _____	*Check one:* ❏ Over the last 180 days before filing this petition, I have lived in this district longer than in any other district. ❏ I have another reason. Explain. (See 28 U.S.C. § 1408.) _____ _____ _____ _____

Part 2: Tell the Court About Your Bankruptcy Case

7. The chapter of the Bankruptcy Code you are choosing to file under

Check one. (For a brief description of each, see *Notice Required by 11 U.S.C. § 342(b) for Individuals Filing for Bankruptcy* (Form 2010)). Also, go to the top of page 1 and check the appropriate box.

❏ Chapter 7

❏ Chapter 11

❏ Chapter 12

❏ Chapter 13

8. How you will pay the fee

❏ **I will pay the entire fee when I file my petition.** Please check with the clerk's office in your local court for more details about how you may pay. Typically, if you are paying the fee yourself, you may pay with cash, cashier's check, or money order. If your attorney is submitting your payment on your behalf, your attorney may pay with a credit card or check with a pre-printed address.

❏ **I need to pay the fee in installments.** If you choose this option, sign and attach the *Application for Individuals to Pay The Filing Fee in Installments* (Official Form 103A).

❏ **I request that my fee be waived** (You may request this option only if you are filing for Chapter 7. By law, a judge may, but is not required to, waive your fee, and may do so only if your income is less than 150% of the official poverty line that applies to your family size and you are unable to pay the fee in installments). If you choose this option, you must fill out the *Application to Have the Chapter 7 Filing Fee Waived* (Official Form 103B) and file it with your petition.

9. Have you filed for bankruptcy within the last 8 years?

❏ No

❏ Yes. District _____ When _____ Case number _____
                                   MM / DD / YYYY

            District _____ When _____ Case number _____
                                   MM / DD / YYYY

            District _____ When _____ Case number _____
                                   MM / DD / YYYY

10. Are any bankruptcy cases pending or being filed by a spouse who is not filing this case with you, or by a business partner, or by an affiliate?

❏ No

❏ Yes. Debtor _____ Relationship to you _____

        District _____ When _____ Case number, if known_____
                              MM / DD / YYYY

        Debtor _____ Relationship to you _____

        District _____ When _____ Case number, if known_____
                              MM / DD / YYYY

11. Do you rent your residence?

❏ No. Go to line 12.

❏ Yes. Has your landlord obtained an eviction judgment against you?

      ❏ No. Go to line 12.

      ❏ Yes. Fill out *Initial Statement About an Eviction Judgment Against You* (Form 101A) and file it as part of this bankruptcy petition.

Part 3:   Report About Any Businesses You Own as a Sole Proprietor

12. Are you a sole proprietor of any full- or part-time business?

A sole proprietorship is a business you operate as an individual, and is not a separate legal entity such as a corporation, partnership, or LLC.

If you have more than one sole proprietorship, use a separate sheet and attach it to this petition.

  ❑ No. Go to Part 4.

  ❑ Yes. Name and location of business

    _____
    Name of business, if any

    _____
    Number   Street

    _____

    _____
    City   State   ZIP Code

    Check the appropriate box to describe your business:

    ❑ Health Care Business (as defined in 11 U.S.C. § 101(27A))

    ❑ Single Asset Real Estate (as defined in 11 U.S.C. § 101(51B))

    ❑ Stockbroker (as defined in 11 U.S.C. § 101(53A))

    ❑ Commodity Broker (as defined in 11 U.S.C. § 101(6))

    ❑ None of the above

13. Are you filing under Chapter 11 of the Bankruptcy Code and are you a *small business debtor*?

For a definition of *small business debtor*, see 11 U.S.C. § 101(51D).

If you are filing under Chapter 11, the court must know whether you are a small business debtor so that it can set appropriate deadlines. If you indicate that you are a small business debtor, you must attach your most recent balance sheet, statement of operations, cash-flow statement, and federal income tax return or if any of these documents do not exist, follow the procedure in 11 U.S.C. § 1116(1)(B).

  ❑ No.   I am not filing under Chapter 11.

  ❑ No.   I am filing under Chapter 11, but I am NOT a small business debtor according to the definition in the Bankruptcy Code.

  ❑ Yes. I am filing under Chapter 11 and I am a small business debtor according to the definition in the Bankruptcy Code.

Part 4:   Report if You Own or Have Any Hazardous Property or Any Property That Needs Immediate Attention

14. Do you own or have any property that poses or is alleged to pose a threat of imminent and identifiable hazard to public health or safety? Or do you own any property that needs immediate attention?

For example, do you own perishable goods, or livestock that must be fed, or a building that needs urgent repairs?

  ❑ No

  ❑ Yes.   What is the hazard? _____

                                 _____

        If immediate attention is needed, why is it needed? _____

                                 _____

        Where is the property? _____
                              Number   Street

                              _____

                              _____
                              City   State   ZIP Code

Part 5:   Explain Your Efforts to Receive a Briefing About Credit Counseling

15. Tell the court whether you have received a briefing about credit counseling.

The law requires that you receive a briefing about credit counseling before you file for bankruptcy. You must truthfully check one of the following choices. If you cannot do so, you are not eligible to file.

If you file anyway, the court can dismiss your case, you will lose whatever filing fee you paid, and your creditors can begin collection activities again.

About Debtor 1:

You must check one:

❑ **I received a briefing from an approved credit counseling agency within the 180 days before I filed this bankruptcy petition, and I received a certificate of completion.**

Attach a copy of the certificate and the payment plan, if any, that you developed with the agency.

❑ **I received a briefing from an approved credit counseling agency within the 180 days before I filed this bankruptcy petition, but I do not have a certificate of completion.**

Within 14 days after you file this bankruptcy petition, you MUST file a copy of the certificate and payment plan, if any.

❑ **I certify that I asked for credit counseling services from an approved agency, but was unable to obtain those services during the 7 days after I made my request, and exigent circumstances merit a 30-day temporary waiver of the requirement.**

To ask for a 30-day temporary waiver of the requirement, attach a separate sheet explaining what efforts you made to obtain the briefing, why you were unable to obtain it before you filed for bankruptcy, and what exigent circumstances required you to file this case.

Your case may be dismissed if the court is dissatisfied with your reasons for not receiving a briefing before you filed for bankruptcy.

If the court is satisfied with your reasons, you must still receive a briefing within 30 days after you file. You must file a certificate from the approved agency, along with a copy of the payment plan you developed, if any. If you do not do so, your case may be dismissed.

Any extension of the 30-day deadline is granted only for cause and is limited to a maximum of 15 days.

❑ **I am not required to receive a briefing about credit counseling because of:**

    ❑ **Incapacity.** I have a mental illness or a mental deficiency that makes me incapable of realizing or making rational decisions about finances.

    ❑ **Disability.** My physical disability causes me to be unable to participate in a briefing in person, by phone, or through the internet, even after I reasonably tried to do so.

    ❑ **Active duty.** I am currently on active military duty in a military combat zone.

If you believe you are not required to receive a briefing about credit counseling, you must file a motion for waiver of credit counseling with the court.

About Debtor 2 (Spouse Only in a Joint Case):

You must check one:

❑ **I received a briefing from an approved credit counseling agency within the 180 days before I filed this bankruptcy petition, and I received a certificate of completion.**

Attach a copy of the certificate and the payment plan, if any, that you developed with the agency.

❑ **I received a briefing from an approved credit counseling agency within the 180 days before I filed this bankruptcy petition, but I do not have a certificate of completion.**

Within 14 days after you file this bankruptcy petition, you MUST file a copy of the certificate and payment plan, if any.

❑ **I certify that I asked for credit counseling services from an approved agency, but was unable to obtain those services during the 7 days after I made my request, and exigent circumstances merit a 30-day temporary waiver of the requirement.**

To ask for a 30-day temporary waiver of the requirement, attach a separate sheet explaining what efforts you made to obtain the briefing, why you were unable to obtain it before you filed for bankruptcy, and what exigent circumstances required you to file this case.

Your case may be dismissed if the court is dissatisfied with your reasons for not receiving a briefing before you filed for bankruptcy.

If the court is satisfied with your reasons, you must still receive a briefing within 30 days after you file. You must file a certificate from the approved agency, along with a copy of the payment plan you developed, if any. If you do not do so, your case may be dismissed.

Any extension of the 30-day deadline is granted only for cause and is limited to a maximum of 15 days.

❑ **I am not required to receive a briefing about credit counseling because of:**

    ❑ **Incapacity.** I have a mental illness or a mental deficiency that makes me incapable of realizing or making rational decisions about finances.

    ❑ **Disability.** My physical disability causes me to be unable to participate in a briefing in person, by phone, or through the internet, even after I reasonably tried to do so.

    ❑ **Active duty.** I am currently on active military duty in a military combat zone.

If you believe you are not required to receive a briefing about credit counseling, you must file a motion for waiver of credit counseling with the court.

Part 6: Answer These Questions for Reporting Purposes

16. What kind of debts do you have?

16a. Are your debts primarily consumer debts? *Consumer debts* are defined in 11 U.S.C. § 101(8) as "incurred by an individual primarily for a personal, family, or household purpose."

❑ No. Go to line 16b.
❑ Yes. Go to line 17.

16b. Are your debts primarily business debts? *Business debts* are debts that you incurred to obtain money for a business or investment or through the operation of the business or investment.

❑ No. Go to line 16c.
❑ Yes. Go to line 17.

16c. State the type of debts you owe that are not consumer debts or business debts.

_____

17. Are you filing under Chapter 7?

Do you estimate that after any exempt property is excluded and administrative expenses are paid that funds will be available for distribution to unsecured creditors?

❑ No. I am not filing under Chapter 7. Go to line 18.

❑ Yes. I am filing under Chapter 7. Do you estimate that after any exempt property is excluded and administrative expenses are paid that funds will be available to distribute to unsecured creditors?

    ❑ No
    ❑ Yes

18. How many creditors do you estimate that you owe?

❑ 1-49	❑ 1,000-5,000	❑ 25,001-50,000
❑ 50-99	❑ 5,001-10,000	❑ 50,001-100,000
❑ 100-199	❑ 10,001-25,000	❑ More than 100,000
❑ 200-999		

19. How much do you estimate your assets to be worth?

❑ $0-$50,000	❑ $1,000,001-$10 million	❑ $500,000,001-$1 billion
❑ $50,001-$100,000	❑ $10,000,001-$50 million	❑ $1,000,000,001-$10 billion
❑ $100,001-$500,000	❑ $50,000,001-$100 million	❑ $10,000,000,001-$50 billion
❑ $500,001-$1 million	❑ $100,000,001-$500 million	❑ More than $50 billion

20. How much do you estimate your liabilities to be?

❑ $0-$50,000	❑ $1,000,001-$10 million	❑ $500,000,001-$1 billion
❑ $50,001-$100,000	❑ $10,000,001-$50 million	❑ $1,000,000,001-$10 billion
❑ $100,001-$500,000	❑ $50,000,001-$100 million	❑ $10,000,000,001-$50 billion
❑ $500,001-$1 million	❑ $100,000,001-$500 million	❑ More than $50 billion

Part 7: Sign Below

For you

I have examined this petition, and I declare under penalty of perjury that the information provided is true and correct.

If I have chosen to file under Chapter 7, I am aware that I may proceed, if eligible, under Chapter 7, 11,12, or 13 of title 11, United States Code. I understand the relief available under each chapter, and I choose to proceed under Chapter 7.

If no attorney represents me and I did not pay or agree to pay someone who is not an attorney to help me fill out this document, I have obtained and read the notice required by 11 U.S.C. § 342(b).

I request relief in accordance with the chapter of title 11, United States Code, specified in this petition.

I understand making a false statement, concealing property, or obtaining money or property by fraud in connection with a bankruptcy case can result in fines up to $250,000, or imprisonment for up to 20 years, or both. 18 U.S.C. §§ 152, 1341, 1519, and 3571.

✗ _____   ✗ _____
    Signature of Debtor 1   Signature of Debtor 2

    Executed on _____   Executed on _____
                 MM / DD / YYYY   MM / DD / YYYY

For your attorney, if you are represented by one

If you are not represented by an attorney, you do not need to file this page.

I, the attorney for the debtor(s) named in this petition, declare that I have informed the debtor(s) about eligibility to proceed under Chapter 7, 11, 12, or 13 of title 11, United States Code, and have explained the relief available under each chapter for which the person is eligible. I also certify that I have delivered to the debtor(s) the notice required by 11 U.S.C. § 342(b) and, in a case in which § 707(b)(4)(D) applies, certify that I have no knowledge after an inquiry that the information in the schedules filed with the petition is incorrect.

✘ _____   Date _____

    Signature of Attorney for Debtor   MM / DD / YYYY

_____

Printed name

_____

Firm name

_____

Number   Street

_____

_____

City   State   ZIP Code

Contact phone _____   Email address _____

_____

Bar number   State

For you if you are filing this bankruptcy without an attorney **If you are represented by an attorney, you do not need to file this page.**	The law allows you, as an individual, to represent yourself in bankruptcy court, but **you should understand that many people find it extremely difficult to represent themselves successfully. Because bankruptcy has long-term financial and legal consequences, you are strongly urged to hire a qualified attorney.** To be successful, you must correctly file and handle your bankruptcy case. The rules are very technical, and a mistake or inaction may affect your rights. For example, your case may be dismissed because you did not file a required document, pay a fee on time, attend a meeting or hearing, or cooperate with the court, case trustee, U.S. trustee, bankruptcy administrator, or audit firm if your case is selected for audit. If that happens, you could lose your right to file another case, or you may lose protections, including the benefit of the automatic stay. You must list all your property and debts in the schedules that you are required to file with the court. Even if you plan to pay a particular debt outside of your bankruptcy, you must list that debt in your schedules. If you do not list a debt, the debt may not be discharged. If you do not list property or properly claim it as exempt, you may not be able to keep the property. The judge can also deny you a discharge of all your debts if you do something dishonest in your bankruptcy case, such as destroying or hiding property, falsifying records, or lying. Individual bankruptcy cases are randomly audited to determine if debtors have been accurate, truthful, and complete. **Bankruptcy fraud is a serious crime; you could be fined and imprisoned.** If you decide to file without an attorney, the court expects you to follow the rules as if you had hired an attorney. The court will not treat you differently because you are filing for yourself. To be successful, you must be familiar with the United States Bankruptcy Code, the Federal Rules of Bankruptcy Procedure, and the local rules of the court in which your case is filed. You must also be familiar with any state exemption laws that apply.

Are you aware that filing for bankruptcy is a serious action with long-term financial and legal consequences?

❑ No
❑ Yes

Are you aware that bankruptcy fraud is a serious crime and that if your bankruptcy forms are inaccurate or incomplete, you could be fined or imprisoned?

❑ No
❑ Yes

Did you pay or agree to pay someone who is not an attorney to help you fill out your bankruptcy forms?
❑ No
❑ Yes. Name of Person_____.
   Attach *Bankruptcy Petition Preparer's Notice, Declaration, and Signature* (Official Form 119).

By signing here, I acknowledge that I understand the risks involved in filing without an attorney. I have read and understood this notice, and I am aware that filing a bankruptcy case without an attorney may cause me to lose my rights or property if I do not properly handle the case.

✖ _____	✖ _____
Signature of Debtor 1	Signature of Debtor 2

Date _____
        MM / DD / YYYY
	Date _____
	        MM / DD / YYYY

Contact phone _____	Contact phone _____
Cell phone _____	Cell phone _____
Email address _____	Email address _____

B 1C (Official Form 1, Exhibit C) (9/01)

[If, to the best of the debtor's knowledge, the debtor owns or has possession of property that poses or is alleged to pose a threat of imminent and identifiable harm to the public health or safety, attach this Exhibit "C" to the petition.]

UNITED STATES BANKRUPTCY COURT

In re _____ ,) Case No. _____

                Debtor   )

)

) Chapter _____

EXHIBIT "C" TO VOLUNTARY PETITION

    1. Identify and briefly describe all real or personal property owned by or in possession of the debtor that, to the best of the debtor's knowledge, poses or is alleged to pose a threat of imminent and identifiable harm to the public health or safety (attach additional sheets if necessary):

    2. With respect to each parcel of real property or item of personal property identified in question 1, describe the nature and location of the dangerous condition, whether environmental or otherwise, that poses or is alleged to pose a threat of imminent and identifiable harm to the public health or safety (attach additional sheets if necessary):

B 1D (Official Form 1, Exhibit D) (12/09)

UNITED STATES BANKRUPTCY COURT

In re_____   Case No._____
         Debtor   (if known)

EXHIBIT D - INDIVIDUAL DEBTOR'S STATEMENT OF COMPLIANCE WITH CREDIT COUNSELING REQUIREMENT

Warning: You must be able to check truthfully one of the five statements regarding credit counseling listed below. If you cannot do so, you are not eligible to file a bankruptcy case, and the court can dismiss any case you do file. If that happens, you will lose whatever filing fee you paid, and your creditors will be able to resume collection activities against you. If your case is dismissed and you file another bankruptcy case later, you may be required to pay a second filing fee and you may have to take extra steps to stop creditors' collection activities.

Every individual debtor must file this Exhibit D. If a joint petition is filed, each spouse must complete and file a separate Exhibit D. Check one of the five statements below and attach any documents as directed.

❑ 1. Within the 180 days **before the filing of my bankruptcy case**, I received a briefing from a credit counseling agency approved by the United States trustee or bankruptcy administrator that outlined the opportunities for available credit counseling and assisted me in performing a related budget analysis, and I have a certificate from the agency describing the services provided to me. *Attach a copy of the certificate and a copy of any debt repayment plan developed through the agency.*

❑ 2. Within the 180 days **before the filing of my bankruptcy case**, I received a briefing from a credit counseling agency approved by the United States trustee or bankruptcy administrator that outlined the opportunities for available credit counseling and assisted me in performing a related budget analysis, but I do not have a certificate from the agency describing the services provided to me. *You must file a copy of a certificate from the agency describing the services provided to you and a copy of any debt repayment plan developed through the agency no later than 14 days after your bankruptcy case is filed.*

❏ 3. I certify that I requested credit counseling services from an approved agency but was unable to obtain the services during the seven days from the time I made my request, and the following exigent circumstances merit a temporary waiver of the credit counseling requirement so I can file my bankruptcy case now. *[Summarize exigent circumstances here.]*

If your certification is satisfactory to the court, you must still obtain the credit counseling briefing within the first 30 days after you file your bankruptcy petition and promptly file a certificate from the agency that provided the counseling, together with a copy of any debt management plan developed through the agency. Failure to fulfill these requirements may result in dismissal of your case. Any extension of the 30-day deadline can be granted only for cause and is limited to a maximum of 15 days. Your case may also be dismissed if the court is not satisfied with your reasons for filing your bankruptcy case without first receiving a credit counseling briefing.

❏ 4. I am not required to receive a credit counseling briefing because of: *[Check the applicable statement.]* *[Must be accompanied by a motion for determination by the court.]*

❏ Incapacity. (Defined in 11 U.S.C. § 109(h)(4) as impaired by reason of mental illness or mental deficiency so as to be incapable of realizing and making rational decisions with respect to financial responsibilities.);
❏ Disability. (Defined in 11 U.S.C. § 109(h)(4) as physically impaired to the extent of being unable, after reasonable effort, to participate in a credit counseling briefing in person, by telephone, or through the Internet.);
❏ Active military duty in a military combat zone.

❏ 5. The United States trustee or bankruptcy administrator has determined that the credit counseling requirement of 11 U.S.C. § 109(h) does not apply in this district.

I certify under penalty of perjury that the information provided above is true and correct.

Signature of Debtor: _____

Date: _____

Official Form 202

Declaration Under Penalty of Perjury for Non-Individual Debtors   12/15

An individual who is authorized to act on behalf of a non-individual debtor, such as a corporation or partnership, must sign and submit this form for the schedules of assets and liabilities, any other document that requires a declaration that is not included in the document, and any amendments of those documents. This form must state the individual's position or relationship to the debtor, the identity of the document, and the date. Bankruptcy Rules 1008 and 9011.

WARNING -- Bankruptcy fraud is a serious crime. Making a false statement, concealing property, or obtaining money or property by fraud in connection with a bankruptcy case can result in fines up to $500,000 or imprisonment for up to 20 years, or both. 18 U.S.C. §§ 152, 1341, 1519, and 3571.

Declaration and signature

I am the president, another officer, or an authorized agent of the corporation; a member or an authorized agent of the partnership; or another individual serving as a representative of the debtor in this case.

I have examined the information in the documents checked below and I have a reasonable belief that the information is true and correct:

☐ *Schedule A/B: Assets–Real and Personal Property* (Official Form 206A/B)

☐ *Schedule D: Creditors Who Have Claims Secured by Property* (Official Form 206D)

☐ *Schedule E/F: Creditors Who Have Unsecured Claims* (Official Form 206E/F)

☐ *Schedule G: Executory Contracts and Unexpired Leases* (Official Form 206G)

☐ *Schedule H: Codebtors* (Official Form 206H)

☐ *Summary of Assets and Liabilities for Non-Individuals* (Official Form 206Sum)

☐ Amended *Schedule* ____

☐ *Chapter 11 or Chapter 9 Cases: List of Creditors Who Have the 20 Largest Unsecured Claims and Are Not Insiders* (Official Form 204)

☐ Other document that requires a declaration_____

I declare under penalty of perjury that the foregoing is true and correct.

Executed on _____   **X**_____
                MM / DD / YYYY   Signature of individual signing on behalf of debtor

                                                 _____
                                                 Printed name

                                                 _____
                                                 Position or relationship to debtor

Fill in this information to identify your case:

Debtor 1 _____
        First Name   Middle Name   Last Name

Debtor 2 _____
(Spouse, if filing) First Name   Middle Name   Last Name

United States Bankruptcy Court for the: _____ District of _____

Case number _____
(If known)

☐ Check if this is an
amended filing

Official Form 103A

Application for Individuals to Pay the Filing Fee in Installments   12/15

Be as complete and accurate as possible. If two married people are filing together, both are equally responsible for supplying correct information.

1. Which chapter of the Bankruptcy Code are you choosing to file under?

   ☐ Chapter 7
   ☐ Chapter 11
   ☐ Chapter 12
   ☐ Chapter 13

2. You may apply to pay the filing fee in up to four installments. Fill in the amounts you propose to pay and the dates you plan to pay them. Be sure all dates are business days. Then add the payments you propose to pay.

   You must propose to pay the entire fee no later than 120 days after you file this bankruptcy case. If the court approves your application, the court will set your final payment timetable.

   You propose to pay...

   $ _____   ☐ With the filing of the petition
                       ☐ On or before this date........ _____
                                                         MM / DD /YYYY

   $ _____   On or before this date .... _____
                                                         MM / DD /YYYY

   $ _____   On or before this date .... _____
                                                         MM / DD /YYYY

   + $ _____ On or before this date .... _____
                                                         MM / DD /YYYY

   Total $ _____   ◄ Your total must equal the entire fee for the chapter you checked in line 1.

Part 2:   Sign Below

By signing here, you state that you are unable to pay the full filing fee at once, that you want to pay the fee in installments, and that you understand that:

▪ You must pay your entire filing fee before you make any more payments or transfer any more property to an attorney, bankruptcy petition preparer, or anyone else for services in connection with your bankruptcy case.

▪ You must pay the entire fee no later than 120 days after you first file for bankruptcy, unless the court later extends your deadline. Your debts will not be discharged until your entire fee is paid.

▪ If you do not make any payment when it is due, your bankruptcy case may be dismissed, and your rights in other bankruptcy proceedings may be affected.

✗ _____   ✗ _____   ✗ _____
Signature of Debtor 1   Signature of Debtor 2   Your attorney's name and signature, if you used one

Date _____   Date _____   Date _____
     MM / DD / YYYY   MM / DD / YYYY   MM / DD / YYYY

Fill in this information to identify the case:

Debtor 1 _____
First Name   Middle Name   Last Name

Debtor 2 _____
(Spouse, if filing) First Name   Middle Name   Last Name

United States Bankruptcy Court for the: _____ District of

Case number _____
(If known)

Chapter filing under:

❑ Chapter 7
❑ Chapter 11
❑ Chapter 12
❑ Chapter 13

Order Approving Payment of Filing Fee in Installments

After considering the *Application for Individuals to Pay the Filing Fee in Installments* (Official Form 103A), the court orders that:

[ ] The debtor(s) may pay the filing fee in installments on the terms proposed in the application.

[ ] The debtor(s) must pay the filing fee according to the following terms:

You must pay…	On or before this date…
$_____	_____ Month / day / year
$_____	_____ Month / day / year
$_____	_____ Month / day / year
+ $_____	_____ Month / day / year
Total $_____	

Until the filing fee is paid in full, the debtor(s) must not make any additional payment or transfer any additional property to an attorney or to anyone else for services in connection with this case.

_____   **By the court:** _____
Month / day / year   United States Bankruptcy Judge

Fill in this information to identify your case:

Debtor 1 _____
First Name   Middle Name   Last Name

Debtor 2
(Spouse, if filing) _____
First Name   Middle Name   Last Name

United States Bankruptcy Court for the: _____ District of _____

Case number _____
(If known)

☐ Check if this is an
amended filing

Official Form 103B

Application to Have the Chapter 7 Filing Fee Waived   12/15

Be as complete and accurate as possible. If two married people are filing together, both are equally responsible for supplying correct information. If more space is needed, attach a separate sheet to this form. On the top of any additional pages, write your name and case number (if known).

Part 1:	Tell the Court About Your Family and Your Family's Income

1. What is the size of your family?

Your family includes you, your spouse, and any dependents listed on *Schedule J: Your Expenses* (Official Form 106J).

Check all that apply:

☐ You
☐ Your spouse
☐ Your dependents _____
How many dependents?

_____
Total number of people

2. Fill in your family's average monthly income.

Include your spouse's income if your spouse is living with you, even if your spouse is not filing.

Do not include your spouse's income if you are separated and your spouse is not filing with you.

Add your income and your spouse's income. Include the value (if known) of any non-cash governmental assistance that you receive, such as food stamps (benefits under the Supplemental Nutrition Assistance Program) or housing subsidies.

If you have already filled out *Schedule I: Your Income*, see line 10 of that schedule.

Subtract any non-cash governmental assistance that you included above.

Your family's average monthly net income

That person's average monthly net income (take-home pay)

You .... $_____

Your spouse .... **+** $_____

Subtotal............ $_____

— $_____

Total................ $_____

3. Do you receive non-cash governmental assistance?

☐ No
☐ Yes. Describe............

Type of assistance
_____

4. Do you expect your family's average monthly net income to increase or decrease by more than 10% during the next 6 months?

☐ No
☐ Yes. Explain. ....
_____

5. Tell the court why you are unable to pay the filing fee in installments within 120 days. If you have some additional circumstances that cause you to not be able to pay your filing fee in installments, explain them.

_____

Debtor 1 _____   Case number *(if known)* _____
          First Name   Middle Name   Last Name

6. **Estimate your average monthly expenses.**

   Include amounts paid by any government assistance that you reported on line 2. $_____

   If you have already filled out *Schedule J, Your Expenses,* copy line 22 from that form.

7. **Do these expenses cover anyone who is not included in your family as reported in line 1?**

   ☐ No
   ☐ Yes. Identify who........ [   ]

8. **Does anyone other than you regularly pay any of these expenses?**

   If you have already filled out *Schedule I: Your Income,* copy the total from line 11.

   ☐ No
   ☐ Yes. How much do you regularly receive as contributions? $_____ monthly

9. **Do you expect your average monthly expenses to increase or decrease by more than 10% during the next 6 months?**

   ☐ No
   ☐ Yes. Explain .... [   ]

If you have already filled out *Schedule A/B: Property (Official Form 106A/B)* attach copies to this application and go to Part 4.

10. **How much cash do you have?**

    Examples: Money you have in your wallet, in your home, and on hand when you file this application

    Cash: $_____

11. **Bank accounts and other deposits of money?**

    Examples: Checking, savings, money market, or other financial accounts; certificates of deposit; shares in banks, credit unions, brokerage houses, and other similar institutions. If you have more than one account with the same institution, list each. Do not include 401(k) and IRA accounts.

	Institution name:	Amount:
Checking account:	_____	$_____
Savings account:	_____	$_____
Other financial accounts:	_____	$_____
Other financial accounts:	_____	$_____

12. **Your home?** (if you own it outright or are purchasing it)

    Examples: House, condominium, manufactured home, or mobile home

    Number   Street
    _____
    City   State   ZIP Code

    Current value: $_____
    Amount you owe on mortgage and liens: $_____

13. **Other real estate?**

    Number   Street
    _____
    City   State   ZIP Code

    Current value: $_____
    Amount you owe on mortgage and liens: $_____

14. **The vehicles you own?**

    Examples: Cars, vans, trucks, sports utility vehicles, motorcycles, tractors, boats

    Make: _____
    Model: _____
    Year: _____
    Mileage _____

    Current value: $_____
    Amount you owe on liens: $_____

    Make: _____
    Model: _____
    Year: _____
    Mileage _____

    Current value: $_____
    Amount you owe on liens: $_____

15. Other assets?

Do not include household items and clothing.

Describe the other assets:

Current value: $_____

Amount you owe on liens: $_____

16. Money or property due you?

Examples: Tax refunds, past due or lump sum alimony, spousal support, child support, maintenance, divorce or property settlements, Social Security benefits, workers' compensation, personal injury recovery

Who owes you the money or property?

_____

_____

How much is owed?

$_____

$_____

Do you believe you will likely receive payment in the next 180 days?

☐ No

☐ Yes. Explain:

_____

Part 4: Answer These Additional Questions

17. Have you paid anyone for services for this case, including filling out this application, the bankruptcy filing package, or the schedules?

☐ No
☐ Yes. **Whom did you pay?** *Check all that apply:*

  ☐ An attorney

  ☐ A bankruptcy petition preparer, paralegal, or typing service

  ☐ Someone else _____

How much did you pay?

$_____

18. Have you promised to pay or do you expect to pay someone for services for your bankruptcy case?

☐ No
☐ Yes. **Whom do you expect to pay?** *Check all that apply:*

  ☐ An attorney

  ☐ A bankruptcy petition preparer, paralegal, or typing service

  ☐ Someone else _____

How much do you expect to pay?

$_____

19. Has anyone paid someone on your behalf for services for this case?

☐ No
☐ Yes. **Who was paid on your behalf?**
Check all that apply:

  ☐ An attorney

  ☐ A bankruptcy petition preparer, paralegal, or typing service

  ☐ Someone else _____

Who paid?
Check all that apply:

  ☐ Parent

  ☐ Brother or sister

  ☐ Friend

  ☐ Pastor or clergy

  ☐ Someone else _____

How much did someone else pay?

$_____

20. Have you filed for bankruptcy within the last 8 years?

☐ No
☐ Yes. District _____ When _____ Case number _____
                              MM/ DD/ YYYY

District _____ When _____ Case number _____
                              MM/ DD/ YYYY

District _____ When _____ Case number _____
                              MM/ DD/ YYYY

Part 5: Sign Below

By signing here under penalty of perjury, I declare that I cannot afford to pay the filing fee either in full or in installments. I also declare that the information I provided in this application is true and correct.

✗ _____   ✗ _____
   Signature of Debtor 1   Signature of Debtor 2

Date _____   Date _____
     MM / DD / YYYY   MM / DD / YYYY

Fill in this information to identify the case:

Debtor 1 _____
           First Name   Middle Name   Last Name

Debtor 2 _____
(Spouse, if filing) First Name   Middle Name   Last Name

United States Bankruptcy Court for the: _____ District of _

Case number _____
(If known)

Order on the Application to Have the Chapter 7 Filing Fee Waived

After considering the debtor's *Application to Have the Chapter 7 Filing Fee Waived* (Official Form 103B), the court orders that the application is:

[ ] **Granted.** However, the court may order the debtor to pay the fee in the future if developments in administering the bankruptcy case show that the waiver was unwarranted.

[ ] **Denied.** The debtor must pay the filing fee according to the following terms:

You must pay…	On or before this date…
$_____	_____ Month / day / year
$_____	_____ Month / day / year
$_____	_____ Month / day / year
+ $_____	_____ Month / day / year

Total

If the debtor would like to propose a different payment timetable, the debtor must file a motion promptly with a payment proposal. The debtor may use *Application for Individuals to Pay the Filing Fee in Installments* (Official Form 103A) for this purpose. The court will consider it.

The debtor must pay the entire filing fee before making any more payments or transferring any more property to an attorney, bankruptcy petition preparer, or anyone else in connection with the bankruptcy case. The debtor must also pay the entire filing fee to receive a discharge. If the debtor does not make any payment when it is due, the bankruptcy case may be dismissed and the debtor's rights in future bankruptcy cases may be affected.

[ ] **Scheduled for hearing.**

A hearing to consider the debtor's application will be held

on _____ at _____ AM / PM at _____.
   Month / day / year   Address of courthouse

If the debtor does not appear at this hearing, the court may deny the application.

_____   By the court: _____
Month / day / year   United States Bankruptcy Judge

☐ Check if this is an
   amended filing

Official Form 106Sum

Summary of Your Assets and Liabilities and Certain Statistical Information   12/15

Be as complete and accurate as possible. If two married people are filing together, both are equally responsible for supplying correct information. Fill out all of your schedules first; then complete the information on this form. If you are filing amended schedules after you file your original forms, you must fill out a new *Summary* and check the box at the top of this page.

Part 1:   Summarize Your Assets

Your assets
Value of what you own

1. *Schedule A/B: Property* (Official Form 106A/B)
   1a. Copy line 55, Total real estate, from *Schedule A/B* .... $ _____

   1b. Copy line 62, Total personal property, from *Schedule A/B* .... $ _____

   1c. Copy line 63, Total of all property on *Schedule A/B* .... $ _____

Part 2:   Summarize Your Liabilities

Your liabilities
Amount you owe

2. *Schedule D: Creditors Who Have Claims Secured by Property* (Official Form 106D)
   2a. Copy the total you listed in Column A, *Amount of claim,* at the bottom of the last page of Part 1 of *Schedule D* .... $ _____

3. *Schedule E/F: Creditors Who Have Unsecured Claims* (Official Form 106E/F)
   3a. Copy the total claims from Part 1 (priority unsecured claims) from line 6e of *Schedule E/F* .... $ _____

   3b. Copy the total claims from Part 2 (nonpriority unsecured claims) from line 6j of *Schedule E/F* ....   **+** $ _____

   Your total liabilities $ _____

Part 3:   Summarize Your Income and Expenses

4. *Schedule I: Your Income* (Official Form 106I)
   Copy your combined monthly income from line 12 of *Schedule I* .... $ _____

5. *Schedule J: Your Expenses* (Official Form 106J)
   Copy your monthly expenses from line 22c of *Schedule J* .... $ _____

Part 4: Answer These Questions for Administrative and Statistical Records

6. **Are you filing for bankruptcy under Chapters 7, 11, or 13?**

    ❏ No. You have nothing to report on this part of the form. Check this box and submit this form to the court with your other schedules.

    ❏ Yes

7. **What kind of debt do you have?**

    ❏ Your debts are primarily consumer debts. *Consumer debts* are those "incurred by an individual primarily for a personal, family, or household purpose." 11 U.S.C. § 101(8). Fill out lines 8-9g for statistical purposes. 28 U.S.C. § 159.

    ❏ Your debts are not primarily consumer debts. You have nothing to report on this part of the form. Check this box and submit this form to the court with your other schedules.

8. **From the** *Statement of Your Current Monthly Income*: Copy your total current monthly income from Official Form 122A-1 Line 11; **OR**, Form 122B Line 11; **OR**, Form 122C-1 Line 14.

    $ _____

9. Copy the following special categories of claims from Part 4, line 6 of *Schedule E/F*:

                                                                    Total claim

    From Part 4 on *Schedule E/F*, copy the following:

    9a. Domestic support obligations (Copy line 6a.) $_____

    9b. Taxes and certain other debts you owe the government. (Copy line 6b.) $_____

    9c. Claims for death or personal injury while you were intoxicated. (Copy line 6c.) $_____

    9d. Student loans. (Copy line 6f.) $_____

    9e. Obligations arising out of a separation agreement or divorce that you did not report as priority claims. (Copy line 6g.) $_____

    9f. Debts to pension or profit-sharing plans, and other similar debts. (Copy line 6h.)   + $_____

    9g. **Total.** Add lines 9a through 9f. $_____

Fill in this information to identify your case and this filing:

Debtor 1 _____
           First Name   Middle Name   Last Name

Debtor 2 _____
(Spouse, if filing) First Name   Middle Name   Last Name

United States Bankruptcy Court for the: _____ District of _____

Case number _____

❑ Check if this is an
   amended filing

Official Form 106A/B

Schedule A/B: Property   12/15

In each category, separately list and describe items. List an asset only once. If an asset fits in more than one category, list the asset in the category where you think it fits best. Be as complete and accurate as possible. If two married people are filing together, both are equally responsible for supplying correct information. If more space is needed, attach a separate sheet to this form. On the top of any additional pages, write your name and case number (if known). Answer every question.

Part 1:   Describe Each Residence, Building, Land, or Other Real Estate You Own or Have an Interest In

1. **Do you own or have any legal or equitable interest in any residence, building, land, or similar property?**

   ❑ No. Go to Part 2.
   ❑ Yes. Where is the property?

What is the property? Check all that apply.

❑ Single-family home
❑ Duplex or multi-unit building
❑ Condominium or cooperative
❑ Manufactured or mobile home
❑ Land
❑ Investment property
❑ Timeshare
❑ Other _____

1.1. _____
     Street address, if available, or other description

_____

_____
City   State   ZIP Code

_____
County

Do not deduct secured claims or exemptions. Put the amount of any secured claims on *Schedule D: Creditors Who Have Claims Secured by Property.*

Current value of the entire property?   **Current value of the portion you own?**

$_____ $_____

Describe the nature of your ownership interest (such as fee simple, tenancy by the entireties, or a life estate), if known.

_____

Who has an interest in the property? Check one.

❑ Debtor 1 only
❑ Debtor 2 only
❑ Debtor 1 and Debtor 2 only
❑ At least one of the debtors and another

❑ Check if this is community property
   (see instructions)

Other information you wish to add about this item, such as local property identification number: _____

If you own or have more than one, list here:

What is the property? Check all that apply.

❑ Single-family home
❑ Duplex or multi-unit building
❑ Condominium or cooperative
❑ Manufactured or mobile home
❑ Land
❑ Investment property
❑ Timeshare
❑ Other _____

1.2. _____
     Street address, if available, or other description

_____

_____
City   State   ZIP Code

_____
County

Do not deduct secured claims or exemptions. Put the amount of any secured claims on *Schedule D: Creditors Who Have Claims Secured by Property.*

Current value of the entire property?   **Current value of the portion you own?**

$_____ $_____

Describe the nature of your ownership interest (such as fee simple, tenancy by the entireties, or a life estate), if known.

_____

Who has an interest in the property? Check one.

❑ Debtor 1 only
❑ Debtor 2 only
❑ Debtor 1 and Debtor 2 only
❑ At least one of the debtors and another

❑ Check if this is community property
   (see instructions)

Other information you wish to add about this item, such as local property identification number: _____

Debtor 1 _____   Case number (*if known*)_____
        First Name   Middle Name   Last Name

1.3. _____
     Street address, if available, or other description

     _____

     _____
     City   State   ZIP Code

     _____
     County

What is the property? Check all that apply.

❑ Single-family home
❑ Duplex or multi-unit building
❑ Condominium or cooperative
❑ Manufactured or mobile home
❑ Land
❑ Investment property
❑ Timeshare
❑ Other _____

Who has an interest in the property? Check one.

❑ Debtor 1 only
❑ Debtor 2 only
❑ Debtor 1 and Debtor 2 only
❑ At least one of the debtors and another

Other information you wish to add about this item, such as local property identification number: _____

Do not deduct secured claims or exemptions. Put the amount of any secured claims on *Schedule D: Creditors Who Have Claims Secured by Property.*

Current value of the entire property?   **Current value of the portion you own?**

$_____ $_____

Describe the nature of your ownership interest (such as fee simple, tenancy by the entireties, or a life estate), if known.

_____

❑ **Check if this is community property** (see instructions)

2. Add the dollar value of the portion you own for all of your entries from Part 1, including any entries for pages you have attached for Part 1. Write that number here. .... → $_____

Part 2:   Describe Your Vehicles

Do you own, lease, or have legal or equitable interest in any vehicles, whether they are registered or not? Include any vehicles you own that someone else drives. If you lease a vehicle, also report it on *Schedule G: Executory Contracts and Unexpired Leases.*

3. **Cars, vans, trucks, tractors, sport utility vehicles, motorcycles**

❑ No
❑ Yes

3.1. Make: _____
      Model: _____
      Year: _____
      Approximate mileage: _____
      Other information:
      _____

Who has an interest in the property? Check one.

❑ Debtor 1 only
❑ Debtor 2 only
❑ Debtor 1 and Debtor 2 only
❑ At least one of the debtors and another

❑ **Check if this is community property** (see instructions)

Do not deduct secured claims or exemptions. Put the amount of any secured claims on *Schedule D: Creditors Who Have Claims Secured by Property.*

Current value of the entire property?   **Current value of the portion you own?**

$_____ $_____

If you own or have more than one, describe here:

3.2. Make: _____
      Model: _____
      Year: _____
      Approximate mileage: _____
      Other information:
      _____

Who has an interest in the property? Check one.

❑ Debtor 1 only
❑ Debtor 2 only
❑ Debtor 1 and Debtor 2 only
❑ At least one of the debtors and another

❑ **Check if this is community property** (see instructions)

Do not deduct secured claims or exemptions. Put the amount of any secured claims on *Schedule D: Creditors Who Have Claims Secured by Property.*

Current value of the entire property?   **Current value of the portion you own?**

$_____ $_____

Official Form 106A/B   **Schedule A/B: Property**   page **2**

3.3. Make: _____

Model: _____

Year: _____

Approximate mileage: _____

Other information:

Who has an interest in the property? Check one.

❑ Debtor 1 only

❑ Debtor 2 only

❑ Debtor 1 and Debtor 2 only

❑ At least one of the debtors and another

❑ **Check if this is community property** (see instructions)

Do not deduct secured claims or exemptions. Put the amount of any secured claims on *Schedule D: Creditors Who Have Claims Secured by Property.*

Current value of the entire property?   **Current value of the portion you own?**

$_____ $_____

3.4. Make: _____

Model: _____

Year: _____

Approximate mileage: _____

Other information:

Who has an interest in the property? Check one.

❑ Debtor 1 only

❑ Debtor 2 only

❑ Debtor 1 and Debtor 2 only

❑ At least one of the debtors and another

❑ **Check if this is community property** (see instructions)

Do not deduct secured claims or exemptions. Put the amount of any secured claims on *Schedule D: Creditors Who Have Claims Secured by Property.*

Current value of the entire property?   **Current value of the portion you own?**

$_____ $_____

4. **Watercraft, aircraft, motor homes, ATVs and other recreational vehicles, other vehicles, and accessories**

Examples: Boats, trailers, motors, personal watercraft, fishing vessels, snowmobiles, motorcycle accessories

❑ No

❑ Yes

4.1. Make: _____

Model: _____

Year: _____

Other information:

Who has an interest in the property? Check one.

❑ Debtor 1 only

❑ Debtor 2 only

❑ Debtor 1 and Debtor 2 only

❑ At least one of the debtors and another

❑ **Check if this is community property** (see instructions)

Do not deduct secured claims or exemptions. Put the amount of any secured claims on *Schedule D: Creditors Who Have Claims Secured by Property.*

Current value of the entire property?   **Current value of the portion you own?**

$_____ $_____

If you own or have more than one, list here:

4.2. Make: _____

Model: _____

Year: _____

Other information:

Who has an interest in the property? Check one.

❑ Debtor 1 only

❑ Debtor 2 only

❑ Debtor 1 and Debtor 2 only

❑ At least one of the debtors and another

❑ **Check if this is community property** (see instructions)

Do not deduct secured claims or exemptions. Put the amount of any secured claims on *Schedule D: Creditors Who Have Claims Secured by Property.*

Current value of the entire property?   **Current value of the portion you own?**

$_____ $_____

5. **Add the dollar value of the portion you own for all of your entries from Part 2, including any entries for pages you have attached for Part 2. Write that number here** ....➔ $_____

Part 3: Describe Your Personal and Household Items

Do you own or have any legal or equitable interest in any of the following items?

Current value of the portion you own?
Do not deduct secured claims or exemptions.

6. **Household goods and furnishings**

    Examples: Major appliances, furniture, linens, china, kitchenware

    ❑ No
    ❑ Yes. Describe......... $_____

7. **Electronics**

    Examples: Televisions and radios; audio, video, stereo, and digital equipment; computers, printers, scanners; music collections; electronic devices including cell phones, cameras, media players, games

    ❑ No
    ❑ Yes. Describe.......... $_____

8. **Collectibles of value**

    Examples: Antiques and figurines; paintings, prints, or other artwork; books, pictures, or other art objects; stamp, coin, or baseball card collections; other collections, memorabilia, collectibles

    ❑ No
    ❑ Yes. Describe.......... $_____

9. **Equipment for sports and hobbies**

    Examples: Sports, photographic, exercise, and other hobby equipment; bicycles, pool tables, golf clubs, skis; canoes and kayaks; carpentry tools; musical instruments

    ❑ No
    ❑ Yes. Describe.......... $_____

10. **Firearms**

    Examples: Pistols, rifles, shotguns, ammunition, and related equipment

    ❑ No
    ❑ Yes. Describe.......... $_____

11. **Clothes**

    Examples: Everyday clothes, furs, leather coats, designer wear, shoes, accessories

    ❑ No
    ❑ Yes. Describe.......... $_____

12. **Jewelry**

    Examples: Everyday jewelry, costume jewelry, engagement rings, wedding rings, heirloom jewelry, watches, gems, gold, silver

    ❑ No
    ❑ Yes. Describe.......... $_____

13. **Non-farm animals**

    Examples: Dogs, cats, birds, horses

    ❑ No
    ❑ Yes. Describe.......... $_____

14. **Any other personal and household items you did not already list, including any health aids you did not list**

    ❑ No
    ❑ Yes. Give specific information. .... $_____

15. **Add the dollar value of all of your entries from Part 3, including any entries for pages you have attached for Part 3. Write that number here** .... ➜ $_____

Part 4: Describe Your Financial Assets

Do you own or have any legal or equitable interest in any of the following?

Current value of the portion you own?
Do not deduct secured claims or exemptions.

16. Cash

Examples: Money you have in your wallet, in your home, in a safe deposit box, and on hand when you file your petition

❑ No
❑ Yes...   Cash: .... $_____

17. Deposits of money

Examples: Checking, savings, or other financial accounts; certificates of deposit; shares in credit unions, brokerage houses, and other similar institutions. If you have multiple accounts with the same institution, list each.

❑ No
❑ Yes ....   Institution name:

17.1. Checking account:	$_____
17.2. Checking account:	$_____
17.3. Savings account:	$_____
17.4. Savings account:	$_____
17.5. Certificates of deposit:	$_____
17.6. Other financial account:	$_____
17.7. Other financial account:	$_____
17.8. Other financial account:	$_____
17.9. Other financial account:	$_____

18. Bonds, mutual funds, or publicly traded stocks

Examples: Bond funds, investment accounts with brokerage firms, money market accounts

❑ No
❑ Yes ....   Institution or issuer name:

_____ $_____
_____ $_____
_____ $_____

19. Non-publicly traded stock and interests in incorporated and unincorporated businesses, including an interest in an LLC, partnership, and joint venture

❑ No   Name of entity: % of ownership:
❑ Yes. Give specific
information about
them........................

Name of entity:	% of ownership:	
_____	0% %	$_____
_____	0% %	$_____
_____	0% %	$_____

20. **Government and corporate bonds and other negotiable and non-negotiable instruments**

   Negotiable instruments include personal checks, cashiers' checks, promissory notes, and money orders.
   Non-negotiable instruments are those you cannot transfer to someone by signing or delivering them.

   ❏ No
   ❏ Yes. Give specific   Issuer name:
   information about
   them......................   _____ $_____
                              _____ $_____
                              _____ $_____

21. **Retirement or pension accounts**

   Examples: Interests in IRA, ERISA, Keogh, 401(k), 403(b), thrift savings accounts, or other pension or profit-sharing plans

   ❏ No
   ❏ Yes. List each   Type of account: Institution name:
   account separately.
                          401(k) or similar plan: _____ $_____
                          Pension plan: _____ $_____
                          IRA: _____ $_____
                          Retirement account: _____ $_____
                          Keogh: _____ $_____
                          Additional account: _____ $_____
                          Additional account: _____ $_____

22. **Security deposits and prepayments**

   Your share of all unused deposits you have made so that you may continue service or use from a company
   Examples: Agreements with landlords, prepaid rent, public utilities (electric, gas, water), telecommunications
   companies, or others

   ❏ No
   ❏ Yes.......................   Institution name or individual:
                          Electric: _____ $_____
                          Gas: _____ $_____
                          Heating oil: _____ $_____
                          Security deposit on rental unit: _____ $_____
                          Prepaid rent: _____ $_____
                          Telephone: _____ $_____
                          Water: _____ $_____
                          Rented furniture: _____ $_____
                          Other: _____ $_____

23. **Annuities** (A contract for a periodic payment of money to you, either for life or for a number of years)

   ❏ No
   ❏ Yes.......................   Issuer name and description:
                          _____ $_____
                          _____ $_____
                          _____ $_____

24. **Interests in an education IRA, in an account in a qualified ABLE program, or under a qualified state tuition program.**
26 U.S.C. §§ 530(b)(1), 529A(b), and 529(b)(1).

❑ No

❑ Yes ....   Institution name and description. Separately file the records of any interests.11 U.S.C. § 521(c):

_____ $_____

_____ $_____

_____ $_____

25. **Trusts, equitable or future interests in property (other than anything listed in line 1), and rights or powers exercisable for your benefit**

❑ No

❑ Yes. Give specific
information about them.... $_____

26. **Patents, copyrights, trademarks, trade secrets, and other intellectual property**
Examples: Internet domain names, websites, proceeds from royalties and licensing agreements

❑ No

❑ Yes. Give specific
information about them.... $_____

27. **Licenses, franchises, and other general intangibles**
Examples: Building permits, exclusive licenses, cooperative association holdings, liquor licenses, professional licenses

❑ No

❑ Yes. Give specific
information about them.... $_____

Money or property owed to you?   **Current value of the
portion you own?**
Do not deduct secured
claims or exemptions.

28. **Tax refunds owed to you**

❑ No

❑ Yes. Give specific information
about them, including whether   Federal: $_____
you already filed the returns   State: $_____
and the tax years. ....   Local: $_____

29. **Family support**
Examples: Past due or lump sum alimony, spousal support, child support, maintenance, divorce settlement, property settlement

❑ No

❑ Yes. Give specific information.............

Alimony: $_____
Maintenance: $_____
Support: $_____
Divorce settlement: $_____
Property settlement: $_____

30. **Other amounts someone owes you**
Examples: Unpaid wages, disability insurance payments, disability benefits, sick pay, vacation pay, workers' compensation,
Social Security benefits; unpaid loans you made to someone else

❑ No

❑ Yes. Give specific information.............

$_____

31. Interests in insurance policies

Examples: Health, disability, or life insurance; health savings account (HSA); credit, homeowner's, or renter's insurance

❑ No

❑ Yes. Name the insurance company
of each policy and list its value. ...

Company name:	Beneficiary:	Surrender or refund value:
_____	_____	$_____
_____	_____	$_____
_____	_____	$_____

32. Any interest in property that is due you from someone who has died

If you are the beneficiary of a living trust, expect proceeds from a life insurance policy, or are currently entitled to receive property because someone has died.

❑ No

❑ Yes. Give specific information............. [   ] $_____

33. Claims against third parties, whether or not you have filed a lawsuit or made a demand for payment

Examples: Accidents, employment disputes, insurance claims, or rights to sue

❑ No

❑ Yes. Describe each claim. .... [   ] $_____

34. Other contingent and unliquidated claims of every nature, including counterclaims of the debtor and rights to set off claims

❑ No

❑ Yes. Describe each claim. .... [   ] $_____

35. Any financial assets you did not already list

❑ No

❑ Yes. Give specific information............ [   ] $_____

36. Add the dollar value of all of your entries from Part 4, including any entries for pages you have attached for Part 4. Write that number here .... ➜ [$_____]

Part 5:   Describe Any Business-Related Property You Own or Have an Interest In. List any real estate in Part 1.

37. Do you own or have any legal or equitable interest in any business-related property?

❑ No. Go to Part 6.

❑ Yes. Go to line 38.

Current value of the portion you own?

Do not deduct secured claims or exemptions.

38. Accounts receivable or commissions you already earned

❑ No

❑ Yes. Describe....... [   ] $_____

39. Office equipment, furnishings, and supplies

Examples: Business-related computers, software, modems, printers, copiers, fax machines, rugs, telephones, desks, chairs, electronic devices

❑ No

❑ Yes. Describe....... [   ] $_____

40. Machinery, fixtures, equipment, supplies you use in business, and tools of your trade

❑ No
❑ Yes. Describe.......

$_____

41. Inventory

❑ No
❑ Yes. Describe.......

$_____

42. Interests in partnerships or joint ventures

❑ No
❑ Yes. Describe....... Name of entity: % of ownership:

_____ _____% $_____
_____ _____% $_____
_____ _____% $_____

43. Customer lists, mailing lists, or other compilations

❑ No
❑ Yes. **Do your lists include personally identifiable information** (as defined in 11 U.S.C. § 101(41A))**?**

    ❑ No
    ❑ Yes. Describe........

$_____

44. Any business-related property you did not already list

❑ No
❑ Yes. Give specific
information .... _____ $_____
_____ $_____
_____ $_____
_____ $_____
_____ $_____
_____ $_____

45. Add the dollar value of all of your entries from Part 5, including any entries for pages you have attached
for Part 5. Write that number here .... ➔ $_____

Part 6: **Describe Any Farm- and Commercial Fishing-Related Property You Own or Have an Interest In.**
If you own or have an interest in farmland, list it in Part 1.

46. Do you own or have any legal or equitable interest in any farm- or commercial fishing-related property?

❑ No. Go to Part 7.
❑ Yes. Go to line 47.

    **Current value of the
portion you own?**
Do not deduct secured claims
or exemptions.

47. Farm animals

Examples: Livestock, poultry, farm-raised fish

❑ No
❑ Yes.........................

$_____

48. **Crops—either growing or harvested**

   ❑ No
   ❑ Yes. Give specific
      information. .... [   ] $_____

49. **Farm and fishing equipment, implements, machinery, fixtures, and tools of trade**
   ❑ No
   ❑ Yes .... [   ] $_____

50. **Farm and fishing supplies, chemicals, and feed**

   ❑ No
   ❑ Yes .... [   ] $_____

51. **Any farm- and commercial fishing-related property you did not already list**
   ❑ No
   ❑ Yes. Give specific
      information. .... [   ] $_____

52. **Add the dollar value of all of your entries from Part 6, including any entries for pages you have attached
    for Part 6. Write that number here** ....   ➔ $_____

Part 7:   Describe All Property You Own or Have an Interest in That You Did Not List Above

53. **Do you have other property of any kind you did not already list?**
   Examples: Season tickets, country club membership

   ❑ No
   ❑ Yes. Give specific
      information. .... [   ] $_____
                                                                                                         $_____
                                                                                                         $_____

54. **Add the dollar value of all of your entries from Part 7. Write that number here** ....   ➔ $_____

Part 8:   List the Totals of Each Part of this Form

55. **Part 1: Total real estate, line 2** ....   ➔ $_____

56. **Part 2: Total vehicles, line 5** $_____

57. **Part 3: Total personal and household items, line 15** $_____

58. **Part 4: Total financial assets, line 36** $_____

59. **Part 5: Total business-related property, line 45** $_____

60. **Part 6: Total farm- and fishing-related property, line 52** $_____

61. **Part 7: Total other property not listed, line 54**   **+** $_____

62. **Total personal property.** Add lines 56 through 61. .... $_____   Copy personal property total ➔ **+** $_____

63. **Total of all property on Schedule A/B.** Add line 55 + line 62. .... $_____

Debtor 1 _____
               First Name   Middle Name   Last Name

Debtor 2 _____
(Spouse, if filing) First Name   Middle Name   Last Name

United States Bankruptcy Court for the: _____ District of _____

Case number _____
(If known)

☐ Check if this is an
    amended filing

Official Form 106C

Schedule C: The Property You Claim as Exempt   04/16

Be as complete and accurate as possible. If two married people are filing together, both are equally responsible for supplying correct information. Using the property you listed on *Schedule A/B: Property* (Official Form 106A/B) as your source, list the property that you claim as exempt. If more space is needed, fill out and attach to this page as many copies of *Part 2: Additional Page* as necessary. On the top of any additional pages, write your name and case number (if known).

For each item of property you claim as exempt, you must specify the amount of the exemption you claim. One way of doing so is to state a specific dollar amount as exempt. Alternatively, you may claim the full fair market value of the property being exempted up to the amount of any applicable statutory limit. Some exemptions—such as those for health aids, rights to receive certain benefits, and tax-exempt retirement funds—may be unlimited in dollar amount. However, if you claim an exemption of 100% of fair market value under a law that limits the exemption to a particular dollar amount and the value of the property is determined to exceed that amount, your exemption would be limited to the applicable statutory amount.

Part 1: Identify the Property You Claim as Exempt

1. **Which set of exemptions are you claiming?** *Check one only, even if your spouse is filing with you.*

   ☐ You are claiming state and federal nonbankruptcy exemptions. 11 U.S.C. § 522(b)(3)

   ☐ You are claiming federal exemptions. 11 U.S.C. § 522(b)(2)

2. **For any property you list on *Schedule A/B* that you claim as exempt, fill in the information below.**

Brief description of the property and line on *Schedule A/B* that lists this property	Current value of the portion you own Copy the value from *Schedule A/B*	Amount of the exemption you claim *Check only one box for each exemption.*	Specific laws that allow exemption
Brief description: _____ Line from *Schedule A/B*: _____	$_____	☐ $ _____ ☐ 100% of fair market value, up to any applicable statutory limit	_____
Brief description: _____ Line from *Schedule A/B*: _____	$_____	☐ $ _____ ☐ 100% of fair market value, up to any applicable statutory limit	_____
Brief description: _____ Line from *Schedule A/B*: _____	$_____	☐ $ _____ ☐ 100% of fair market value, up to any applicable statutory limit	_____

3. **Are you claiming a homestead exemption of more than $160,375?**

   (Subject to adjustment on 4/01/19 and every 3 years after that for cases filed on or after the date of adjustment.)

   ☐ No

   ☐ Yes. Did you acquire the property covered by the exemption within 1,215 days before you filed this case?

        ☐ No

        ☐ Yes

Part 2: Additional Page

Brief description of the property and line on *Schedule A/B* that lists this property	Current value of the portion you own Copy the value from *Schedule A/B*	Amount of the exemption you claim *Check only one box for each exemption*	Specific laws that allow exemption
Brief description: _____ Line from *Schedule A/B*: _____	$_____	❏ $ _____ ❏ 100% of fair market value, up to any applicable statutory limit	_____
Brief description: _____ Line from *Schedule A/B*: _____	$_____	❏ $ _____ ❏ 100% of fair market value, up to any applicable statutory limit	_____
Brief description: _____ Line from *Schedule A/B*: _____	$_____	❏ $ _____ ❏ 100% of fair market value, up to any applicable statutory limit	_____
Brief description: _____ Line from *Schedule A/B*: _____	$_____	❏ $ _____ ❏ 100% of fair market value, up to any applicable statutory limit	_____
Brief description: _____ Line from *Schedule A/B*: _____	$_____	❏ $ _____ ❏ 100% of fair market value, up to any applicable statutory limit	_____
Brief description: _____ Line from *Schedule A/B*: _____	$_____	❏ $ _____ ❏ 100% of fair market value, up to any applicable statutory limit	_____
Brief description: _____ Line from *Schedule A/B*: _____	$_____	❏ $ _____ ❏ 100% of fair market value, up to any applicable statutory limit	_____
Brief description: _____ Line from *Schedule A/B*: _____	$_____	❏ $ _____ ❏ 100% of fair market value, up to any applicable statutory limit	_____
Brief description: _____ Line from *Schedule A/B*: _____	$_____	❏ $ _____ ❏ 100% of fair market value, up to any applicable statutory limit	_____
Brief description: _____ Line from *Schedule A/B*: _____	$_____	❏ $ _____ ❏ 100% of fair market value, up to any applicable statutory limit	_____
Brief description: _____ Line from *Schedule A/B*: _____	$_____	❏ $ _____ ❏ 100% of fair market value, up to any applicable statutory limit	_____
Brief description: _____ Line from *Schedule A/B*: _____	$_____	❏ $ _____ ❏ 100% of fair market value, up to any applicable statutory limit	_____

Fill in this information to identify your case:

Debtor 1 _____
First Name   Middle Name   Last Name

Debtor 2 _____
(Spouse, if filing) First Name   Middle Name   Last Name

United States Bankruptcy Court for the: _____ District of _____

Case number _____
(If known)

☐ Check if this is an
   amended filing

Official Form 106D

Schedule D: Creditors Who Have Claims Secured by Property   12/15

Be as complete and accurate as possible. If two married people are filing together, both are equally responsible for supplying correct information. If more space is needed, copy the Additional Page, fill it out, number the entries, and attach it to this form. On the top of any additional pages, write your name and case number (if known).

1. **Do any creditors have claims secured by your property?**

   ☐ No. Check this box and submit this form to the court with your other schedules. You have nothing else to report on this form.

   ☐ Yes. Fill in all of the information below.

Part 1:   List All Secured Claims

2. **List all secured claims.** If a creditor has more than one secured claim, list the creditor separately for each claim. If more than one creditor has a particular claim, list the other creditors in Part 2. As much as possible, list the claims in alphabetical order according to the creditor's name.

	Column A **Amount of claim** Do not deduct the value of collateral.	Column B **Value of collateral** that supports this claim	Column C **Unsecured** portion If any

2.1 _____

Describe the property that secures the claim:

Column A: $_____ Column B: $_____ Column C: $_____

Creditor's Name

Number   Street

_____

_____
City   State   ZIP Code

As of the date you file, the claim is: Check all that apply.
☐ Contingent
☐ Unliquidated
☐ Disputed

Who owes the debt? Check one.

☐ Debtor 1 only
☐ Debtor 2 only
☐ Debtor 1 and Debtor 2 only
☐ At least one of the debtors and another

☐ Check if this claim relates to a
   community debt

Date debt was incurred _____

Nature of lien. Check all that apply.

☐ An agreement you made (such as mortgage or secured
   car loan)
☐ Statutory lien (such as tax lien, mechanic's lien)
☐ Judgment lien from a lawsuit
☐ Other (including a right to offset) _____

Last 4 digits of account number ___ ___ ___ ___

2.2 _____

Describe the property that secures the claim:

Column A: $_____ Column B: $_____ Column C: $_____

Creditor's Name

Number   Street

_____

_____
City   State   ZIP Code

As of the date you file, the claim is: Check all that apply.
☐ Contingent
☐ Unliquidated
☐ Disputed

Who owes the debt? Check one.

☐ Debtor 1 only
☐ Debtor 2 only
☐ Debtor 1 and Debtor 2 only
☐ At least one of the debtors and another

☐ Check if this claim relates to a
   community debt

Date debt was incurred _____

Nature of lien. Check all that apply.

☐ An agreement you made (such as mortgage or secured
   car loan)
☐ Statutory lien (such as tax lien, mechanic's lien)
☐ Judgment lien from a lawsuit
☐ Other (including a right to offset) _____

Last 4 digits of account number ___ ___ ___ ___

Add the dollar value of your entries in Column A on this page. Write that number here: $_____

| Part 1: | **Additional Page**
After listing any entries on this page, number them beginning with 2.3, followed by 2.4, and so forth. | *Column A*
Amount of claim
Do not deduct the value of collateral. | *Column B*
Value of collateral that supports this claim | *Column C*
Unsecured portion
If any |

☐

_____
Creditor's Name

_____
Number   Street

_____

_____
City   State   ZIP Code

Who owes the debt? Check one.

☐ Debtor 1 only
☐ Debtor 2 only
☐ Debtor 1 and Debtor 2 only
☐ At least one of the debtors and another

☐ **Check if this claim relates to a community debt**

Date debt was incurred _____

Describe the property that secures the claim:

[ ]

As of the date you file, the claim is: Check all that apply.
☐ Contingent
☐ Unliquidated
☐ Disputed

Nature of lien. Check all that apply.
☐ An agreement you made (such as mortgage or secured car loan)
☐ Statutory lien (such as tax lien, mechanic's lien)
☐ Judgment lien from a lawsuit
☐ Other (including a right to offset) _____

Last 4 digits of account number ___ ___ ___ ___

$_____ $_____ $_____

☐

_____
Creditor's Name

_____
Number   Street

_____

_____
City   State   ZIP Code

Who owes the debt? Check one.

☐ Debtor 1 only
☐ Debtor 2 only
☐ Debtor 1 and Debtor 2 only
☐ At least one of the debtors and another

☐ **Check if this claim relates to a community debt**

Date debt was incurred _____

Describe the property that secures the claim:

[ ]

As of the date you file, the claim is: Check all that apply.
☐ Contingent
☐ Unliquidated
☐ Disputed

Nature of lien. Check all that apply.
☐ An agreement you made (such as mortgage or secured car loan)
☐ Statutory lien (such as tax lien, mechanic's lien)
☐ Judgment lien from a lawsuit
☐ Other (including a right to offset) _____

Last 4 digits of account number ___ ___ ___ ___

$_____ $_____ $_____

☐

_____
Creditor's Name

_____
Number   Street

_____

_____
City   State   ZIP Code

Who owes the debt? Check one.

☐ Debtor 1 only
☐ Debtor 2 only
☐ Debtor 1 and Debtor 2 only
☐ At least one of the debtors and another

☐ **Check if this claim relates to a community debt**

Date debt was incurred _____

Describe the property that secures the claim:

[ ]

As of the date you file, the claim is: Check all that apply.
☐ Contingent
☐ Unliquidated
☐ Disputed

Nature of lien. Check all that apply.
☐ An agreement you made (such as mortgage or secured car loan)
☐ Statutory lien (such as tax lien, mechanic's lien)
☐ Judgment lien from a lawsuit
☐ Other (including a right to offset) _____

Last 4 digits of account number ___ ___ ___ ___

$_____ $_____ $_____

Add the dollar value of your entries in Column A on this page. Write that number here: $_____

If this is the last page of your form, add the dollar value totals from all pages.
Write that number here: $_____

Debtor 1 _____   Case number (*if known*)_____
         First Name   Middle Name   Last Name

Use this page only if you have others to be notified about your bankruptcy for a debt that you already listed in Part 1. For example, if a collection agency is trying to collect from you for a debt you owe to someone else, list the creditor in Part 1, and then list the collection agency here. Similarly, if you have more than one creditor for any of the debts that you listed in Part 1, list the additional creditors here. If you do not have additional persons to be notified for any debts in Part 1, do not fill out or submit this page.

☐ _____   On which line in Part 1 did you enter the creditor? _____
   Name

                                                            Last 4 digits of account number ___ ___ ___ ___
   _____
   Number   Street

   _____

   _____
   City   State   ZIP Code

☐ _____   On which line in Part 1 did you enter the creditor? _____
   Name

                                                            Last 4 digits of account number ___ ___ ___ ___
   _____
   Number   Street

   _____

   _____
   City   State   ZIP Code

☐ _____   On which line in Part 1 did you enter the creditor? _____
   Name

                                                            Last 4 digits of account number ___ ___ ___ ___
   _____
   Number   Street

   _____

   _____
   City   State   ZIP Code

☐ _____   On which line in Part 1 did you enter the creditor? _____
   Name

                                                            Last 4 digits of account number ___ ___ ___ ___
   _____
   Number   Street

   _____

   _____
   City   State   ZIP Code

☐ _____   On which line in Part 1 did you enter the creditor? _____
   Name

                                                            Last 4 digits of account number ___ ___ ___ ___
   _____
   Number   Street

   _____

   _____
   City   State   ZIP Code

☐ _____   On which line in Part 1 did you enter the creditor? _____
   Name

                                                            Last 4 digits of account number ___ ___ ___ ___
   _____
   Number   Street

   _____

   _____
   City   State   ZIP Code

Debtor 1 _____
First Name   Middle Name   Last Name

Debtor 2 _____
(Spouse, if filing) First Name   Middle Name   Last Name

United States Bankruptcy Court for the: _____ District of _____

Case number _____
(If known)

❑ Check if this is an amended filing

Official Form 106E/F

Schedule E/F: Creditors Who Have Unsecured Claims   12/15

Be as complete and accurate as possible. Use Part 1 for creditors with PRIORITY claims and Part 2 for creditors with NONPRIORITY claims. List the other party to any executory contracts or unexpired leases that could result in a claim. Also list executory contracts on *Schedule A/B: Property* (Official Form 106A/B) and on *Schedule G: Executory Contracts and Unexpired Leases* (Official Form 106G). Do not include any creditors with partially secured claims that are listed in *Schedule D: Creditors Who Have Claims Secured by Property*. If more space is needed, copy the Part you need, fill it out, number the entries in the boxes on the left. Attach the Continuation Page to this page. On the top of any additional pages, write your name and case number (if known).

Part 1:   List All of Your PRIORITY Unsecured Claims

1. Do any creditors have priority unsecured claims against you?

   ❑ No. Go to Part 2.

   ❑ Yes.

2. List all of your priority unsecured claims. If a creditor has more than one priority unsecured claim, list the creditor separately for each claim. For each claim listed, identify what type of claim it is. If a claim has both priority and nonpriority amounts, list that claim here and show both priority and nonpriority amounts. As much as possible, list the claims in alphabetical order according to the creditor's name. If you have more than two priority unsecured claims, fill out the Continuation Page of Part 1. If more than one creditor holds a particular claim, list the other creditors in Part 3.

(For an explanation of each type of claim, see the instructions for this form in the instruction booklet.)

	Total claim	Priority amount	Nonpriority amount

2.1 _____
Priority Creditor's Name

_____
Number   Street

_____

_____
City   State   ZIP Code

Who incurred the debt? Check one.
❑ Debtor 1 only
❑ Debtor 2 only
❑ Debtor 1 and Debtor 2 only
❑ At least one of the debtors and another
❑ Check if this claim is for a community debt

Is the claim subject to offset?
❑ No
❑ Yes

Last 4 digits of account number ___ ___ ___ ___ $_____ $_____ $_____

When was the debt incurred? _____

As of the date you file, the claim is: Check all that apply
❑ Contingent
❑ Unliquidated
❑ Disputed

Type of PRIORITY unsecured claim:
❑ Domestic support obligations
❑ Taxes and certain other debts you owe the government
❑ Claims for death or personal injury while you were intoxicated
❑ Other. Specify _____

2.2 _____
Priority Creditor's Name

_____
Number   Street

_____

_____
City   State   ZIP Code

Who incurred the debt? Check one.
❑ Debtor 1 only
❑ Debtor 2 only
❑ Debtor 1 and Debtor 2 only
❑ At least one of the debtors and another
❑ Check if this claim is for a community debt

Is the claim subject to offset?
❑ No
❑ Yes

Last 4 digits of account number ___ ___ ___ ___ $_____ $_____ $_____

When was the debt incurred? _____

As of the date you file, the claim is: Check all that apply
❑ Contingent
❑ Unliquidated
❑ Disputed

Type of PRIORITY unsecured claim:
❑ Domestic support obligations
❑ Taxes and certain other debts you owe the government
❑ Claims for death or personal injury while you were intoxicated
❑ Other. Specify _____

Part 1:   Your PRIORITY Unsecured Claims — Continuation Page

After listing any entries on this page, number them beginning with 2.3, followed by 2.4, and so forth.

	Total claim	Priority amount	Nonpriority amount

_____
Priority Creditor's Name

_____
Number   Street

_____

_____
City   State   ZIP Code

Who incurred the debt? Check one.

❑ Debtor 1 only
❑ Debtor 2 only
❑ Debtor 1 and Debtor 2 only
❑ At least one of the debtors and another

❑ Check if this claim is for a community debt

Is the claim subject to offset?

❑ No
❑ Yes

Last 4 digits of account number ___ ___ ___ ___ $_____ $_____ $_____

When was the debt incurred? _____

As of the date you file, the claim is: Check all that apply.

❑ Contingent
❑ Unliquidated
❑ Disputed

Type of PRIORITY unsecured claim:

❑ Domestic support obligations
❑ Taxes and certain other debts you owe the government
❑ Claims for death or personal injury while you were intoxicated
❑ Other. Specify _____

_____
Priority Creditor's Name

_____
Number   Street

_____

_____
City   State   ZIP Code

Who incurred the debt? Check one.

❑ Debtor 1 only
❑ Debtor 2 only
❑ Debtor 1 and Debtor 2 only
❑ At least one of the debtors and another

❑ Check if this claim is for a community debt

Is the claim subject to offset?

❑ No
❑ Yes

Last 4 digits of account number ___ ___ ___ ___ $_____ $_____ $_____

When was the debt incurred? _____

As of the date you file, the claim is: Check all that apply.

❑ Contingent
❑ Unliquidated
❑ Disputed

Type of PRIORITY unsecured claim:

❑ Domestic support obligations
❑ Taxes and certain other debts you owe the government
❑ Claims for death or personal injury while you were intoxicated
❑ Other. Specify _____

_____
Priority Creditor's Name

_____
Number   Street

_____

_____
City   State   ZIP Code

Who incurred the debt? Check one.

❑ Debtor 1 only
❑ Debtor 2 only
❑ Debtor 1 and Debtor 2 only
❑ At least one of the debtors and another

❑ Check if this claim is for a community debt

Is the claim subject to offset?

❑ No
❑ Yes

Last 4 digits of account number ___ ___ ___ ___ $_____ $_____ $_____

When was the debt incurred? _____

As of the date you file, the claim is: Check all that apply.

❑ Contingent
❑ Unliquidated
❑ Disputed

Type of PRIORITY unsecured claim:

❑ Domestic support obligations
❑ Taxes and certain other debts you owe the government
❑ Claims for death or personal injury while you were intoxicated
❑ Other. Specify _____

Debtor 1 _____   Case number *(if known)*_____
         First Name   Middle Name   Last Name

3. **Do any creditors have nonpriority unsecured claims against you?**

    ❑ No. You have nothing to report in this part. Submit this form to the court with your other schedules.

    ❑ Yes

4. **List all of your nonpriority unsecured claims in the alphabetical order of the creditor who holds each claim.** If a creditor has more than one nonpriority unsecured claim, list the creditor separately for each claim. For each claim listed, identify what type of claim it is. Do not list claims already included in Part 1. If more than one creditor holds a particular claim, list the other creditors in Part 3.If you have more than three nonpriority unsecured claims fill out the Continuation Page of Part 2.

                                                                                   Total claim

4.1   _____   **Last 4 digits of account number** ___ ___ ___ ___ $_____

     Nonpriority Creditor's Name   **When was the debt incurred?**   _____

     _____

     Number   Street

     _____   **As of the date you file, the claim is:** Check all that apply.

     City   State   ZIP Code

                                         ❑ Contingent

     Who incurred the debt? Check one.   ❑ Unliquidated

     ❑ Debtor 1 only   ❑ Disputed

     ❑ Debtor 2 only

     ❑ Debtor 1 and Debtor 2 only   **Type of NONPRIORITY unsecured claim:**

     ❑ At least one of the debtors and another

                                         ❑ Student loans

     ❑ **Check if this claim is for a community debt**   ❑ Obligations arising out of a separation agreement or divorce that you did not report as priority claims

     Is the claim subject to offset?   ❑ Debts to pension or profit-sharing plans, and other similar debts

     ❑ No   ❑ Other. Specify _____

     ❑ Yes

4.2   _____   **Last 4 digits of account number** ___ ___ ___ ___ $_____

     Nonpriority Creditor's Name   **When was the debt incurred?**   _____

     _____

     Number   Street

     _____   **As of the date you file, the claim is:** Check all that apply.

     City   State   ZIP Code

                                         ❑ Contingent

     Who incurred the debt? Check one.   ❑ Unliquidated

     ❑ Debtor 1 only   ❑ Disputed

     ❑ Debtor 2 only

     ❑ Debtor 1 and Debtor 2 only   **Type of NONPRIORITY unsecured claim:**

     ❑ At least one of the debtors and another

                                         ❑ Student loans

     ❑ **Check if this claim is for a community debt**   ❑ Obligations arising out of a separation agreement or divorce that you did not report as priority claims

     Is the claim subject to offset?   ❑ Debts to pension or profit-sharing plans, and other similar debts

     ❑ No   ❑ Other. Specify _____

     ❑ Yes

4.3   _____   **Last 4 digits of account number** ___ ___ ___ ___ $_____

     Nonpriority Creditor's Name   **When was the debt incurred?**   _____

     _____

     Number   Street

     _____   **As of the date you file, the claim is:** Check all that apply.

     City   State   ZIP Code

                                         ❑ Contingent

     Who incurred the debt? Check one.   ❑ Unliquidated

     ❑ Debtor 1 only   ❑ Disputed

     ❑ Debtor 2 only

     ❑ Debtor 1 and Debtor 2 only   **Type of NONPRIORITY unsecured claim:**

     ❑ At least one of the debtors and another

                                         ❑ Student loans

     ❑ **Check if this claim is for a community debt**   ❑ Obligations arising out of a separation agreement or divorce that you did not report as priority claims

     Is the claim subject to offset?   ❑ Debts to pension or profit-sharing plans, and other similar debts

     ❑ No   ❑ Other. Specify _____

     ❑ Yes

Part 2:   Your NONPRIORITY Unsecured Claims — Continuation Page

After listing any entries on this page, number them beginning with 4.4, followed by 4.5, and so forth.   Total claim

_____

Nonpriority Creditor's Name

_____

Number   Street

_____

City   State   ZIP Code

Who incurred the debt? Check one.

❑ Debtor 1 only
❑ Debtor 2 only
❑ Debtor 1 and Debtor 2 only
❑ At least one of the debtors and another

❑ Check if this claim is for a community debt

Is the claim subject to offset?

❑ No
❑ Yes

Last 4 digits of account number ___ ___ ___ ___ $_____

When was the debt incurred?   _____

As of the date you file, the claim is: Check all that apply.

❑ Contingent
❑ Unliquidated
❑ Disputed

Type of **NONPRIORITY** unsecured claim:

❑ Student loans
❑ Obligations arising out of a separation agreement or divorce that you did not report as priority claims
❑ Debts to pension or profit-sharing plans, and other similar debts
❑ Other. Specify_____

_____

Nonpriority Creditor's Name

_____

Number   Street

_____

City   State   ZIP Code

Who incurred the debt? Check one.

❑ Debtor 1 only
❑ Debtor 2 only
❑ Debtor 1 and Debtor 2 only
❑ At least one of the debtors and another

❑ Check if this claim is for a community debt

Is the claim subject to offset?

❑ No
❑ Yes

Last 4 digits of account number ___ ___ ___ ___ $_____

When was the debt incurred?   _____

As of the date you file, the claim is: Check all that apply.

❑ Contingent
❑ Unliquidated
❑ Disputed

Type of **NONPRIORITY** unsecured claim:

❑ Student loans
❑ Obligations arising out of a separation agreement or divorce that you did not report as priority claims
❑ Debts to pension or profit-sharing plans, and other similar debts
❑ Other. Specify_____

_____

Nonpriority Creditor's Name

_____

Number   Street

_____

City   State   ZIP Code

Who incurred the debt? Check one.

❑ Debtor 1 only
❑ Debtor 2 only
❑ Debtor 1 and Debtor 2 only
❑ At least one of the debtors and another

❑ Check if this claim is for a community debt

Is the claim subject to offset?

❑ No
❑ Yes

$_____

Last 4 digits of account number ___ ___ ___ ___

When was the debt incurred?   _____

As of the date you file, the claim is: Check all that apply.

❑ Contingent
❑ Unliquidated
❑ Disputed

Type of **NONPRIORITY** unsecured claim:

❑ Student loans
❑ Obligations arising out of a separation agreement or divorce that you did not report as priority claims
❑ Debts to pension or profit-sharing plans, and other similar debts
❑ Other. Specify_____

Part 3: **List Others to Be Notified About a Debt That You Already Listed**

5. Use this page only if you have others to be notified about your bankruptcy, for a debt that you already listed in Parts 1 or 2. For example, if a collection agency is trying to collect from you for a debt you owe to someone else, list the original creditor in Parts 1 or 2, then list the collection agency here. Similarly, if you have more than one creditor for any of the debts that you listed in Parts 1 or 2, list the additional creditors here. If you do not have additional persons to be notified for any debts in Parts 1 or 2, do not fill out or submit this page.

_____
Name

_____
Number   Street

_____

_____
City   State   ZIP Code

On which entry in Part 1 or Part 2 did you list the original creditor?

Line _____ of (Check one): ❑ Part 1: Creditors with Priority Unsecured Claims
                              ❑ Part 2: Creditors with Nonpriority Unsecured Claims

Last 4 digits of account number ___ ___ ___ ___

_____
Name

_____
Number   Street

_____

_____
City   State   ZIP Code

On which entry in Part 1 or Part 2 did you list the original creditor?

Line _____ of (Check one): ❑ Part 1: Creditors with Priority Unsecured Claims
                              ❑ Part 2: Creditors with Nonpriority Unsecured Claims

Last 4 digits of account number ___ ___ ___ ___

_____
Name

_____
Number   Street

_____

_____
City   State   ZIP Code

On which entry in Part 1 or Part 2 did you list the original creditor?

Line _____ of (Check one): ❑ Part 1: Creditors with Priority Unsecured Claims
                              ❑ Part 2: Creditors with Nonpriority Unsecured Claims

Last 4 digits of account number ___ ___ ___ ___

_____
Name

_____
Number   Street

_____

_____
City   State   ZIP Code

On which entry in Part 1 or Part 2 did you list the original creditor?

Line _____ of (Check one): ❑ Part 1: Creditors with Priority Unsecured Claims
                              ❑ Part 2: Creditors with Nonpriority Unsecured Claims

Last 4 digits of account number ___ ___ ___ ___

_____
Name

_____
Number   Street

_____

_____
City   State   ZIP Code

On which entry in Part 1 or Part 2 did you list the original creditor?

Line _____ of (Check one): ❑ Part 1: Creditors with Priority Unsecured Claims
                              ❑ Part 2: Creditors with Nonpriority Unsecured Claims

Last 4 digits of account number ___ ___ ___ ___

_____
Name

_____
Number   Street

_____

_____
City   State   ZIP Code

On which entry in Part 1 or Part 2 did you list the original creditor?

Line _____ of (Check one): ❑ Part 1: Creditors with Priority Unsecured Claims
                              ❑ Part 2: Creditors with Nonpriority Unsecured Claims

Last 4 digits of account number ___ ___ ___ ___

_____
Name

_____
Number   Street

_____

_____
City   State   ZIP Code

On which entry in Part 1 or Part 2 did you list the original creditor?

Line _____ of (Check one): ❑ Part 1: Creditors with Priority Unsecured Claims
                              ❑ Part 2: Creditors with Nonpriority Unsecured Claims

Last 4 digits of account number ___ ___ ___ ___

Part 4:	Add the Amounts for Each Type of Unsecured Claim

6. Total the amounts of certain types of unsecured claims. This information is for statistical reporting purposes only. 28 U.S.C. § 159.
   Add the amounts for each type of unsecured claim.

Total claim

Total claims from Part 1

6a. Domestic support obligations

6a. $_____

6b. Taxes and certain other debts you owe the government

6b. $_____

6c. Claims for death or personal injury while you were intoxicated

6c. $_____

6d. **Other.** Add all other priority unsecured claims. Write that amount here.

6d. **+** $_____

6e. **Total.** Add lines 6a through 6d.

6e.
$_____

Total claim

Total claims from Part 2

6f. Student loans

6f. $_____

6g. Obligations arising out of a separation agreement or divorce that you did not report as priority claims

6g. $_____

6h. Debts to pension or profit-sharing plans, and other similar debts

6h. $_____

6i. **Other.** Add all other nonpriority unsecured claims. Write that amount here.

6i. **+** $_____

6j. **Total.** Add lines 6f through 6i.

6j.
$_____

Fill in this information to identify your case:

Debtor _____
            First Name   Middle Name   Last Name

Debtor 2 _____
(Spouse If filing) First Name   Middle Name   Last Name

United States Bankruptcy Court for the: _____ District of _____

Case number _____
(If known)

❏ Check if this is an
   amended filing

Official Form 106G

Schedule G: Executory Contracts and Unexpired Leases   12/15

Be as complete and accurate as possible. If two married people are filing together, both are equally responsible for supplying correct information. If more space is needed, copy the additional page, fill it out, number the entries, and attach it to this page. On the top of any additional pages, write your name and case number (if known).

1. **Do you have any executory contracts or unexpired leases?**
   ❏ No. Check this box and file this form with the court with your other schedules. You have nothing else to report on this form.
   ❏ Yes. Fill in all of the information below even if the contracts or leases are listed on *Schedule A/B: Property* (Official Form 106A/B).

2. **List separately each person or company with whom you have the contract or lease. Then state what each contract or lease is for (for example, rent, vehicle lease, cell phone).** See the instructions for this form in the instruction booklet for more examples of executory contracts and unexpired leases.

Person or company with whom you have the contract or lease   **State what the contract or lease is for**

2.1 _____
    Name

    _____
    Number   Street

    _____
    City   State   ZIP Code

2.2 _____
    Name

    _____
    Number   Street

    _____
    City   State   ZIP Code

2.3 _____
    Name

    _____
    Number   Street

    _____
    City   State   ZIP Code

2.4 _____
    Name

    _____
    Number   Street

    _____
    City   State   ZIP Code

2.5 _____
    Name

    _____
    Number   Street

    _____
    City   State   ZIP Code

Additional Page if You Have More Contracts or Leases

Person or company with whom you have the contract or lease   **What the contract or lease is for**

2.2 _____
  Name

  _____
  Number   Street

  _____
  City   State   ZIP Code

2._ _____
  Name

  _____
  Number   Street

  _____
  City   State   ZIP Code

2._ _____
  Name

  _____
  Number   Street

  _____
  City   State   ZIP Code

2._ _____
  Name

  _____
  Number   Street

  _____
  City   State   ZIP Code

2._ _____
  Name

  _____
  Number   Street

  _____
  City   State   ZIP Code

2._ _____
  Name

  _____
  Number   Street

  _____
  City   State   ZIP Code

2._ _____
  Name

  _____
  Number   Street

  _____
  City   State   ZIP Code

2._ _____
  Name

  _____
  Number   Street

  _____
  City   State   ZIP Code

Debtor 1 _____
            First Name   Middle Name   Last Name

Debtor 2 _____
(Spouse, if filing) First Name   Middle Name   Last Name

United States Bankruptcy Court for the: _____ District of _____

Case number _____
(If known)

☐ Check if this is an amended filing

Official Form 106H

Schedule H: Your Codebtors

12/15

Codebtors are people or entities who are also liable for any debts you may have. Be as complete and accurate as possible. If two married people are filing together, both are equally responsible for supplying correct information. If more space is needed, copy the Additional Page, fill it out, and number the entries in the boxes on the left. Attach the Additional Page to this page. On the top of any Additional Pages, write your name and case number (if known). Answer every question.

1. **Do you have any codebtors?** (If you are filing a joint case, do not list either spouse as a codebtor.)

    ☐ No

    ☐ Yes

2. **Within the last 8 years, have you lived in a community property state or territory?** (*Community property states and territories* include Arizona, California, Idaho, Louisiana, Nevada, New Mexico, Puerto Rico, Texas, Washington, and Wisconsin.)

    ☐ No. Go to line 3.

    ☐ Yes. Did your spouse, former spouse, or legal equivalent live with you at the time?

        ☐ No

        ☐ Yes. In which community state or territory did you live? _____. Fill in the name and current address of that person.

        _____
        Name of your spouse, former spouse, or legal equivalent

        _____
        Number   Street

        _____
        City   State   ZIP Code

3. In Column 1, list all of your codebtors. Do not include your spouse as a codebtor if your spouse is filing with you. List the person shown in line 2 again as a codebtor only if that person is a guarantor or cosigner. Make sure you have listed the creditor on *Schedule D* (Official Form 106D), *Schedule E/F* (Official Form 106E/F), or *Schedule G* (Official Form 106G). Use *Schedule D, Schedule E/F, or Schedule G* to fill out Column 2.

    Column 1: **Your codebtor**   *Column 2:* **The creditor to whom you owe the debt**

                                                  Check all schedules that apply:

    3.1 _____

    Name

    _____
    Number   Street

    _____
    City   State   ZIP Code

    ☐ Schedule D, line _____
    ☐ Schedule E/F, line _____
    ☐ Schedule G, line _____

    3.2 _____

    Name

    _____
    Number   Street

    _____
    City   State   ZIP Code

    ☐ Schedule D, line _____
    ☐ Schedule E/F, line _____
    ☐ Schedule G, line _____

    3.3 _____

    Name

    _____
    Number   Street

    _____
    City   State   ZIP Code

    ☐ Schedule D, line _____
    ☐ Schedule E/F, line _____
    ☐ Schedule G, line _____

Debtor 1 _____   Case number (if known)_____
　　　　　　First Name　　Middle Name　　Last Name

Additional Page to List More Codebtors

Column 1: **Your codebtor**

Column 2: **The creditor to whom you owe the debt**

Check all schedules that apply:

3._

Name

Number   Street

City   State   ZIP Code

❑ Schedule D, line _____
❑ Schedule E/F, line _____
❑ Schedule G, line _____

3._

Name

Number   Street

City   State   ZIP Code

❑ Schedule D, line _____
❑ Schedule E/F, line _____
❑ Schedule G, line _____

3._

Name

Number   Street

City   State   ZIP Code

❑ Schedule D, line _____
❑ Schedule E/F, line _____
❑ Schedule G, line _____

3._

Name

Number   Street

City   State   ZIP Code

❑ Schedule D, line _____
❑ Schedule E/F, line _____
❑ Schedule G, line _____

3._

Name

Number   Street

City   State   ZIP Code

❑ Schedule D, line _____
❑ Schedule E/F, line _____
❑ Schedule G, line _____

3._

Name

Number   Street

City   State   ZIP Code

❑ Schedule D, line _____
❑ Schedule E/F, line _____
❑ Schedule G, line _____

3._

Name

Number   Street

City   State   ZIP Code

❑ Schedule D, line _____
❑ Schedule E/F, line _____
❑ Schedule G, line _____

3._

Name

Number   Street

City   State   ZIP Code

❑ Schedule D, line _____
❑ Schedule E/F, line _____
❑ Schedule G, line _____

Fill in this information to identify your case:

Debtor 1 _____
         First Name   Middle Name   Last Name

Debtor 2 _____
(Spouse, if filing) First Name   Middle Name   Last Name

United States Bankruptcy Court for the: _____ District of _____

Case number _____
(If known)

Check if this is:

❑ An amended filing

❑ A supplement showing postpetition chapter 13 income as of the following date:

_____
MM / DD / YYYY

Official Form 106I _____

Schedule I: Your Income

12/15

Be as complete and accurate as possible. If two married people are filing together (Debtor 1 and Debtor 2), both are equally responsible for supplying correct information. If you are married and not filing jointly, and your spouse is living with you, include information about your spouse. If you are separated and your spouse is not filing with you, do not include information about your spouse. If more space is needed, attach a separate sheet to this form. On the top of any additional pages, write your name and case number (if known). Answer every question.

Part 1: Describe Employment

1. **Fill in your employment information.**

   If you have more than one job, attach a separate page with information about additional employers.

   Include part-time, seasonal, or self-employed work.

   Occupation may include student or homemaker, if it applies.

	Debtor 1	Debtor 2 or non-filing spouse
Employment status	❑ Employed ❑ Not employed	❑ Employed ❑ Not employed
Occupation	_____	_____
Employer's name	_____	_____
Employer's address	_____ Number Street	_____ Number Street
	_____	_____
	_____	_____
	_____ City State ZIP Code	_____ City State ZIP Code
How long employed there?	_____	_____

Part 2: Give Details About Monthly Income

Estimate monthly income as of the date you file this form. If you have nothing to report for any line, write $0 in the space. Include your non-filing spouse unless you are separated.

If you or your non-filing spouse have more than one employer, combine the information for all employers for that person on the lines below. If you need more space, attach a separate sheet to this form.

		For Debtor 1	For Debtor 2 or non-filing spouse
2.	**List monthly gross wages, salary, and commissions** (before all payroll deductions). If not paid monthly, calculate what the monthly wage would be.	2. $_____	$_____
3.	**Estimate and list monthly overtime pay.**	3. +$_____	+$_____
4.	**Calculate gross income.** Add line 2 + line 3.	4. $_____	$_____

Debtor 1 _____   Case number (if known)_____
         First Name   Middle Name   Last Name

	For Debtor 1	For Debtor 2 or non-filing spouse
Copy line 4 here... → 4.	$_____	$_____

5. List all payroll deductions:

		For Debtor 1	For Debtor 2 or non-filing spouse
5a. Tax, Medicare, and Social Security deductions	5a.	$_____	$_____
5b. Mandatory contributions for retirement plans	5b.	$_____	$_____
5c. Voluntary contributions for retirement plans	5c.	$_____	$_____
5d. Required repayments of retirement fund loans	5d.	$_____	$_____
5e. Insurance	5e.	$_____	$_____
5f. Domestic support obligations	5f.	$_____	$_____
5g. Union dues	5g.	$_____	$_____
5h. Other deductions. Specify: _____	5h.	+ $_____	+ $_____
6. Add the payroll deductions. Add lines 5a + 5b + 5c + 5d + 5e +5f + 5g + 5h.	6.	$_____	$_____
7. Calculate total monthly take-home pay. Subtract line 6 from line 4.	7.	$_____	$_____

8. List all other income regularly received:

8a. **Net income from rental property and from operating a business, profession, or farm**

Attach a statement for each property and business showing gross receipts, ordinary and necessary business expenses, and the total monthly net income.

		For Debtor 1	For Debtor 2 or non-filing spouse
	8a.	$_____	$_____
8b. Interest and dividends	8b.	$_____	$_____

8c. **Family support payments that you, a non-filing spouse, or a dependent regularly receive**

Include alimony, spousal support, child support, maintenance, divorce settlement, and property settlement.

		For Debtor 1	For Debtor 2 or non-filing spouse
	8c.	$_____	$_____
8d. Unemployment compensation	8d.	$_____	$_____
8e. Social Security	8e.	$_____	$_____

8f. **Other government assistance that you regularly receive**

Include cash assistance and the value (if known) of any non-cash assistance that you receive, such as food stamps (benefits under the Supplemental Nutrition Assistance Program) or housing subsidies.

Specify: _____

		For Debtor 1	For Debtor 2 or non-filing spouse
	8f.	$_____	$_____
8g. Pension or retirement income	8g.	$_____	$_____
8h. Other monthly income. Specify: _____	8h.	+ $_____	+ $_____
9. Add all other income. Add lines 8a + 8b + 8c + 8d + 8e + 8f +8g + 8h.	9.	$_____	$_____
10. Calculate monthly income. Add line 7 + line 9. Add the entries in line 10 for Debtor 1 and Debtor 2 or non-filing spouse.	10.	$_____ +	$_____ = $_____

11. **State all other regular contributions to the expenses that you list in *Schedule J*.**

Include contributions from an unmarried partner, members of your household, your dependents, your roommates, and other friends or relatives.

Do not include any amounts already included in lines 2-10 or amounts that are not available to pay expenses listed in *Schedule J*.

Specify: _____   11. + $_____

12. **Add the amount in the last column of line 10 to the amount in line 11.** The result is the combined monthly income.

Write that amount on the *Summary of Your Assets and Liabilities and Certain Statistical Information*, if it applies   12. $_____

Combined monthly income

13. **Do you expect an increase or decrease within the year after you file this form?**

☐ No.

☐ Yes. Explain: _____

Debtor 1 _____
First Name   Middle Name   Last Name

Debtor 2
(Spouse, if filing) First Name   Middle Name   Last Name

United States Bankruptcy Court for the: _____ District of _____

Case number _____
(If known)

Check if this is:

☐ An amended filing
☐ A supplement showing postpetition chapter 13 expenses as of the following date:
_____
MM / DD / YYYY

Official Form 106J

Schedule J: Your Expenses

12/15

Be as complete and accurate as possible. If two married people are filing together, both are equally responsible for supplying correct information. If more space is needed, attach another sheet to this form. On the top of any additional pages, write your name and case number (if known). Answer every question.

Part 1: Describe Your Household

1. **Is this a joint case?**

   ☐ No. Go to line 2.
   ☐ Yes. **Does Debtor 2 live in a separate household?**

      ☐ No
      ☐ Yes. Debtor 2 must file Official Form 106J-2, *Expenses for Separate Household of Debtor 2.*

2. **Do you have dependents?**

   Do not list Debtor 1 and Debtor 2.

   Do not state the dependents' names.

   ☐ No
   ☐ Yes. Fill out this information for each dependent..........................

Dependent's relationship to Debtor 1 or Debtor 2	Dependent's age	Does dependent live with you?
_____	_____	☐ No ☐ Yes
_____	_____	☐ No ☐ Yes
_____	_____	☐ No ☐ Yes
_____	_____	☐ No ☐ Yes
_____	_____	☐ No ☐ Yes

3. **Do your expenses include expenses of people other than yourself and your dependents?**

   ☐ No
   ☐ Yes

Part 2: Estimate Your Ongoing Monthly Expenses

Estimate your expenses as of your bankruptcy filing date unless you are using this form as a supplement in a Chapter 13 case to report expenses as of a date after the bankruptcy is filed. If this is a supplemental *Schedule J*, check the box at the top of the form and fill in the applicable date.

Include expenses paid for with non-cash government assistance if you know the value of such assistance and have included it on *Schedule I: Your Income* (Official Form 106I.)

Your expenses

4. **The rental or home ownership expenses for your residence.** Include first mortgage payments and any rent for the ground or lot.

   4. $_____

   If not included in line 4:

   4a. Real estate taxes   4a. $_____

   4b. Property, homeowner's, or renter's insurance   4b. $_____

   4c. Home maintenance, repair, and upkeep expenses   4c. $_____

   4d. Homeowner's association or condominium dues   4d. $_____

Your expenses

5. **Additional mortgage payments for your residence**, such as home equity loans   5. $_____

6. **Utilities:**

    6a. Electricity, heat, natural gas   6a. $_____

    6b. Water, sewer, garbage collection   6b. $_____

    6c. Telephone, cell phone, Internet, satellite, and cable services   6c. $_____

    6d. Other. Specify: _____   6d. $_____

7. **Food and housekeeping supplies**   7. $_____

8. **Childcare and children's education costs**   8. $_____

9. **Clothing, laundry, and dry cleaning**   9. $_____

10. **Personal care products and services**   10. $_____

11. **Medical and dental expenses**   11. $_____

12. **Transportation.** Include gas, maintenance, bus or train fare.
Do not include car payments.   12. $_____

13. **Entertainment, clubs, recreation, newspapers, magazines, and books**   13. $_____

14. **Charitable contributions and religious donations**   14. $_____

15. **Insurance.**
Do not include insurance deducted from your pay or included in lines 4 or 20.

    15a. Life insurance   15a. $_____

    15b. Health insurance   15b. $_____

    15c. Vehicle insurance   15c. $_____

    15d. Other insurance. Specify:_____   15d. $_____

16. **Taxes.** Do not include taxes deducted from your pay or included in lines 4 or 20.
Specify: _____   16. $_____

17. **Installment or lease payments:**

    17a. Car payments for Vehicle 1   17a. $_____

    17b. Car payments for Vehicle 2   17b. $_____

    17c. Other. Specify:_____   17c. $_____

    17d. Other. Specify:_____   17d. $_____

18. **Your payments of alimony, maintenance, and support that you did not report as deducted from
your pay on line 5, *Schedule I, Your Income* (Official Form 106I).**   18. $_____

19. **Other payments you make to support others who do not live with you.**
Specify:_____   19. $_____

20. **Other real property expenses not included in lines 4 or 5 of this form or on *Schedule I: Your Income*.**

    20a. Mortgages on other property   20a. $_____

    20b. Real estate taxes   20b. $_____

    20c. Property, homeowner's, or renter's insurance   20c. $_____

    20d. Maintenance, repair, and upkeep expenses   20d. $_____

    20e. Homeowner's association or condominium dues   20e. $_____

21. **Other**. Specify: _____   21.   **+**$_____

22. **Calculate your monthly expenses.**

    22a. Add lines 4 through 21.   22a. $_____

    22b. Copy line 22 (monthly expenses for Debtor 2), if any, from Official Form 106J-2   22b. $_____

    22c. Add line 22a and 22b. The result is your monthly expenses.   22c. $_____

23. **Calculate your monthly net income.**

    23a.   Copy line 12 (*your combined monthly income*) from *Schedule I.*   23a. $_____

    23b.   Copy your monthly expenses from line 22c above.   23b.   **–** $_____

    23c.   Subtract your monthly expenses from your monthly income.
        The result is your *monthly net income.*   23c. $_____

24. **Do you expect an increase or decrease in your expenses within the year after you file this form?**

    For example, do you expect to finish paying for your car loan within the year or do you expect your mortgage payment to increase or decrease because of a modification to the terms of your mortgage?

    ❏ No.
    ❏ Yes.   Explain here:

Fill in this information to identify your case:

Debtor 1 _____
         First Name   Middle Name   Last Name

Debtor 2 _____
(Spouse, if filing) First Name   Middle Name   Last Name

United States Bankruptcy Court for the: _____ District of _____

Case number _____
(If known)

☐ Check if this is an
  amended filing

Official Form 106Dec

Declaration About an Individual Debtor's Schedules   12/15

If two married people are filing together, both are equally responsible for supplying correct information.

You must file this form whenever you file bankruptcy schedules or amended schedules. Making a false statement, concealing property, or obtaining money or property by fraud in connection with a bankruptcy case can result in fines up to $250,000, or imprisonment for up to 20 years, or both. 18 U.S.C. §§ 152, 1341, 1519, and 3571.

Sign Below

Did you pay or agree to pay someone who is NOT an attorney to help you fill out bankruptcy forms?

☐ No

☐ Yes. Name of person_____. Attach *Bankruptcy Petition Preparer's Notice, Declaration, and*
                                                                          Signature (Official Form 119).

Under penalty of perjury, I declare that I have read the summary and schedules filed with this declaration and that they are true and correct.

✗ _____   ✗ _____
Signature of Debtor 1   Signature of Debtor 2

Date _____   Date _____
     MM / DD / YYYY   MM / DD / YYYY

Debtor 1 _____
          First Name   Middle Name   Last Name

Debtor 2 _____
(Spouse, if filing) First Name   Middle Name   Last Name

United States Bankruptcy Court for the: _____ District of _____

Case number _____
(If known)

❑ Check if this is an
   amended filing

Official Form 107

Statement of Financial Affairs for Individuals Filing for Bankruptcy   04/16

Be as complete and accurate as possible. If two married people are filing together, both are equally responsible for supplying correct information. If more space is needed, attach a separate sheet to this form. On the top of any additional pages, write your name and case number (if known). Answer every question.

| Part 1: | Give Details About Your Marital Status and Where You Lived Before |

1. What is your current marital status?

❑ Married
❑ Not married

2. During the last 3 years, have you lived anywhere other than where you live now?

❑ No
❑ Yes. List all of the places you lived in the last 3 years. Do not include where you live now.

Debtor 1:	Dates Debtor 1 lived there	Debtor 2:	Dates Debtor 2 lived there
		❑ Same as Debtor 1	❑ Same as Debtor 1
_____ Number Street	From _____ To _____	_____ Number Street	From _____ To _____
_____ City State ZIP Code		_____ City State ZIP Code	
		❑ Same as Debtor 1	❑ Same as Debtor 1
_____ Number Street	From _____ To _____	_____ Number Street	From _____ To _____
_____ City State ZIP Code		_____ City State ZIP Code	

3. Within the last 8 years, did you ever live with a spouse or legal equivalent in a community property state or territory? (*Community property states and territories* include Arizona, California, Idaho, Louisiana, Nevada, New Mexico, Puerto Rico, Texas, Washington, and Wisconsin.)

❑ No
❑ Yes. Make sure you fill out *Schedule H: Your Codebtors* (Official Form 106H).

| Part 2: | Explain the Sources of Your Income |

4. **Did you have any income from employment or from operating a business during this year or the two previous calendar years?**

   Fill in the total amount of income you received from all jobs and all businesses, including part-time activities.

   If you are filing a joint case and you have income that you receive together, list it only once under Debtor 1.

   ☐ No
   ☐ Yes. Fill in the details.

	Debtor 1		Debtor 2	
	Sources of income Check all that apply.	Gross income (before deductions and exclusions)	Sources of income Check all that apply.	Gross income (before deductions and exclusions)
From January 1 of current year until the date you filed for bankruptcy:	☐ Wages, commissions, bonuses, tips ☐ Operating a business	$_____	☐ Wages, commissions, bonuses, tips ☐ Operating a business	$_____
For last calendar year: (January 1 to December 31, _____) YYYY	☐ Wages, commissions, bonuses, tips ☐ Operating a business	$_____	☐ Wages, commissions, bonuses, tips ☐ Operating a business	$_____
For the calendar year before that: (January 1 to December 31, _____) YYYY	☐ Wages, commissions, bonuses, tips ☐ Operating a business	$_____	☐ Wages, commissions, bonuses, tips ☐ Operating a business	$_____

5. **Did you receive any other income during this year or the two previous calendar years?**

   Include income regardless of whether that income is taxable. Examples of *other income* are alimony; child support; Social Security, unemployment, and other public benefit payments; pensions; rental income; interest; dividends; money collected from lawsuits; royalties; and gambling and lottery winnings. If you are filing a joint case and you have income that you received together, list it only once under Debtor 1.

   List each source and the gross income from each source separately. Do not include income that you listed in line 4.

   ☐ No
   ☐ Yes. Fill in the details.

	Debtor 1		Debtor 2	
	Sources of income Describe below.	Gross income from each source (before deductions and exclusions)	Sources of income Describe below.	Gross income from each source (before deductions and exclusions)
From January 1 of current year until the date you filed for bankruptcy:	_____ _____ _____	$_____ $_____ $_____	_____ _____ _____	$_____ $_____ $_____
For last calendar year: (January 1 to December 31, _____) YYYY	_____ _____ _____	$_____ $_____ $_____	_____ _____ _____	$_____ $_____ $_____
For the calendar year before that: (January 1 to December 31, _____) YYYY	_____ _____ _____	$_____ $_____ $_____	_____ _____ _____	$_____ $_____ $_____

Part 3: List Certain Payments You Made Before You Filed for Bankruptcy

6. **Are either Debtor 1's or Debtor 2's debts primarily consumer debts?**

   ❑ No. **Neither Debtor 1 nor Debtor 2 has primarily consumer debts.** *Consumer debts* are defined in 11 U.S.C. § 101(8) as "incurred by an individual primarily for a personal, family, or household purpose."

   During the 90 days before you filed for bankruptcy, did you pay any creditor a total of $6,425* or more?

   ❑ No. Go to line 7.

   ❑ Yes. List below each creditor to whom you paid a total of $6,425* or more in one or more payments and the total amount you paid that creditor. Do not include payments for domestic support obligations, such as child support and alimony. Also, do not include payments to an attorney for this bankruptcy case.

   * Subject to adjustment on 4/01/19 and every 3 years after that for cases filed on or after the date of adjustment.

   ❑ Yes. **Debtor 1 or Debtor 2 or both have primarily consumer debts.**

   During the 90 days before you filed for bankruptcy, did you pay any creditor a total of $600 or more?

   ❑ No. Go to line 7.

   ❑ Yes. List below each creditor to whom you paid a total of $600 or more and the total amount you paid that creditor. Do not include payments for domestic support obligations, such as child support and alimony. Also, do not include payments to an attorney for this bankruptcy case.

	Dates of payment	Total amount paid	Amount you still owe	Was this payment for...
_____ Creditor's Name	_____	$_____	$_____	❑ Mortgage ❑ Car
_____ Number Street	_____			❑ Credit card ❑ Loan repayment
_____	_____			❑ Suppliers or vendors
_____ City State ZIP Code				❑ Other _____
_____ Creditor's Name	_____	$_____	$_____	❑ Mortgage ❑ Car
_____ Number Street	_____			❑ Credit card ❑ Loan repayment
_____	_____			❑ Suppliers or vendors
_____ City State ZIP Code				❑ Other _____
_____ Creditor's Name	_____	$_____	$_____	❑ Mortgage ❑ Car
_____ Number Street	_____			❑ Credit card ❑ Loan repayment
_____	_____			❑ Suppliers or vendors
_____ City State ZIP Code				❑ Other _____

7. **Within 1 year before you filed for bankruptcy, did you make a payment on a debt you owed anyone who was an insider?**
   Insiders include your relatives; any general partners; relatives of any general partners; partnerships of which you are a general partner;
   corporations of which you are an officer, director, person in control, or owner of 20% or more of their voting securities; and any managing
   agent, including one for a business you operate as a sole proprietor. 11 U.S.C. § 101. Include payments for domestic support obligations,
   such as child support and alimony.

   ☐ No
   ☐ Yes. List all payments to an insider.

	Dates of payment	Total amount paid	Amount you still owe	Reason for this payment
_____ Insider's Name	_____	$_____	$_____	
_____ Number Street	_____			
_____	_____			
_____ City State ZIP Code				
_____ Insider's Name	_____	$_____	$_____	
_____ Number Street	_____			
_____	_____			
_____ City State ZIP Code				

8. **Within 1 year before you filed for bankruptcy, did you make any payments or transfer any property on account of a debt that benefited an insider?**
   Include payments on debts guaranteed or cosigned by an insider.

   ☐ No
   ☐ Yes. List all payments that benefited an insider.

	Dates of payment	Total amount paid	Amount you still owe	Reason for this payment Include creditor's name
_____ Insider's Name	_____	$_____	$_____	
_____ Number Street	_____			
_____	_____			
_____ City State ZIP Code				
_____ Insider's Name	_____	$_____	$_____	
_____ Number Street	_____			
_____	_____			
_____ City State ZIP Code				

Part 4: Identify Legal Actions, Repossessions, and Foreclosures

9. **Within 1 year before you filed for bankruptcy, were you a party in any lawsuit, court action, or administrative proceeding?**
List all such matters, including personal injury cases, small claims actions, divorces, collection suits, paternity actions, support or custody modifications, and contract disputes.

☐ No
☐ Yes. Fill in the details.

	Nature of the case	Court or agency	Status of the case
Case title_____ _____ Case number _____		Court Name _____ Number　Street _____ City　　　State　ZIP Code _____	☐ Pending ☐ On appeal ☐ Concluded
Case title_____ _____ Case number _____		Court Name _____ Number　Street _____ City　　　State　ZIP Code _____	☐ Pending ☐ On appeal ☐ Concluded

10. **Within 1 year before you filed for bankruptcy, was any of your property repossessed, foreclosed, garnished, attached, seized, or levied?**
Check all that apply and fill in the details below.

☐ No. Go to line 11.
☐ Yes. Fill in the information below.

	Describe the property	Date	Value of the property
_____ Creditor's Name _____ Number　Street _____ _____ City　　State　ZIP Code	 **Explain what happened** ☐ Property was repossessed. ☐ Property was foreclosed. ☐ Property was garnished. ☐ Property was attached, seized, or levied.	_____	$_____
_____ Creditor's Name _____ Number　Street _____ _____ City　　State　ZIP Code	 **Explain what happened** ☐ Property was repossessed. ☐ Property was foreclosed. ☐ Property was garnished. ☐ Property was attached, seized, or levied.	_____	$_____

11. Within 90 days before you filed for bankruptcy, did any creditor, including a bank or financial institution, set off any amounts from your accounts or refuse to make a payment because you owed a debt?

❏ No

❏ Yes. Fill in the details.

	Describe the action the creditor took	Date action was taken	Amount
_____ Creditor's Name			
_____ Number Street		_____	$_____
_____			
_____ City State ZIP Code	Last 4 digits of account number: XXXX–___ ___ ___ ___		

12. Within 1 year before you filed for bankruptcy, was any of your property in the possession of an assignee for the benefit of creditors, a court-appointed receiver, a custodian, or another official?

❏ No

❏ Yes

Part 5: List Certain Gifts and Contributions

13. Within 2 years before you filed for bankruptcy, did you give any gifts with a total value of more than $600 per person?

❏ No

❏ Yes. Fill in the details for each gift.

Gifts with a total value of more than $600 per person	Describe the gifts	Dates you gave the gifts	Value
_____ Person to Whom You Gave the Gift		_____	$_____
_____		_____	$_____
_____ Number Street			
_____ City State ZIP Code			
Person's relationship to you _____			

Gifts with a total value of more than $600 per person	Describe the gifts	Dates you gave the gifts	Value
_____ Person to Whom You Gave the Gift		_____	$_____
_____		_____	$_____
_____ Number Street			
_____ City State ZIP Code			
Person's relationship to you _____			

14. **Within 2 years before you filed for bankruptcy, did you give any gifts or contributions with a total value of more than $600 to any charity?**

☐ No
☐ Yes. Fill in the details for each gift or contribution.

Gifts or contributions to charities that total more than $600	Describe what you contributed	Date you contributed	Value
_____ Charity's Name		_____	$_____
_____		_____	$_____
_____ Number Street			
_____ City State ZIP Code			

Part 6:   List Certain Losses

15. **Within 1 year before you filed for bankruptcy or since you filed for bankruptcy, did you lose anything because of theft, fire, other disaster, or gambling?**

☐ No
☐ Yes. Fill in the details.

Describe the property you lost and how the loss occurred	Describe any insurance coverage for the loss Include the amount that insurance has paid. List pending insurance claims on line 33 of *Schedule A/B: Property*.	Date of your loss	Value of property lost
		_____	$_____

Part 7:   List Certain Payments or Transfers

16. **Within 1 year before you filed for bankruptcy, did you or anyone else acting on your behalf pay or transfer any property to anyone you consulted about seeking bankruptcy or preparing a bankruptcy petition?**
Include any attorneys, bankruptcy petition preparers, or credit counseling agencies for services required in your bankruptcy.

☐ No
☐ Yes. Fill in the details.

	Description and value of any property transferred	Date payment or transfer was made	Amount of payment
_____ Person Who Was Paid			
_____ Number Street		_____	$_____
_____		_____	$_____
_____ City State ZIP Code			
_____ Email or website address			
_____ Person Who Made the Payment, if Not You			

	Description and value of any property transferred	Date payment or transfer was made	Amount of payment

Person Who Was Paid _____

Number   Street _____

_____

City   State   ZIP Code

_____

Email or website address

_____

Person Who Made the Payment, if Not You

$_____

$_____

17. Within 1 year before you filed for bankruptcy, did you or anyone else acting on your behalf pay or transfer any property to anyone who promised to help you deal with your creditors or to make payments to your creditors?
Do not include any payment or transfer that you listed on line 16.

☐ No
☐ Yes. Fill in the details.

	Description and value of any property transferred	Date payment or transfer was made	Amount of payment

Person Who Was Paid _____

Number   Street _____

_____

City   State   ZIP Code

$_____

$_____

18. Within 2 years before you filed for bankruptcy, did you sell, trade, or otherwise transfer any property to anyone, other than property transferred in the ordinary course of your business or financial affairs?
Include both outright transfers and transfers made as security (such as the granting of a security interest or mortgage on your property).
Do not include gifts and transfers that you have already listed on this statement.

☐ No
☐ Yes. Fill in the details.

	Description and value of property transferred	Describe any property or payments received or debts paid in exchange	Date transfer was made

Person Who Received Transfer _____

Number   Street _____

_____

City   State   ZIP Code

Person's relationship to you _____

Person Who Received Transfer _____

Number   Street _____

_____

City   State   ZIP Code

Person's relationship to you _____

19. **Within 10 years before you filed for bankruptcy, did you transfer any property to a self-settled trust or similar device of which you are a beneficiary?** (These are often called *asset-protection devices*.)

❑ No
❑ Yes. Fill in the details.

	Description and value of the property transferred	Date transfer was made
Name of trust _____		_____

Part 8: List Certain Financial Accounts, Instruments, Safe Deposit Boxes, and Storage Units

20. **Within 1 year before you filed for bankruptcy, were any financial accounts or instruments held in your name, or for your benefit, closed, sold, moved, or transferred?**
    Include checking, savings, money market, or other financial accounts; certificates of deposit; shares in banks, credit unions, brokerage houses, pension funds, cooperatives, associations, and other financial institutions.

❑ No
❑ Yes. Fill in the details.

	Last 4 digits of account number	Type of account or instrument	Date account was closed, sold, moved, or transferred	Last balance before closing or transfer
Name of Financial Institution Number Street City State ZIP Code	XXXX–__ __ __ __	❑ Checking ❑ Savings ❑ Money market ❑ Brokerage ❑ Other_____	_____	$_____
Name of Financial Institution Number Street City State ZIP Code	XXXX–__ __ __ __	❑ Checking ❑ Savings ❑ Money market ❑ Brokerage ❑ Other_____	_____	$_____

21. **Do you now have, or did you have within 1 year before you filed for bankruptcy, any safe deposit box or other depository for securities, cash, or other valuables?**

❑ No
❑ Yes. Fill in the details.

	Who else had access to it?	Describe the contents	Do you still have it?
			❑ No ❑ Yes
Name of Financial Institution Number Street City State ZIP Code	Name Number Street City State ZIP Code		

22. Have you stored property in a storage unit or place other than your home within 1 year before you filed for bankruptcy?

❑ No
❑ Yes. Fill in the details.

	Who else has or had access to it?	Describe the contents	Do you still have it?
			❑ No
_____	_____		❑ Yes
Name of Storage Facility	Name		
_____	_____		
Number Street	Number Street		
_____	_____		
	City State ZIP Code		
City State ZIP Code			

Part 9:   Identify Property You Hold or Control for Someone Else

23. Do you hold or control any property that someone else owns? Include any property you borrowed from, are storing for, or hold in trust for someone.

❑ No
❑ Yes. Fill in the details.

	Where is the property?	Describe the property	Value
			$_____
_____			
Owner's Name			
_____	_____		
Number Street	Number Street		
	_____		
_____	City State ZIP Code		
City State ZIP Code			

Part 10:   Give Details About Environmental Information

For the purpose of Part 10, the following definitions apply:

▪ *Environmental law* means any federal, state, or local statute or regulation concerning pollution, contamination, releases of hazardous or toxic substances, wastes, or material into the air, land, soil, surface water, groundwater, or other medium, including statutes or regulations controlling the cleanup of these substances, wastes, or material.

▪ *Site* means any location, facility, or property as defined under any environmental law, whether you now own, operate, or utilize it or used to own, operate, or utilize it, including disposal sites.

▪ *Hazardous material* means anything an environmental law defines as a hazardous waste, hazardous substance, toxic substance, hazardous material, pollutant, contaminant, or similar term.

Report all notices, releases, and proceedings that you know about, regardless of when they occurred.

24. Has any governmental unit notified you that you may be liable or potentially liable under or in violation of an environmental law?

❑ No
❑ Yes. Fill in the details.

	Governmental unit	Environmental law, if you know it	Date of notice
			_____
_____	_____		
Name of site	Governmental unit		
_____	_____		
Number Street	Number Street		
_____	_____		
	City State ZIP Code		
_____			
City State ZIP Code			

25. Have you notified any governmental unit of any release of hazardous material?

❑ No

❑ Yes. Fill in the details.

	Governmental unit	Environmental law, if you know it	Date of notice
Name of site	Governmental unit		_____
Number Street	Number Street		
	City State ZIP Code		
City State ZIP Code			

26. Have you been a party in any judicial or administrative proceeding under any environmental law? Include settlements and orders.

❑ No

❑ Yes. Fill in the details.

	Court or agency	Nature of the case	Status of the case
Case title_____			❑ Pending
	Court Name		❑ On appeal
	Number Street		❑ Concluded
Case number	City State ZIP Code		

Part 11: Give Details About Your Business or Connections to Any Business

---

27. Within 4 years before you filed for bankruptcy, did you own a business or have any of the following connections to any business?

❑ A sole proprietor or self-employed in a trade, profession, or other activity, either full-time or part-time

❑ A member of a limited liability company (LLC) or limited liability partnership (LLP)

❑ A partner in a partnership

❑ An officer, director, or managing executive of a corporation

❑ An owner of at least 5% of the voting or equity securities of a corporation

❑ No. None of the above applies. Go to Part 12.

❑ Yes. Check all that apply above and fill in the details below for each business.

	Describe the nature of the business	Employer Identification number Do not include Social Security number or ITIN.
Business Name		EIN: __ __ – __ __ __ __ __ __ __
Number Street	Name of accountant or bookkeeper	Dates business existed
		From _____ To _____
City State ZIP Code	Describe the nature of the business	Employer Identification number Do not include Social Security number or ITIN.
Business Name		EIN: __ __ – __ __ __ __ __ __ __
Number Street	Name of accountant or bookkeeper	Dates business existed
		From _____ To _____
City State ZIP Code		

| | Describe the nature of the business | Employer Identification number
Do not include Social Security number or ITIN. |
|---|---|---|
| **Business Name** | | EIN: __ __ – __ __ __ __ __ __ __ |
| **Number   Street** | Name of accountant or bookkeeper | Dates business existed |
| | | |
| **City   State   ZIP Code** | | From _____ To _____ |

28. Within 2 years before you filed for bankruptcy, did you give a financial statement to anyone about your business? Include all financial institutions, creditors, or other parties.

❏ No
❏ Yes. Fill in the details below.

Date issued

_____   _____
Name   **MM / DD / YYYY**

_____
Number   Street

_____

_____
City   State   ZIP Code

Part 12:   Sign Below

I have read the answers on this *Statement of Financial Affairs* and any attachments, and I declare under penalty of perjury that the answers are true and correct. I understand that making a false statement, concealing property, or obtaining money or property by fraud in connection with a bankruptcy case can result in fines up to $250,000, or imprisonment for up to 20 years, or both.
18 U.S.C. §§ 152, 1341, 1519, and 3571.

✘ _____   ✘ _____

   Signature of Debtor 1   Signature of Debtor 2

   Date _____   Date _____

Did you attach additional pages to *Your Statement of Financial Affairs for Individuals Filing for Bankruptcy* (Official Form 107)?

❏ No
❏ Yes

Did you pay or agree to pay someone who is not an attorney to help you fill out bankruptcy forms?

❏ No
❏ Yes. Name of person_____. Attach the *Bankruptcy Petition Preparer's Notice, Declaration, and Signature* (Official Form 119).

Fill in this information to identify your case:

Debtor 1 _____
         First Name   Middle Name   Last Name

Debtor 2 _____
(Spouse, if filing) First Name   Middle Name   Last Name

United States Bankruptcy Court for the: _____ District of _____

Case number _____
(If known)

☐ Check if this is an
   amended filing

Official Form 108

Statement of Intention for Individuals Filing Under Chapter 7   12/15

If you are an individual filing under chapter 7, you must fill out this form if:
- creditors have claims secured by your property, or
- you have leased personal property and the lease has not expired.

You must file this form with the court within 30 days after you file your bankruptcy petition or by the date set for the meeting of creditors, whichever is earlier, unless the court extends the time for cause. You must also send copies to the creditors and lessors you list on the form.

If two married people are filing together in a joint case, both are equally responsible for supplying correct information. Both debtors must sign and date the form.

Be as complete and accurate as possible. If more space is needed, attach a separate sheet to this form. On the top of any additional pages, write your name and case number (if known).

Part 1:   List Your Creditors Who Have Secured Claims

1. For any creditors that you listed in Part 1 of *Schedule D: Creditors Who Have Claims Secured by Property* (Official Form 106D), fill in the information below.

Identify the creditor and the property that is collateral	What do you intend to do with the property that secures a debt?	Did you claim the property as exempt on Schedule C?
Creditor's name: Description of property securing debt:	☐ Surrender the property. ☐ Retain the property and redeem it. ☐ Retain the property and enter into a *Reaffirmation Agreement*. ☐ Retain the property and [explain]: _____ _____	☐ No ☐ Yes
Creditor's name: Description of property securing debt:	☐ Surrender the property. ☐ Retain the property and redeem it. ☐ Retain the property and enter into a *Reaffirmation Agreement*. ☐ Retain the property and [explain]: _____ _____	☐ No ☐ Yes
Creditor's name: Description of property securing debt:	☐ Surrender the property. ☐ Retain the property and redeem it. ☐ Retain the property and enter into a *Reaffirmation Agreement*. ☐ Retain the property and [explain]: _____ _____	☐ No ☐ Yes
Creditor's name: Description of property securing debt:	☐ Surrender the property. ☐ Retain the property and redeem it. ☐ Retain the property and enter into a *Reaffirmation Agreement*. ☐ Retain the property and [explain]: _____ _____	☐ No ☐ Yes

Part 2:   List Your Unexpired Personal Property Leases

For any unexpired personal property lease that you listed in *Schedule G: Executory Contracts and Unexpired Leases* (Official Form 106G), fill in the information below. Do not list real estate leases. *Unexpired leases* are leases that are still in effect; the lease period has not yet ended. You may assume an unexpired personal property lease if the trustee does not assume it. 11 U.S.C. § 365(p)(2).

Describe your unexpired personal property leases	Will the lease be assumed?
Lessor's name: Description of leased property:	☐ No ☐ Yes
Lessor's name: Description of leased property:	☐ No ☐ Yes
Lessor's name: Description of leased property:	☐ No ☐ Yes
Lessor's name: Description of leased property:	☐ No ☐ Yes
Lessor's name: Description of leased property:	☐ No ☐ Yes
Lessor's name: Description of leased property:	☐ No ☐ Yes
Lessor's name: Description of leased property:	☐ No ☐ Yes

Part 3:   Sign Below

Under penalty of perjury, I declare that I have indicated my intention about any property of my estate that secures a debt and any personal property that is subject to an unexpired lease.

✗ _____   ✗ _____
Signature of Debtor 1   Signature of Debtor 2

Date _____   Date _____
     MM / DD / YYYY   MM / DD / YYYY

Fill in this information to identify your case:

Debtor 1 _____
          First Name   Middle Name   Last Name

Debtor 2 _____
(Spouse, if filing) First Name   Middle Name   Last Name

United States Bankruptcy Court for the: _____ District of _____

Case number _____
(If known)

Check one box only as directed in this form and in Form 122A-1Supp:

❑ 1. There is no presumption of abuse.

❑ 2. The calculation to determine if a presumption of abuse applies will be made under *Chapter 7 Means Test Calculation* (Official Form 122A–2).

❑ 3. The Means Test does not apply now because of qualified military service but it could apply later.

❑ Check if this is an amended filing

Official Form 122A–1

Chapter 7 Statement of Your Current Monthly Income   12/15

Be as complete and accurate as possible. If two married people are filing together, both are equally responsible for being accurate. If more space is needed, attach a separate sheet to this form. Include the line number to which the additional information applies. On the top of any additional pages, write your name and case number (if known). If you believe that you are exempted from a presumption of abuse because you do not have primarily consumer debts or because of qualifying military service, complete and file *Statement of Exemption from Presumption of Abuse Under § 707(b)(2)* (Official Form 122A-1Supp) with this form.

Part 1: Calculate Your Current Monthly Income

1. **What is your marital and filing status?** Check one only.

   ❑ **Not married.** Fill out Column A, lines 2-11.

   ❑ **Married and your spouse is filing with you.** Fill out both Columns A and B, lines 2-11.

   ❑ **Married and your spouse is NOT filing with you. You and your spouse are:**

      ❑ **Living in the same household and are not legally separated.** Fill out both Columns A and B, lines 2-11.

      ❑ **Living separately or are legally separated.** Fill out Column A, lines 2-11; do not fill out Column B. By checking this box, you declare under penalty of perjury that you and your spouse are legally separated under nonbankruptcy law that applies or that you and your spouse are living apart for reasons that do not include evading the Means Test requirements. 11 U.S.C. § 707(b)(7)(B).

   Fill in the average monthly income that you received from all sources, derived during the 6 full months before you file this bankruptcy case. 11 U.S.C. § 101(10A). For example, if you are filing on September 15, the 6-month period would be March 1 through August 31. If the amount of your monthly income varied during the 6 months, add the income for all 6 months and divide the total by 6. Fill in the result. Do not include any income amount more than once. For example, if both spouses own the same rental property, put the income from that property in one column only. If you have nothing to report for any line, write $0 in the space.

	Column A Debtor 1	Column B Debtor 2 or non-filing spouse
2. **Your gross wages, salary, tips, bonuses, overtime, and commissions** (before all payroll deductions).	$_____	$_____
3. **Alimony and maintenance payments.** Do not include payments from a spouse if Column B is filled in.	$_____	$_____
4. **All amounts from any source which are regularly paid for household expenses of you or your dependents, including child support.** Include regular contributions from an unmarried partner, members of your household, your dependents, parents, and roommates. Include regular contributions from a spouse only if Column B is not filled in. Do not include payments you listed on line 3.	$_____	$_____

5. **Net income from operating a business, profession, or farm**

	Debtor 1	Debtor 2			
Gross receipts (before all deductions)	$_____	$_____			
Ordinary and necessary operating expenses	– $_____	– $_____			
Net monthly income from a business, profession, or farm	$_____	$_____	Copy here ➜	$_____	$_____

6. **Net income from rental and other real property**

	Debtor 1	Debtor 2			
Gross receipts (before all deductions)	$_____	$_____			
Ordinary and necessary operating expenses	– $_____	– $_____			
Net monthly income from rental or other real property	$_____	$_____	Copy here ➜	$_____	$_____

7. **Interest, dividends, and royalties** | | $_____ | $_____ |

	Column A Debtor 1	Column B Debtor 2 or non-filing spouse
8. **Unemployment compensation**	$_____	$_____

Do not enter the amount if you contend that the amount received was a benefit under the Social Security Act. Instead, list it here: .... ↓

For you .... $_____

For your spouse... $_____

	Column A Debtor 1	Column B
9. **Pension or retirement income.** Do not include any amount received that was a benefit under the Social Security Act.	$_____	$_____

10. **Income from all other sources not listed above.** Specify the source and amount. Do not include any benefits received under the Social Security Act or payments received as a victim of a war crime, a crime against humanity, or international or domestic terrorism. If necessary, list other sources on a separate page and put the total below.

	Column A	Column B
_____	$_____	$_____
_____	$_____	$_____
Total amounts from separate pages, if any.	+ $_____	+ $_____

11. **Calculate your total current monthly income.** Add lines 2 through 10 for each column. Then add the total for Column A to the total for Column B.

$_____ + $_____ = $_____
Total current
monthly income

Part 2: Determine Whether the Means Test Applies to You

12. **Calculate your current monthly income for the year.** Follow these steps:

12a. Copy your total current monthly income from line 11. .... Copy line 11 here → $_____

Multiply by 12 (the number of months in a year). x 12

12b. The result is your annual income for this part of the form. 12b. $_____

13. **Calculate the median family income that applies to you.** Follow these steps:

Fill in the state in which you live. [ ]

Fill in the number of people in your household. [ ]

Fill in the median family income for your state and size of household. .... 13. $_____

To find a list of applicable median income amounts, go online using the link specified in the separate instructions for this form. This list may also be available at the bankruptcy clerk's office.

14. **How do the lines compare?**

14a. ❑ Line 12b is less than or equal to line 13. On the top of page 1, check box 1, *There is no presumption of abuse.* Go to Part 3.

14b. ❑ Line 12b is more than line 13. On the top of page 1, check box 2, *The presumption of abuse is determined by Form 122A–2.* Go to Part 3 and fill out Form 122A–2.

Part 3: Sign Below

By signing here, I declare under penalty of perjury that the information on this statement and in any attachments is true and correct.

✗ _____   ✗ _____
Signature of Debtor 1   Signature of Debtor 2

Date _____   Date _____
MM / DD / YYYY   MM / DD / YYYY

If you checked line 14a, do NOT fill out or file Form 122A–2.

If you checked line 14b, fill out Form 122A–2 and file it with this form.

Fill in this information to identify your case:

Debtor 1 _____
First Name   Middle Name   Last Name

Debtor 2 _____
(Spouse, if filing) First Name   Middle Name   Last Name

United States Bankruptcy Court for the: _____ District of _____

Case number _____
(If known)

Official Form 122A–2

Chapter 7 Means Test Calculation   04/16

To fill out this form, you will need your completed copy of *Chapter 7 Statement of Your Current Monthly Income* (Official Form 122A-1).

Be as complete and accurate as possible. If two married people are filing together, both are equally responsible for being accurate. If more space is needed, attach a separate sheet to this form. Include the line number to which the additional information applies. On the top of any additional pages, write your name and case number (if known).

Part 1:	Determine Your Adjusted Income

1. Copy your total current monthly income. .... Copy line 11 from Official Form 122A-1 here ➔ .... $_____

2. **Did you fill out Column B in Part 1 of Form 122A–1?**

   ❑ No. Fill in $0 for the total on line 3.

   ❑ Yes. Is your spouse filing with you?

       ❑ No. Go to line 3.

       ❑ Yes. Fill in $0 for the total on line 3.

3. **Adjust your current monthly income by subtracting any part of your spouse's income not used to pay for the household expenses of you or your dependents.** Follow these steps:

   On line 11, Column B of Form 122A–1, was any amount of the income you reported for your spouse NOT regularly used for the household expenses of you or your dependents?

   ❑ No. Fill in 0 for the total on line 3.

   ❑ Yes. Fill in the information below:

State each purpose for which the income was used For example, the income is used to pay your spouse's tax debt or to support people other than you or your dependents	Fill in the amount you are subtracting from your spouse's income
_____	$_____
_____	$_____
_____	+ $_____
Total.	$_____ Copy total here ➔ — $_____

4. **Adjust your current monthly income.** Subtract the total on line 3 from line 1. $_____

Part 2:	**Calculate Your Deductions from Your Income**

The Internal Revenue Service (IRS) issues National and Local Standards for certain expense amounts. Use these amounts to answer the questions in lines 6-15. To find the IRS standards, go online using the link specified in the separate instructions for this form. This information may also be available at the bankruptcy clerk's office.

Deduct the expense amounts set out in lines 6-15 regardless of your actual expense. In later parts of the form, you will use some of your actual expenses if they are higher than the standards. Do not deduct any amounts that you subtracted from your spouse's income in line 3 and do not deduct any operating expenses that you subtracted from income in lines 5 and 6 of Form 122A–1.

If your expenses differ from month to month, enter the average expense.

Whenever this part of the form refers to *you*, it means both you and your spouse if Column B of Form 122A–1 is filled in.

5. **The number of people used in determining your deductions from income**

    Fill in the number of people who could be claimed as exemptions on your federal income tax return, plus the number of any additional dependents whom you support. This number may be different from the number of people in your household.

National Standards   You must use the IRS National Standards to answer the questions in lines 6-7.

6. **Food, clothing, and other items:** Using the number of people you entered in line 5 and the IRS National Standards, fill in the dollar amount for food, clothing, and other items. $_____

7. **Out-of-pocket health care allowance:** Using the number of people you entered in line 5 and the IRS National Standards, fill in the dollar amount for out-of-pocket health care. The number of people is split into two categories—people who are under 65 and people who are 65 or older—because older people have a higher IRS allowance for health care costs. If your actual expenses are higher than this IRS amount, you may deduct the additional amount on line 22.

People who are under 65 years of age

    7a.   Out-of-pocket health care allowance per person $_____

    7b.   Number of people who are under 65   X _____

    7c.   **Subtotal.** Multiply line 7a by line 7b. $_____   Copy here➡ $_____

People who are 65 years of age or older

    7d.   Out-of-pocket health care allowance per person $_____

    7e.   Number of people who are 65 or older   X _____

    7f.   **Subtotal.** Multiply line 7d by line 7e. $_____   Copy here➡ + $_____

    7g.   **Total.** Add lines 7c and 7f... $_____   Copy total here➡ $_____

Local Standards   You must use the IRS Local Standards to answer the questions in lines 8-15.

Based on information from the IRS, the U.S. Trustee Program has divided the IRS Local Standard for housing for bankruptcy purposes into two parts:

■ Housing and utilities – Insurance and operating expenses
■ Housing and utilities – Mortgage or rent expenses

To answer the questions in lines 8-9, use the U.S. Trustee Program chart.

To find the chart, go online using the link specified in the separate instructions for this form.
This chart may also be available at the bankruptcy clerk's office.

8. **Housing and utilities – Insurance and operating expenses:** Using the number of people you entered in line 5, fill in the dollar amount listed for your county for insurance and operating expenses. .... $_____

9. **Housing and utilities – Mortgage or rent expenses:**

   9a. Using the number of people you entered in line 5, fill in the dollar amount listed for your county for mortgage or rent expenses.. $_____

   9b. Total average monthly payment for all mortgages and other debts secured by your home.

   To calculate the total average monthly payment, add all amounts that are contractually due to each secured creditor in the 60 months after you file for bankruptcy. Then divide by 60.

Name of the creditor	Average monthly payment
_____	$_____
_____	$_____
_____	+ $_____
Total average monthly payment	$_____

   Copy here➡ – $_____   Repeat this amount on line 33a.

   9c. Net mortgage or rent expense.
   Subtract line 9b (*total average monthly payment*) from line 9a (*mortgage or rent expense*). If this amount is less than $0, enter $0. .... $_____ Copy here➡ $_____

10. **If you claim that the U.S. Trustee Program's division of the IRS Local Standard for housing is incorrect and affects the calculation of your monthly expenses, fill in any additional amount you claim.** $_____

    Explain why: _____
    _____

11. **Local transportation expenses:** Check the number of vehicles for which you claim an ownership or operating expense.

    ☐ 0. Go to line 14.
    ☐ 1. Go to line 12.
    ☐ 2 or more. Go to line 12.

12. **Vehicle operation expense:** Using the IRS Local Standards and the number of vehicles for which you claim the operating expenses, fill in the *Operating Costs* that apply for your Census region or metropolitan statistical area. $_____

13. **Vehicle ownership or lease expense:** Using the IRS Local Standards, calculate the net ownership or lease expense for each vehicle below. You may not claim the expense if you do not make any loan or lease payments on the vehicle. In addition, you may not claim the expense for more than two vehicles.

Vehicle 1   **Describe Vehicle 1:** _____

_____

13a. Ownership or leasing costs using IRS Local Standard. .... $_____

13b. Average monthly payment for all debts secured by Vehicle 1.
Do not include costs for leased vehicles.

To calculate the average monthly payment here and on line 13e, add all amounts that are contractually due to each secured creditor in the 60 months after you filed for bankruptcy. Then divide by 60.

Name of each creditor for Vehicle 1	Average monthly payment
_____	$_____
_____	+ $_____
Total average monthly payment	$_____

Copy here➡   − $_____   Repeat this amount on line 33b.

13c. Net Vehicle 1 ownership or lease expense
Subtract line 13b from line 13a. If this amount is less than $0, enter $0. .... $_____   Copy net Vehicle 1 expense here.....➡ $_____

Vehicle 2   **Describe Vehicle 2:** _____

_____

13d. Ownership or leasing costs using IRS Local Standard. .... $_____

13e. Average monthly payment for all debts secured by Vehicle 2.
Do not include costs for leased vehicles.

Name of each creditor for Vehicle 2	Average monthly payment
_____	$_____
_____	+ $_____
Total average monthly payment	$_____

Copy here➡   − $_____   Repeat this amount on line 33c.

13f. Net Vehicle 2 ownership or lease expense
Subtract line 13e from 13d. If this amount is less than $0, enter $0. .... $_____   Copy net Vehicle 2 expense here ...➡ $_____

14. **Public transportation expense**: If you claimed 0 vehicles in line 11, using the IRS Local Standards, fill in the *Public Transportation* expense allowance regardless of whether you use public transportation. $_____

15. **Additional public transportation expense:** If you claimed 1 or more vehicles in line 11 and if you claim that you may also deduct a public transportation expense, you may fill in what you believe is the appropriate expense, but you may not claim more than the IRS Local Standard for *Public Transportation*. $_____

Other Necessary Expenses   In addition to the expense deductions listed above, you are allowed your monthly expenses for the following IRS categories.

16. **Taxes:** The total monthly amount that you will actually owe for federal, state and local taxes, such as income taxes, self-employment taxes, Social Security taxes, and Medicare taxes. You may include the monthly amount withheld from your pay for these taxes. However, if you expect to receive a tax refund, you must divide the expected refund by 12 and subtract that number from the total monthly amount that is withheld to pay for taxes.

    Do not include real estate, sales, or use taxes.

    $_____

17. **Involuntary deductions:** The total monthly payroll deductions that your job requires, such as retirement contributions, union dues, and uniform costs.

    Do not include amounts that are not required by your job, such as voluntary 401(k) contributions or payroll savings.

    $_____

18. **Life insurance:** The total monthly premiums that you pay for your own term life insurance. If two married people are filing together, include payments that you make for your spouse's term life insurance. Do not include premiums for life insurance on your dependents, for a non-filing spouse's life insurance, or for any form of life insurance other than term.

    $_____

19. **Court-ordered payments:** The total monthly amount that you pay as required by the order of a court or administrative agency, such as spousal or child support payments.

    Do not include payments on past due obligations for spousal or child support. You will list these obligations in line 35.

    $_____

20. **Education:** The total monthly amount that you pay for education that is either required:

    ▪ as a condition for your job, or
    ▪ for your physically or mentally challenged dependent child if no public education is available for similar services.

    $_____

21. **Childcare:** The total monthly amount that you pay for childcare, such as babysitting, daycare, nursery, and preschool.

    Do not include payments for any elementary or secondary school education.

    $_____

22. **Additional health care expenses, excluding insurance costs:** The monthly amount that you pay for health care that is required for the health and welfare of you or your dependents and that is not reimbursed by insurance or paid by a health savings account. Include only the amount that is more than the total entered in line 7.
    Payments for health insurance or health savings accounts should be listed only in line 25.

    $_____

23. **Optional telephones and telephone services:** The total monthly amount that you pay for telecommunication services for you and your dependents, such as pagers, call waiting, caller identification, special long distance, or business cell phone service, to the extent necessary for your health and welfare or that of your dependents or for the production of income, if it is not reimbursed by your employer.

    Do not include payments for basic home telephone, internet and cell phone service. Do not include self-employment expenses, such as those reported on line 5 of Official Form 122A-1, or any amount you previously deducted.

    + $_____

24. **Add all of the expenses allowed under the IRS expense allowances.**
    Add lines 6 through 23.

    $_____

Additional Expense Deductions   These are additional deductions allowed by the Means Test.

Note: Do not include any expense allowances listed in lines 6-24.

25. **Health insurance, disability insurance, and health savings account expenses.** The monthly expenses for health insurance, disability insurance, and health savings accounts that are reasonably necessary for yourself, your spouse, or your dependents.

Health insurance	$_____
Disability insurance	$_____
Health savings account	+ $_____
Total	$_____

Copy total here➜ .... $_____

Do you actually spend this total amount?

❑ No. How much do you actually spend? $_____

❑ Yes

26. **Continuing contributions to the care of household or family members.** The actual monthly expenses that you will continue to pay for the reasonable and necessary care and support of an elderly, chronically ill, or disabled member of your household or member of your immediate family who is unable to pay for such expenses. These expenses may include contributions to an account of a qualified ABLE program. 26 U.S.C. § 529A(b). $_____

27. **Protection against family violence.** The reasonably necessary monthly expenses that you incur to maintain the safety of you and your family under the Family Violence Prevention and Services Act or other federal laws that apply. $_____

By law, the court must keep the nature of these expenses confidential.

28. **Additional home energy costs.** Your home energy costs are included in your insurance and operating expenses on line 8.

If you believe that you have home energy costs that are more than the home energy costs included in expenses on line 8, then fill in the excess amount of home energy costs. $_____

You must give your case trustee documentation of your actual expenses, and you must show that the additional amount claimed is reasonable and necessary.

29. **Education expenses for dependent children who are younger than 18.** The monthly expenses (not more than $160.42* per child) that you pay for your dependent children who are younger than 18 years old to attend a private or public elementary or secondary school. $_____

You must give your case trustee documentation of your actual expenses, and you must explain why the amount claimed is reasonable and necessary and not already accounted for in lines 6-23.

  * Subject to adjustment on 4/01/19, and every 3 years after that for cases begun on or after the date of adjustment.

30. **Additional food and clothing expense.** The monthly amount by which your actual food and clothing expenses are higher than the combined food and clothing allowances in the IRS National Standards. That amount cannot be more than 5% of the food and clothing allowances in the IRS National Standards. $_____

To find a chart showing the maximum additional allowance, go online using the link specified in the separate instructions for this form. This chart may also be available at the bankruptcy clerk's office.

You must show that the additional amount claimed is reasonable and necessary.

31. **Continuing charitable contributions.** The amount that you will continue to contribute in the form of cash or financial instruments to a religious or charitable organization. 26 U.S.C. § 170(c)(1)-(2).   + $_____

32. **Add all of the additional expense deductions.**
Add lines 25 through 31. $_____

Debtor 1 _____   Case number (if known)_____

First Name   Middle Name   Last Name

Deductions for Debt Payment

33. **For debts that are secured by an interest in property that you own, including home mortgages, vehicle loans, and other secured debt, fill in lines 33a through 33e.**

    To calculate the total average monthly payment, add all amounts that are contractually due to each secured creditor in the 60 months after you file for bankruptcy. Then divide by 60.

		Average monthly payment
Mortgages on your home:		
33a. Copy line 9b here ....➔		$_____
Loans on your first two vehicles:		
33b. Copy line 13b here. ....➔		$_____
33c. Copy line 13e here. ....➔		$_____

    33d. List other secured debts:

Name of each creditor for other secured debt	Identify property that secures the debt	Does payment include taxes or insurance?	
_____	_____	❑ No ❑ Yes	$_____
_____	_____	❑ No ❑ Yes	$_____
_____	_____	❑ No ❑ Yes	+ $_____

    33e. Total average monthly payment. Add lines 33a through 33d. .... $_____   Copy total here ➔ $_____

34. **Are any debts that you listed in line 33 secured by your primary residence, a vehicle, or other property necessary for your support or the support of your dependents?**

    ❑ No. Go to line 35.
    ❑ Yes. State any amount that you must pay to a creditor, in addition to the payments listed in line 33, to keep possession of your property (called the *cure amount*). Next, divide by 60 and fill in the information below.

Name of the creditor	Identify property that secures the debt	Total cure amount		Monthly cure amount
_____	_____	$_____	÷ 60 =	$_____
_____	_____	$_____	÷ 60 =	$_____
_____	_____	$_____	÷ 60 =	+ $_____
		Total		$_____ Copy total here ➔ $_____

35. **Do you owe any priority claims such as a priority tax, child support, or alimony — that are past due as of the filing date of your bankruptcy case?** 11 U.S.C. § 507.

    ❑ No. Go to line 36.
    ❑ Yes. Fill in the total amount of all of these priority claims. Do not include current or ongoing priority claims, such as those you listed in line 19.

    Total amount of all past-due priority claims .... $_____ ÷ 60 = $_____

36. **Are you eligible to file a case under Chapter 13?** 11 U.S.C. § 109(e).
For more information, go online using the link for *Bankruptcy Basics* specified in the separate instructions for this form. *Bankruptcy Basics* may also be available at the bankruptcy clerk's office.

- ❑ No.   Go to line 37.
- ❑ Yes. Fill in the following information.

    Projected monthly plan payment if you were filing under Chapter 13 $_____

    Current multiplier for your district as stated on the list issued by the Administrative Office of the United States Courts (for districts in Alabama and North Carolina) or by the Executive Office for United States Trustees (for all other districts).   X _____

    To find a list of district multipliers that includes your district, go online using the link specified in the separate instructions for this form. This list may also be available at the bankruptcy clerk's office.

    Average monthly administrative expense if you were filing under Chapter 13 $_____ Copy total here ➔ $_____

37. **Add all of the deductions for debt payment.**
Add lines 33e through 36. .... $_____

Total Deductions from Income

38. **Add all of the allowed deductions.**

Copy line 24, *All of the expenses allowed under IRS expense allowances* .... $_____

Copy line 32, *All of the additional expense deductions* .... $_____

Copy line 37, *All of the deductions for debt payment* .... + $_____

                          Total deductions $_____   Copy total here .... ➔ $_____

Part 3:   **Determine Whether There Is a Presumption of Abuse**

---

39. **Calculate monthly disposable income for 60 months**

    39a. Copy line 4, *adjusted current monthly income* ..... $_____

    39b. Copy line 38, *Total deductions* ....   − $_____

    39c. Monthly disposable income. 11 U.S.C. § 707(b)(2).
          Subtract line 39b from line 39a. $_____   Copy here ➔ $_____

          For the next 60 months (5 years)..   x 60

    39d. **Total.** Multiply line 39c by 60. .... $_____ Copy here ➔ $_____

40. **Find out whether there is a presumption of abuse.** Check the box that applies:

- ❑ **The line 39d is less than $7,700*.** On the top of page 1 of this form, check box 1, *There is no presumption of abuse.* Go to Part 5.

- ❑ **The line 39d is more than $12,850*.** On the top of page 1 of this form, check box 2, *There is a presumption of abuse.* You may fill out Part 4 if you claim special circumstances. Then go to Part 5.

- ❑ **The line 39d is at least $7,700*, but not more than $12,850*.** Go to line 41.

    * Subject to adjustment on 4/01/19, and every 3 years after that for cases filed on or after the date of adjustment.

41. 41a. **Fill in the amount of your total nonpriority unsecured debt.** If you filled out *A Summary of Your Assets and Liabilities and Certain Statistical Information Schedules* (Official Form 106Sum), you may refer to line 3b on that form.. $_____

                                                          x .25

     41b. **25% of your total nonpriority unsecured debt.** 11 U.S.C. § 707(b)(2)(A)(i)(I). Multiply line 41a by 0.25. .... $_____ Copy here→ $_____

42. **Determine whether the income you have left over after subtracting all allowed deductions is enough to pay 25% of your unsecured, nonpriority debt.**
Check the box that applies:

   ❏ **Line 39d is less than line 41b.** On the top of page 1 of this form, check box 1, *There is no presumption of abuse.* Go to Part 5.

   ❏ **Line 39d is equal to or more than line 41b.** On the top of page 1 of this form, check box 2, *There is a presumption of abuse.* You may fill out Part 4 if you claim special circumstances. Then go to Part 5.

Part 4:   **Give Details About Special Circumstances**

43. **Do you have any special circumstances that justify additional expenses or adjustments of current monthly income for which there is no reasonable alternative?** 11 U.S.C. § 707(b)(2)(B).

   ❏ No. Go to Part 5.

   ❏ Yes. Fill in the following information. All figures should reflect your average monthly expense or income adjustment for each item. You may include expenses you listed in line 25.

      You must give a detailed explanation of the special circumstances that make the expenses or income adjustments necessary and reasonable. You must also give your case trustee documentation of your actual expenses or income adjustments.

Give a detailed explanation of the special circumstances	Average monthly expense or income adjustment
_____	$_____
_____	$_____
_____	$_____
_____	$_____

Part 5:   **Sign Below**

By signing here, I declare under penalty of perjury that the information on this statement and in any attachments is true and correct.

✗ _____   ✗ _____
   Signature of Debtor 1   Signature of Debtor 2

   Date _____   Date _____
       MM / DD / YYYY   MM / DD / YYYY

Fill in this information to identify the case:

Debtor 1 _____
          First Name   Middle Name   Last Name

Debtor 2 _____
(Spouse, if filing) First Name   Middle Name   Last Name

United States Bankruptcy Court for the: _____ District of _____

Case number _____
(If known)

Official Form 423

Certification About a Financial Management Course

12/15

If you are an individual, you must take an approved course about personal financial management if:

- you filed for bankruptcy under chapter 7 or 13, or
- you filed for bankruptcy under chapter 11 and § 1141 (d)(3) applies.

In a joint case, each debtor must take the course. 11 U.S.C. §§ 727(a)(11) and 1328(g).

After you finish the course, the provider will give you a certificate. The provider may notify the court that you have completed the course. If the provider does notify the court, you need not file this form. If the provider does not notify the court, then Debtor 1 and Debtor 2 must each file this form with the certificate number before your debts will be discharged.

- If you filed under chapter 7 and you need to file this form, file it within 60 days after the first date set for the meeting of creditors under § 341 of the Bankruptcy Code.

- If you filed under chapter 11 or 13 and you need to file this form, file it before you make the last payment that your plan requires or before you file a motion for a discharge under § 1141(d)(5)(B) or § 1328(b) of the Bankruptcy Code. Fed. R. Bankr. P. 1007(c).

In some cases, the court can waive the requirement to take the financial management course. To have the requirement waived, you must file a motion with the court and obtain a court order.

Part 1: Tell the Court About the Required Course

You must check one:

❑ **I completed an approved course in personal financial management:**

Date I took the course _____
                         MM / DD / YYYY

Name of approved provider _____

Certificate number _____

❑ **I am not required to complete a course in personal financial management because the court has granted my motion for a waiver of the requirement based on** *(check one)*:

❑ **Incapacity.** I have a mental illness or a mental deficiency that makes me incapable of realizing or making rational decisions about finances.

❑ **Disability.** My physical disability causes me to be unable to complete a course in personal financial management in person, by phone, or through the internet, even after I reasonably tried to do so.

❑ **Active duty.** I am currently on active military duty in a military combat zone.

❑ **Residence.** I live in a district in which the United States trustee (or bankruptcy administrator) has determined that the approved instructional courses cannot adequately meet my needs.

Part 2: Sign Here

I certify that the information I have provided is true and correct.

_____   _____   Date _____
Signature of debtor named on certificate   Printed name of debtor   MM / DD / YYYY

United States Bankruptcy Court for the:

_____ District of _____

Case number (*If known*): _____

Official Form 121

Statement About Your Social Security Numbers

12/15

Use this form to tell the court about any Social Security or federal Individual Taxpayer Identification numbers you have used. Do not file this form as part of the public case file. This form must be submitted separately and must not be included in the court's public electronic records. Please consult local court procedures for submission requirements.

To protect your privacy, the court will not make this form available to the public. You should not include a full Social Security Number or Individual Taxpayer Number on any other document filed with the court. The court will make only the last four digits of your numbers known to the public. However, the full numbers will be available to your creditors, the U.S. Trustee or bankruptcy administrator, and the trustee assigned to your case.

Making a false statement, concealing property, or obtaining money or property by fraud in connection with a bankruptcy case can result in fines up to $250,000, or imprisonment for up to 20 years, or both. 18 U.S.C. §§ 152, 1341, 1519, and 3571.

Part 1: Tell the Court About Yourself and Your spouse if Your Spouse is Filing With You

	For Debtor 1:	For Debtor 2 (Only If Spouse Is Filing):
1. Your name	_____ First name	_____ First name
	_____ Middle name	_____ Middle name
	_____ Last name	_____ Last name

Part 2: Tell the Court About all of Your Social Security or Federal Individual Taxpayer Identification Numbers

2. All Social Security Numbers you have used

— — — — — — — — — —

— — — — — — — — — —

❏ You do not have a Social Security number.

❏ You do not have a Social Security number.

3. All federal Individual Taxpayer Identification Numbers (ITIN) you have used

9 _ _ _ _ _ _ _ _

9 _ _ _ _ _ _ _ _

9 _ _ _ _ _ _ _ _

9 _ _ _ _ _ _ _ _

❏ You do not have an ITIN.

❏ You do not have an ITIN.

Part 3: Sign Below

Under penalty of perjury, I declare that the information I have provided in this form is true and correct.

Under penalty of perjury, I declare that the information I have provided in this form is true and correct.

✗ _____
Signature of Debtor 1

✗ _____
Signature of Debtor 2

Date _____
MM / DD / YYYY

Date _____
MM / DD / YYYY

Information to identify the case:

Debtor 1 _____
First Name   Middle Name   Last Name

Debtor 2 _____
(Spouse, if filing) First Name   Middle Name   Last Name

United States Bankruptcy Court for the: _____ District of _____
(State)

Case number: _____

Last 4 digits of Social Security number or ITIN __ __ __ __

EIN __ __ - __ __ __ __ __ __ __

Last 4 digits of Social Security number or ITIN __ __ __ __

EIN __ __ - __ __ __ __ __ __ __

[Date case filed for chapter 7 _____
MM / DD / YYYY OR

[Date case filed in chapter _____ _____
MM / DD / YYYY

Date case converted to chapter 7 _____]
MM / DD / YYYY

Official Form 309A (For Individuals or Joint Debtors)

Notice of Chapter 7 Bankruptcy Case — No Proof of Claim Deadline   12/15

For the debtors listed above, a case has been filed under chapter 7 of the Bankruptcy Code. An order for relief has been entered.

This notice has important information about the case for creditors, debtors, and trustees, including information about the meeting of creditors and deadlines. Read both pages carefully.

The filing of the case imposed an automatic stay against most collection activities. This means that creditors generally may not take action to collect debts from the debtors or the debtors' property. For example, while the stay is in effect, creditors cannot sue, garnish wages, assert a deficiency, repossess property, or otherwise try to collect from the debtors. Creditors cannot demand repayment from debtors by mail, phone, or otherwise. Creditors who violate the stay can be required to pay actual and punitive damages and attorney's fees. Under certain circumstances, the stay may be limited to 30 days or not exist at all, although debtors can ask the court to extend or impose a stay.

The debtors are seeking a discharge. Creditors who assert that the debtors are not entitled to a discharge of any debts or who want to have a particular debt excepted from discharge may be required to file a complaint in the bankruptcy clerk's office within the deadlines specified in this notice. (See line 9 for more information.)

To protect your rights, consult an attorney. All documents filed in the case may be inspected at the bankruptcy clerk's office at the address listed below or through PACER (Public Access to Court Electronic Records at www.pacer.gov).

The staff of the bankruptcy clerk's office cannot give legal advice.

To help creditors correctly identify debtors, debtors submit full Social Security or Individual Taxpayer Identification Numbers, which may appear on a version of this notice. However, the full numbers must not appear on any document filed with the court.

Do not file this notice with any proof of claim or other filing in the case. Do not include more than the last four digits of a Social Security or Individual Taxpayer Identification Number in any document, including attachments, that you file with the court.

	About Debtor 1:	About Debtor 2:
1. **Debtor's full name**		
2. **All other names used in the last 8 years**		
3. **Address**		If Debtor 2 lives at a different address:
4. **Debtor's attorney** Name and address		Contact phone _____ Email _____
5. **Bankruptcy trustee** Name and address		Contact phone _____ Email _____

For more information, see page 2 ▶

6. **Bankruptcy clerk's office**

Documents in this case may be filed at this address.

You may inspect all records filed in this case at this office or online at www.pacer.gov.

Hours open _____

Contact phone _____

7. **Meeting of creditors**

Debtors must attend the meeting to be questioned under oath. In a joint case, both spouses must attend.

Creditors may attend, but are not required to do so.

_____ at _____

Date   Time

Location:

The meeting may be continued or adjourned to a later date. If so, the date will be on the court docket.

8. **Presumption of abuse**

If the presumption of abuse arises, you may have the right to file a motion to dismiss the case under 11 U.S.C. § 707(b). Debtors may rebut the presumption by showing special circumstances.

[The presumption of abuse does not arise.]

[The presumption of abuse arises.]

[Insufficient information has been filed to permit the clerk to determine whether the presumption of abuse arises. If more complete information is filed and shows that the presumption has arisen, the clerk will notify creditors.]

9. **Deadlines**

The bankruptcy clerk's office must receive these documents and any required filing fee by the following deadlines.

File by the deadline to object to discharge or to challenge whether certain debts are dischargeable:

You must file a complaint:

if you assert that the debtor is not entitled to receive a discharge of any debts under any of the subdivisions of 11 U.S.C. § 727(a)(2) through (7), or

if you want to have a debt excepted from discharge under 11 U.S.C. § 523(a)(2), (4), or (6).

You must file a motion if you assert that the discharge should be denied under § 727(a)(8) or (9).

Filing deadline: _____

Deadline to object to exemptions:

The law permits debtors to keep certain property as exempt. If you believe that the law does not authorize an exemption claimed, you may file an objection.

Filing deadline: 30 days after the *conclusion* of the meeting of creditors

10. **Proof of claim**

Please do not file a proof of claim unless you receive a notice to do so.

No property appears to be available to pay creditors. Therefore, please do not file a proof of claim now. If it later appears that assets are available to pay creditors, the clerk will send you another notice telling you that you may file a proof of claim and stating the deadline.

11. **Creditors with a foreign address**

If you are a creditor receiving a notice mailed to a foreign address, you may file a motion asking the court to extend the deadlines in this notice. Consult an attorney familiar with United States bankruptcy law if you have any questions about your rights in this case.

12. **Exempt property**

The law allows debtors to keep certain property as exempt. Fully exempt property will not be sold and distributed to creditors. Debtors must file a list of property claimed as exempt. You may inspect that list at the bankruptcy clerk's office or online at www.pacer.gov. If you believe that the law does not authorize an exemption that the debtors claim, you may file an objection. The bankruptcy clerk's office must receive the objection by the deadline to object to exemptions in line 9.

Information to identify the case:

Debtor _____ EIN __ __ – __ __ __ __ __ __ __
           Name

United States Bankruptcy Court for the: _____ District of _____
                                                           (State)

Case number: _____

[Date case filed for chapter 7 _____

_____ MM / DD / YYYY OR

[Date case filed in chapter _____

_____ MM / DD / YYYY

Date case converted to chapter 7

_____]
MM / DD / YYYY

Official Form 309C (For Corporations or Partnerships)

Notice of Chapter 7 Bankruptcy Case — No Proof of Claim Deadline   12/15

For the debtor listed above, a case has been filed under chapter 7 of the Bankruptcy Code. An order for relief has been entered.

This notice has important information about the case for creditors, debtors, and trustees, including information about the meeting of creditors and deadlines.

The filing of the case imposed an automatic stay against most collection activities. This means that creditors generally may not take action to collect debts from the debtor or the debtor's property. For example, while the stay is in effect, creditors cannot sue, assert a deficiency, repossess property, or otherwise try to collect from the debtor. Creditors cannot demand repayment from debtors by mail, phone, or otherwise. Creditors who violate the stay can be required to pay actual and punitive damages and attorney's fees.

To protect your rights, consult an attorney. All documents filed in the case may be inspected at the bankruptcy clerk's office at the address listed below or through PACER (Public Access to Court Electronic Records at www.pacer.gov).

The staff of the bankruptcy clerk's office cannot give legal advice.

Do not file this notice with any proof of claim or other filing in the case.

1.	**Debtor's full name**	
2.	**All other names used in the last 8 years**	
3.	**Address**	
4.	**Debtor's attorney** Name and address	Contact phone _____ Email _____
5.	**Bankruptcy trustee** Name and address	Contact phone _____ Email _____
6.	**Bankruptcy clerk's office** Documents in this case may be filed at this address. You may inspect all records filed in this case at this office or online at www.pacer.gov.	Hours open _____ Contact phone _____
7.	**Meeting of creditors** The debtor's representative must attend the meeting to be questioned under oath. Creditors may attend, but are not required to do so.	_____ at _____ Date Time The meeting may be continued or adjourned to a later date. If so, the date will be on the court docket.	Location:
8.	**Proof of claim** Please do not file a proof of claim unless you receive a notice to do so.	No property appears to be available to pay creditors. Therefore, please do not file a proof of claim now. If it later appears that assets are available to pay creditors, the clerk will send you another notice telling you that you may file a proof of claim and stating the deadline.	
9.	**Creditors with a foreign address**	If you are a creditor receiving a notice mailed to a foreign address, you may file a motion asking the court to extend the deadlines in this notice. Consult an attorney familiar with United States bankruptcy law if you have any questions about your rights in this case.	

WISDOM IS THE KEY TO SUCCESS
Get Wise; Get a Smith's Guide™

**Let Smith guide you step-by-step through the courts
and do it right the first time—every time.**

All Smith's Guides are designed for the beginning pro se prisoner
and the practicing pro se litigator alike and are complete
with example pleadings from successful cases.

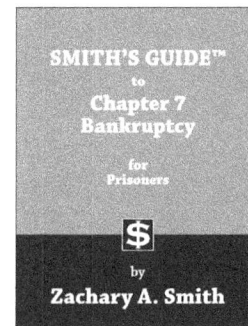

NEW! *SMITH'S GUIDE™ to State Habeas Corpus Relief for State Prisoners*

> Provides detailed information and instructions for seeking relief via state habeas petition and for exhausting state-court remedies before proceeding to federal court to file a §2254 petition or an application to file a second or successive habeas petition. Includes state habeas rules and statutes for all 50 states. [578 pages]

SMITH'S GUIDE™ to Habeas Corpus Relief for State Prisoners
Under 28 U.S.C. §2254

> This book covers the entire process for filing the initial §2254 habeas petition to the final petition for a writ of certiorari in the U.S. Supreme Court. [380 pages]

NEW! *SMITH'S GUIDE™ to Second or Successive Federal Habeas Corpus Relief for State and Federal Prisoners*

> For those seeking to file a second or successive habeas petition under §2244 or §2255, based on newly discovered evidence or retroactive effect of a U.S. Supreme Court case, this book provides detailed instructions for preparing the application. [352 pages]

SMITH'S GUIDE™ to Executive Clemency for State and Federal Prisoners

> For those who have exhausted all legal remedies or have sentences that are too long to serve, this book lays out every aspect of the clemency process, self-development and personal transformation, communication skills, clemency campaign and promotional strategies, and much more. It is also applicable for parole hearings and could make the difference between freedom or additional incarceration. [288 pages]

SMITH'S GUIDE™ to Chapter 7 Bankruptcy for Prisoners

> Get immediate freedom from liens against offender account (including from incarceration reimbursement judgment, halfway house costs, probation/parole intervention fees, and other debt) by filing chapter 7 bankruptcy. Includes blank bankruptcy forms and filing instructions. [422 pages]

All titles available online at Amazon.com

WISDOM IS THE KEY TO SUCCESS
Get Wise; Get a Smith's Guide™

Let Smith guide you step-by-step through the courts and do it right the first time—every time.

All Smith's Guides are designed for the beginning pro se prisoner and the practicing pro se litigator alike and are complete with example pleadings from successful cases.

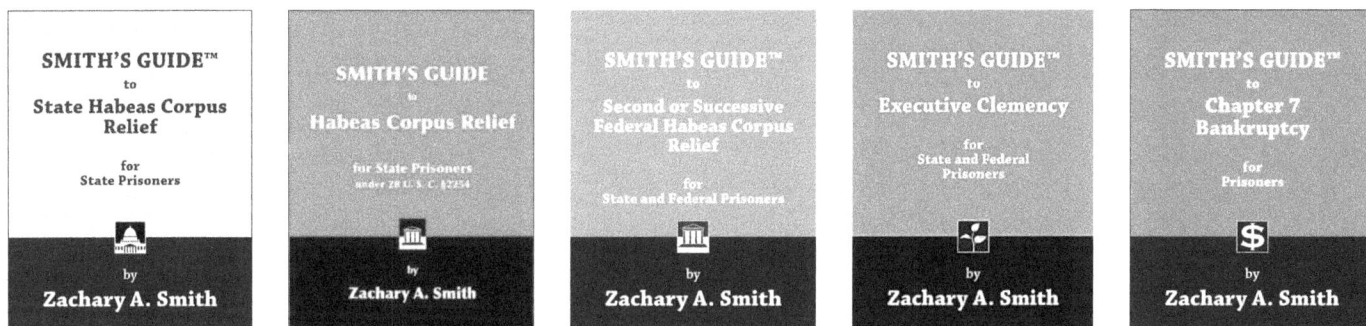

SMITH'S GUIDE™ to State Habeas Corpus Relief for State Prisoners by Zachary A. Smith	SMITH'S GUIDE to Habeas Corpus Relief for State Prisoners under 28 U.S.C. §2254 by Zachary A. Smith	SMITH'S GUIDE™ to Second or Successive Federal Habeas Corpus Relief for State and Federal Prisoners by Zachary A. Smith	SMITH'S GUIDE™ to Executive Clemency for State and Federal Prisoners by Zachary A. Smith	SMITH'S GUIDE™ to Chapter 7 Bankruptcy for Prisoners by Zachary A. Smith

NEW! SMITH'S GUIDE™ to State Habeas Corpus Relief for State Prisoners

Provides detailed information and instructions for seeking relief via state habeas petition and for exhausting state-court remedies before proceeding to federal court to file a §2254 petition or an application to file a second or successive habeas petition. Includes state habeas rules and statutes for all 50 states. [578 pages]

SMITH'S GUIDE™ to Habeas Corpus Relief for State Prisoners Under 28 U.S.C. §2254

This book covers the entire process for filing the initial §2254 habeas petition to the final petition for a writ of certiorari in the U.S. Supreme Court. [380 pages]

NEW! SMITH'S GUIDE™ to Second or Successive Federal Habeas Corpus Relief for State and Federal Prisoners

For those seeking to file a second or successive habeas petition under §2244 or §2255, based on newly discovered evidence or retroactive effect of a U.S. Supreme Court case, this book provides detailed instructions for preparing the application. [352 pages]

SMITH'S GUIDE™ to Executive Clemency for State and Federal Prisoners

For those who have exhausted all legal remedies or have sentences that are too long to serve, this book lays out every aspect of the clemency process, self-development and personal transformation, communication skills, clemency campaign and promotional strategies, and much more. It is also applicable for parole hearings and could make the difference between freedom or additional incarceration. [288 pages]

SMITH'S GUIDE™ to Chapter 7 Bankruptcy for Prisoners

Get immediate freedom from liens against offender account (including from incarceration reimbursement judgment, halfway house costs, probation/parole intervention fees, and other debt) by filing chapter 7 bankruptcy. Includes blank bankruptcy forms and filing instructions. [422 pages]

All titles available online at Amazon.com

www.ingramcontent.com/pod-product-compliance
Lightning Source LLC
Chambersburg PA
CBHW082126210326
41599CB00031B/5888